IMAGES
of America

MEDINA

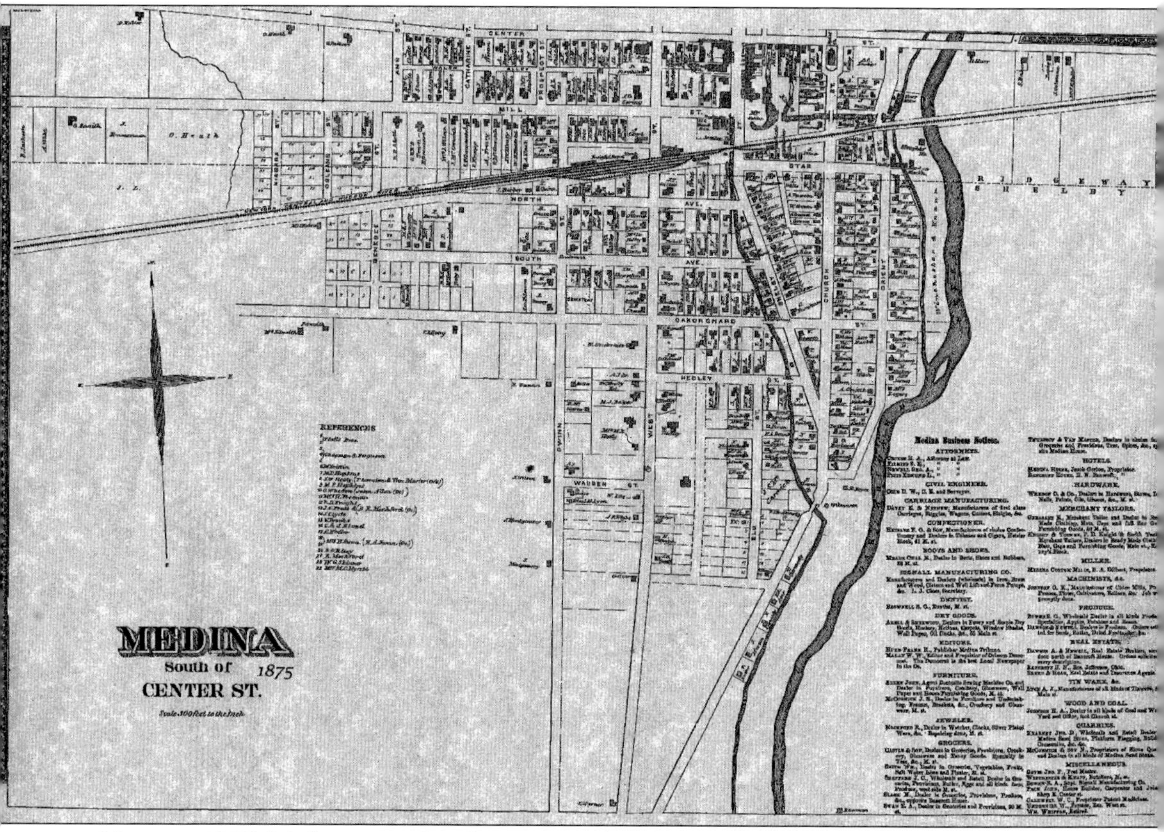

MEDINA, 1875. Medina was a bustling metropolis after the completion of the Erie Canal, and its largest growth spurt occurred between 1825 and the early 20th century. By 1832, Medina had 800 residents, and today there are over 7,000. (Courtesy of Historicaltownmaps.com.)

IMAGES
of America

MEDINA

Avis A. Townsend

ARCADIA
PUBLISHING

ISBN 978-0-7385-3936-2

Published by Arcadia Publishing
Charleston, South Carolina

Printed in the United States of America

Library of Congress Control Number: 2005932037

For all general information contact Arcadia Publishing at:
Telephone 843-853-2070
Fax 843-853-0044
E-mail sales@arcadiapublishing.com
For customer service and orders:
Toll-Free 1-888-313-2665

Visit us on the Internet at www.arcadiapublishing.com

Contents

FOREWORD

I have had interactions with Medina for the past 40 years. As a teenager, I considered Medina "the rival." My school played the Medina Mustangs, with football and basketball causing the most intense rivalry.

As I got older, the stores I had frequented in nearby Lockport gave way to malls, and I missed the old-fashioned stores I would shop in with my mother. Medina's Main Street still had those stores, so when my children were old enough, I would take them there, touring through businesses with wooden floors and creaky stairways, letting them have a glimpse of life in the past before it was gone forever. Who would have known that Medina would not give way to urban renewal and that although merchants changed, the buildings would be kept the same, their façades closely resembling the façades of the early 20th century.

Medina's Apple Grove Inn became the "in" place for wedding receptions, and I celebrated there frequently. When I became social editor of our daily newspaper, I covered the packet boat rides leaving from the Apple Grove's docks—learning a bit about Medina's history, seeing how the original boats were pulled by horses and mules, hearing yarns by Muleskinner Dave, and visiting the fascinating Medina Falls, an area hidden to most who do not know the area. I drove my car under the culvert that lies under the canal, glad to emerge from its low ceiling unscathed.

It only made sense to include Medina as one of the Images of America books I would prepare for Arcadia Publishing. Working on this project has given me more insight to everything Medina has to offer, and I have made many new friends along the way.

—Avis A. Townsend, author

INTRODUCTION

Medina's hub lies along the banks of the Erie Canal. Part of Orleans County, its borders pass Route 31 to the south and Lake Ontario to the north, with the hamlets of Knowlesville and Oak Orchard making use of the waterways that ribbon through the area. It also lies in the middle of two towns, Ridgeway and Shelby. The Ridgeway Town Hall is on West Avenue in Medina, right behind the Medina Historical Society, both sharing the same parking lot. Although Medina is incorporated as a village, its police and fire departments share a building called City Hall. It has an upper dam and a lower dam, a creek that flows under the Erie Canal, and a road that travels under it as well.

Oak Orchard Creek attracted early settlers, offering water power necessary for running lumber mills and gristmills and for producing electricity. After the 1825 opening of the Erie Canal, people flocked to the area in droves. A large natural harbor that is part of the canal allowed packet boats to dock en masse, their occupants seeking food or lodging for the night or just departing the boats to stretch their legs. Entrepreneurs realized they could make money by building hotels, restaurants, and taverns in this vicinity. And Medina was born. People knew this area was perfect for loading fruits and vegetables to be taken west to Buffalo or east to Albany and points farther than that. Medina grew and prospered. Businesses settled on Main Street to be as close to the canal and its shipping capabilities as possible.

An old gorge that once offered a scenic falls was used to create power. As early as 1818, people were diverting water from the falls to create raceways to run mills via waterwheels. When the canal was built, water was rerouted from it as well. Businessman Albert Swett saw the need for more power, and he ordered a 60-foot-tall dam built on the north end of Glenwood Lake, which created more energy. He then began a power company on Main Street called the Swett Electric Light Office, which eventually merged with the powerful Niagara Mohawk Power Corporation. Niagara Mohawk still owns the dam on Glenwood Lake.

Main Street is very long, winding its way from Route 31 to the canal, and the storefronts from the railroad tracks to the canal look much the same today as they did in the early 20th century, with different merchants occupying the spaces. However, some of the original stores were made of wood, and after a huge fire that destroyed much of Main Street, it was decreed that any future buildings be built of brick or stone to keep fire hazards at a minimum.

Founding fathers created a very wide Main Street. Where horses and buggies were formerly tethered on the dirt road, cars and trucks now park diagonally in front of each store on a smoothly paved roadway, with no congestion because of its width. Pedestrian crosswalks have been replaced by signal lights and signs telling people when and where they can cross.

One of the area's most important discoveries was Medina sandstone. Stonecutters found it while carving out a path through rock for the Erie Canal, and as soon as the canal work was completed, they returned to study this new rock and to begin quarrying. Medina sandstone ranges in color from a light gray to a deep, reddish brown. The stone creates a lovely building, and it was used to create Sibley Hall at Cornell University and Anderson Hall and another Sibley Hall at the old University of Rochester campus. It was also used for the federal building in Rochester and on the steps of the state capitol in Albany. On the waterfront, it was used for the harbor breakwater walls in Buffalo and Cleveland and for the pillars of the George Washington Bridge, the Brooklyn Bridge, and the Williamsburg Bridge. Homes and buildings in Medina made of the substance are still standing. History mentions that sandstone was sent to England to be used in Buckingham Palace and to Havana, Cuba, as well.

It is easy to tell which buildings are of Medina sandstone. It is impressive to see, and the blocks of stone are much larger than brick or cobblestones. Medina's City Hall and the armory building were constructed of the red stone, while the Baptist church sports the grayish stone.

Medina boasts two interesting canal phenomena. On Culvert Road, the canal passes over the roadway. Cars pass through a tunnel that has leaked for a hundred years, but the tunnel remains firm. Also, a few miles away, the aqueduct allows the canal to flow over the top of Oak Orchard Creek.

A sawmill was the first business to start up in Medina, with Moore's Tavern following shortly after. The tavern housed overnight passengers from the canal and was a stopping place for the stagecoaches that traveled Ridge Road. Two taverns that began in the late 19th century were the Walsh Hotel and what is now O'Brien's Inn. Both are still standing today, both still taverns almost back to back on adjacent streets. The Walsh was on the railroad tracks and was a hotel for many years. O'Brien's is located on the west side of Main Street next to City Hall, also on the tracks.

Medina was incorporated as a village in 1832, and the population numbered close to 800 people. By 1900, many people had moved on, seeking their fortunes in nearby towns or neighboring states, leaving friends and family behind. In August 1906, a huge undertaking called Old Homecoming Week was conducted by those who stayed, and invitations were sent to anyone who had moved away, inviting them back. The newspaper ran articles, telegraphs were sent, and people returned. There was a major celebration. A parade marched through town, and bunting was hung on the storefronts. Medina had many parades and celebrations after the beginning of the 20th century, including a welcome home for Spanish-American War soldiers, various flower parades, and July Fourth celebrations.

Today's merchants realize they are a part of history, and their buildings reflect the past. The canal has been upgraded and landscaped and welcomes pleasure boats instead of packet boats. The original sandstone buildings are as solid and lovely today as they were a century ago.

One

BEGINNINGS

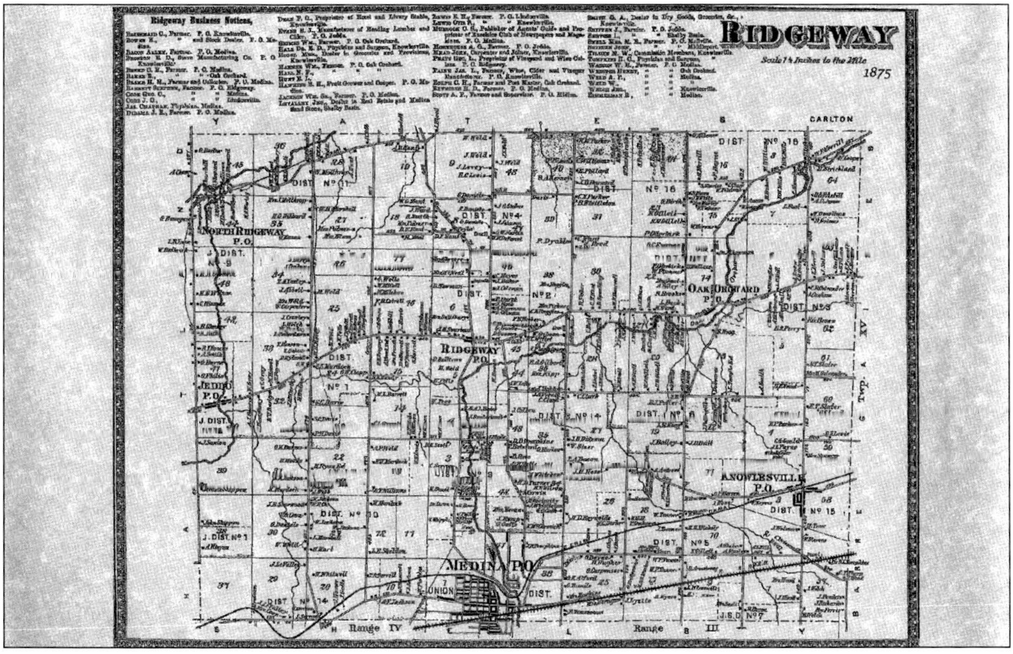

RIDGEWAY EXPANDS. By 1875, Ridgewood had grown with many roads, new houses, and many new inhabitants. It was easy to drive from the Ridge into Medina and find many familiar faces along the way. (Courtesy of Historicaltownmaps.com.)

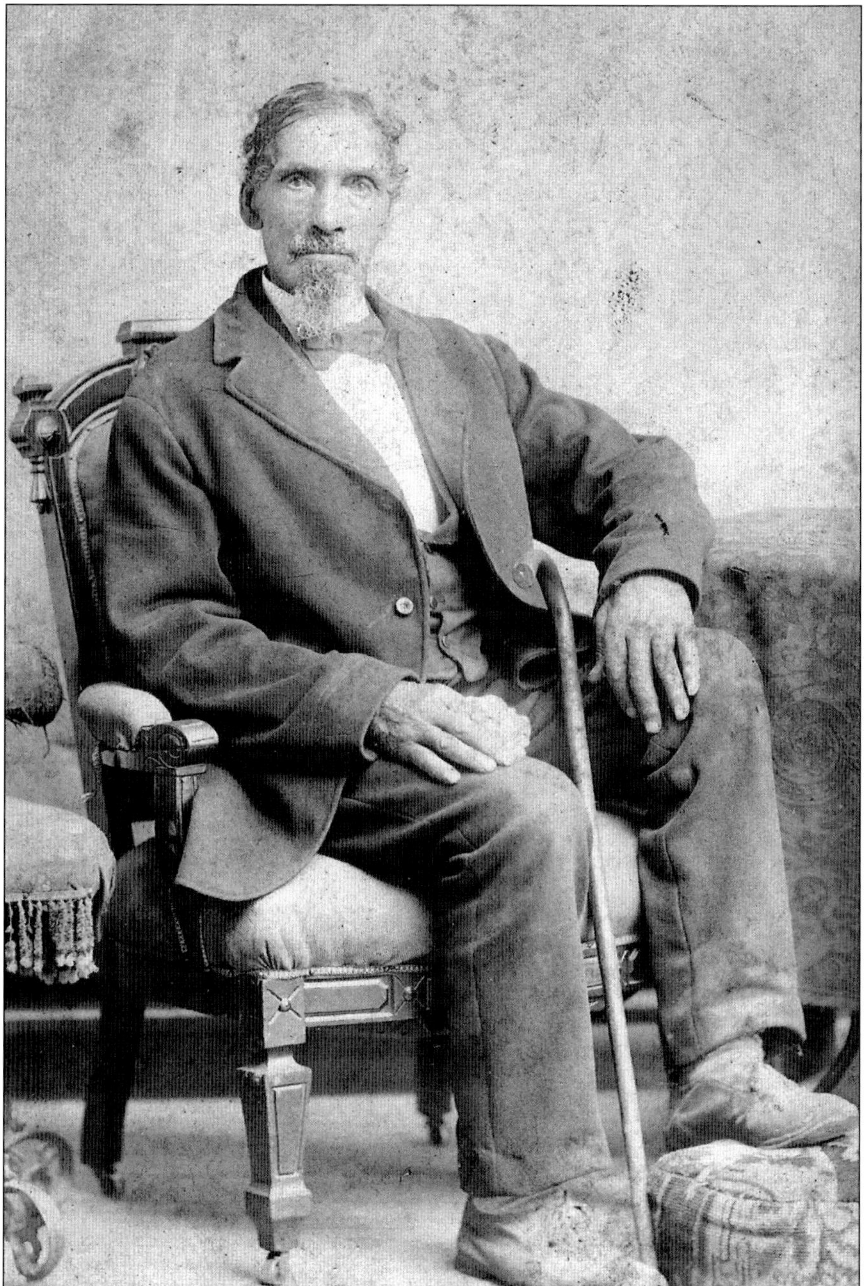

RICHARD GORDINEER. The son of Mohawk Dutchman Jacob Gordineer and a slave, Richard Gordineer was a horse dealer who went from rags to riches in Medina. Born in 1794, he and his mother were sold to Joseph Grant when he was only two months old. They were set free in 1825, and he worked on the Erie Canal until 1839. He became a famed cook and was in great demand for posh weddings. He was the only cart man in Medina for many years, and he became very successful as a horse trader. Betrayed by a friend, Gordineer lost his fortune in 1863. After that he earned money by whitewashing fences, smoking hams, and doing paltry odd jobs. He died penniless at the age of 96 in 1890. (Courtesy of the Orleans County Department of History.)

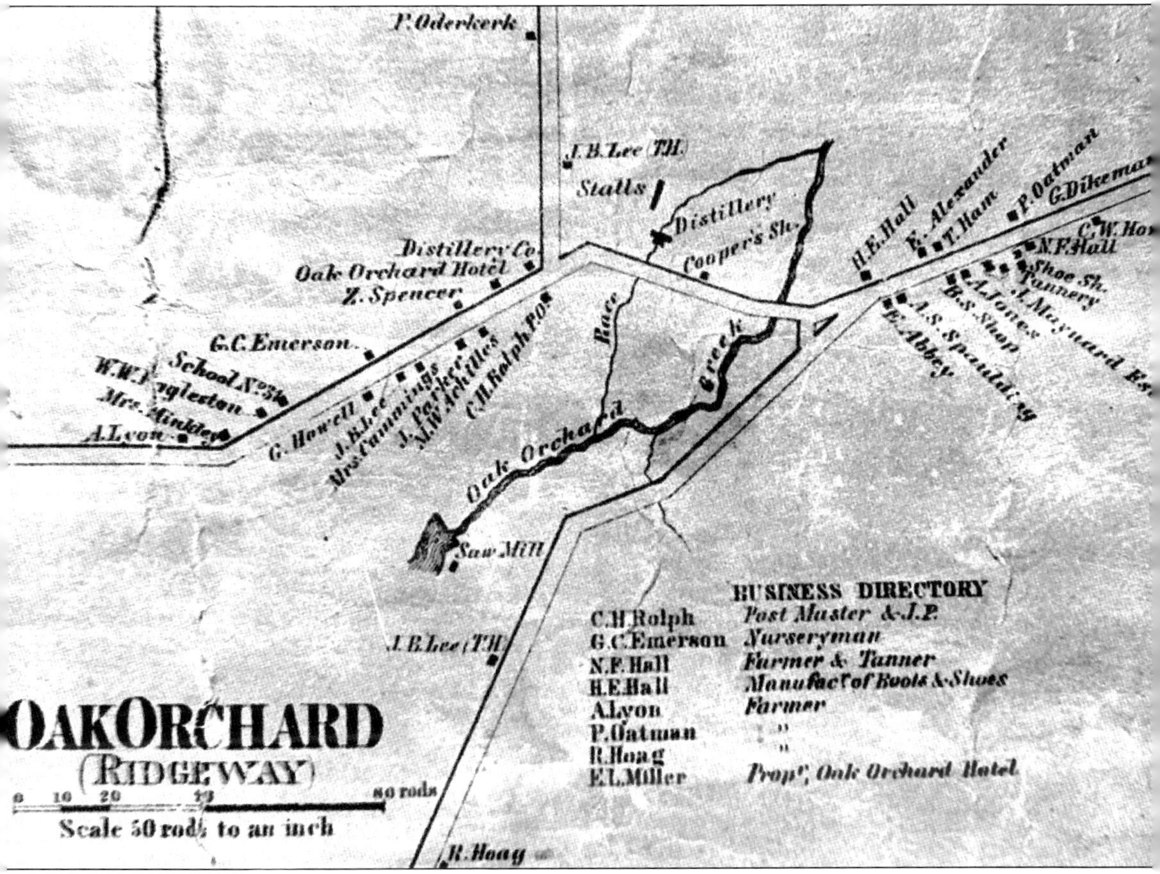

OAK ORCHARD MAP. Ridge Road was the natural trail leading from Batavia to what is now Lewiston, with many people settling as they traveled east. This early map shows the buildings and farms that formed in Oak Orchard on the Ridge before the 20th century. (Courtesy of Richard Nellist.)

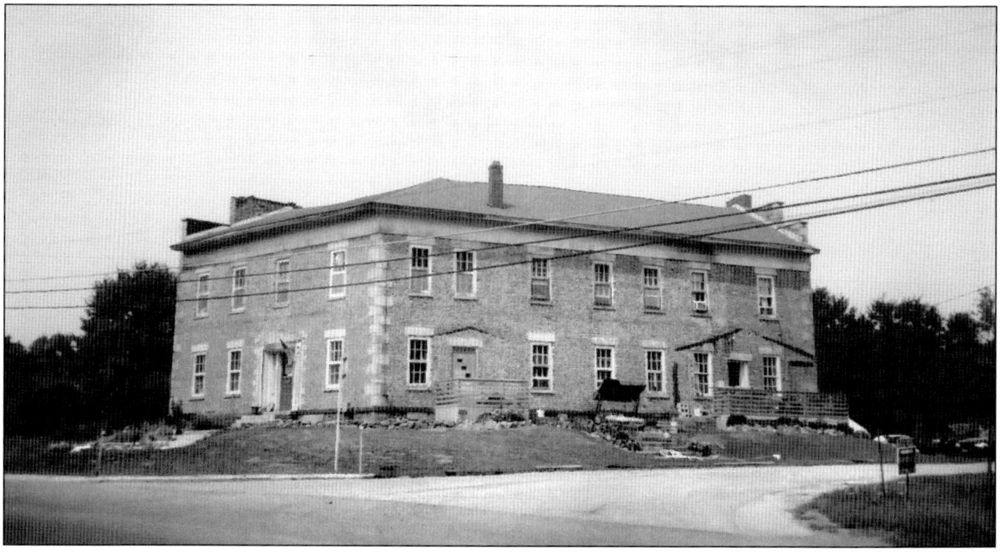

STAGECOACH STOP. This huge cobblestone inn, built in 1817, is still in existence on Ridge Road, except it is an antique shop today. Located west of Oak Orchard Creek, the two-story, 22-room inn was once known as the Spencer House and boasted a fireplace in each room. When it was first built, it did not have a porch, but it did have step gables. The cobblestones are accented by red Medina sandstone. (Courtesy of Richard Nellist.)

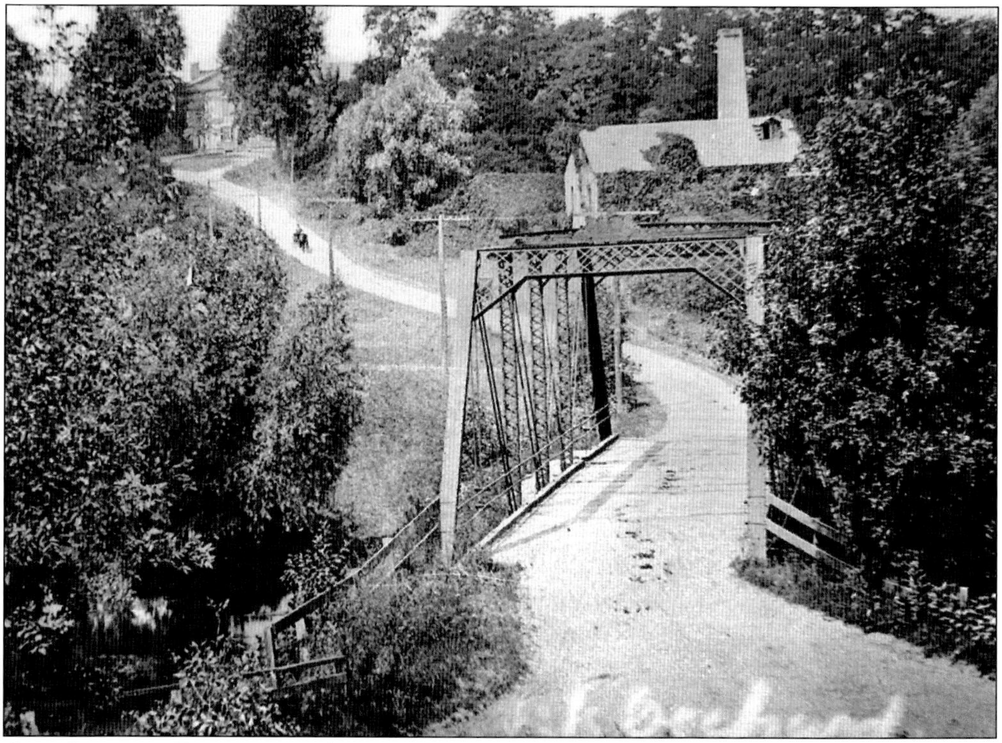

OAK ORCHARD BRIDGE. A solitary buggy begins the trek past the Spencer House Inn (upper left at the top of the hill), toward Lee's Distillery, and across the bridge at Oak Orchard around 1900. (Courtesy of Richard Nellist.)

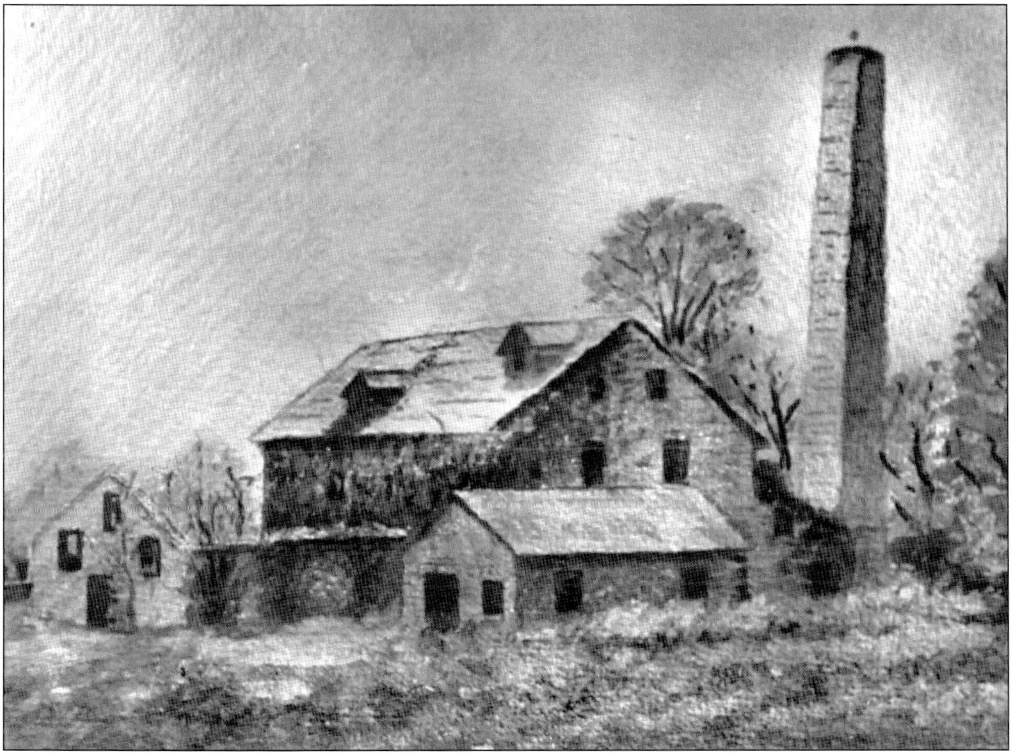

ARTIST'S RENDERING. This painting of Lee's Distillery was exact. Unfortunately, the artist is unknown. The distillery opened in 1838, constructed in the flats at Oak Orchard for John Lee of Albion. The early farmers built distilleries to use up their excess corn and rye. Whiskey was plentiful. (Courtesy of Richard Nellist.)

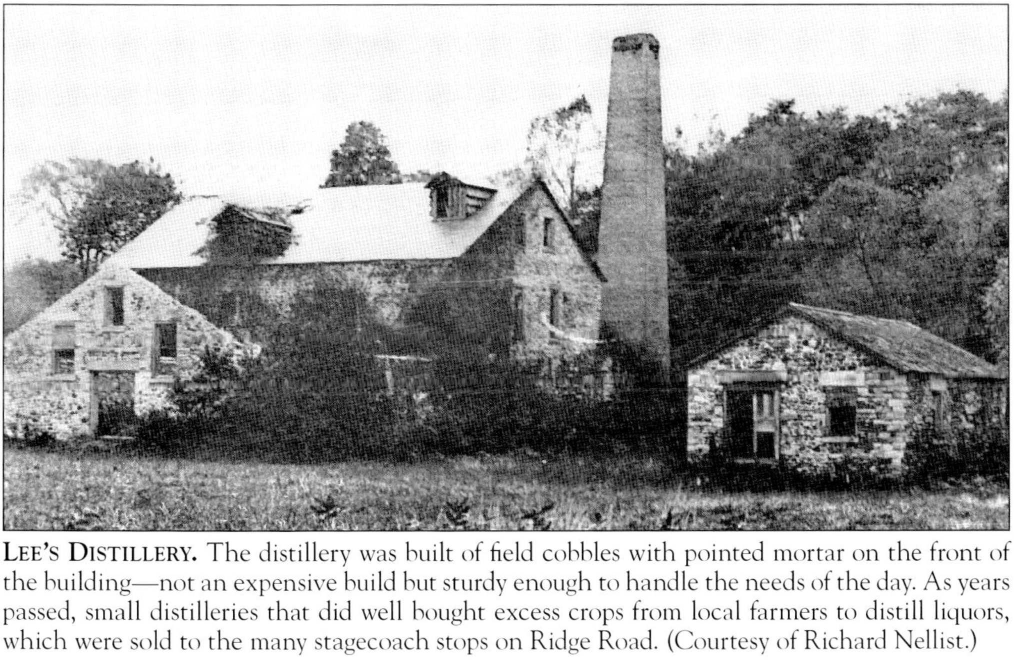

LEE'S DISTILLERY. The distillery was built of field cobbles with pointed mortar on the front of the building—not an expensive build but sturdy enough to handle the needs of the day. As years passed, small distilleries that did well bought excess crops from local farmers to distill liquors, which were sold to the many stagecoach stops on Ridge Road. (Courtesy of Richard Nellist.)

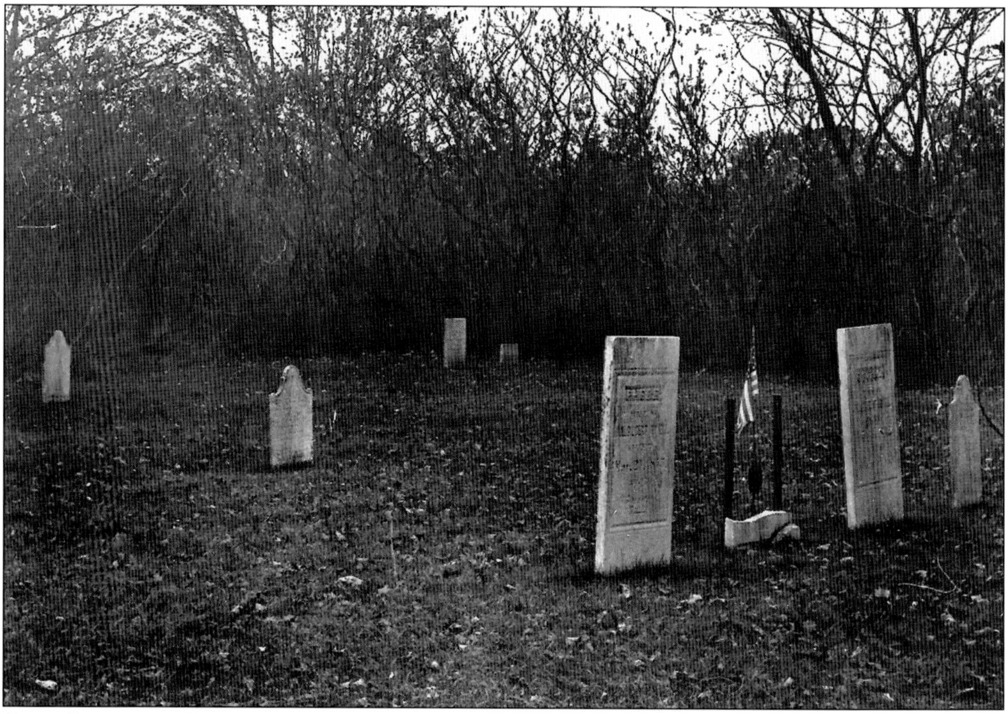

Oak Orchard Cemetery. This Civil War–era cemetery is all but defunct, and there is no access to it today. Most of the graves were moved to other property, and the stones were moved or too broken to identify. (Courtesy of Richard Nellist.)

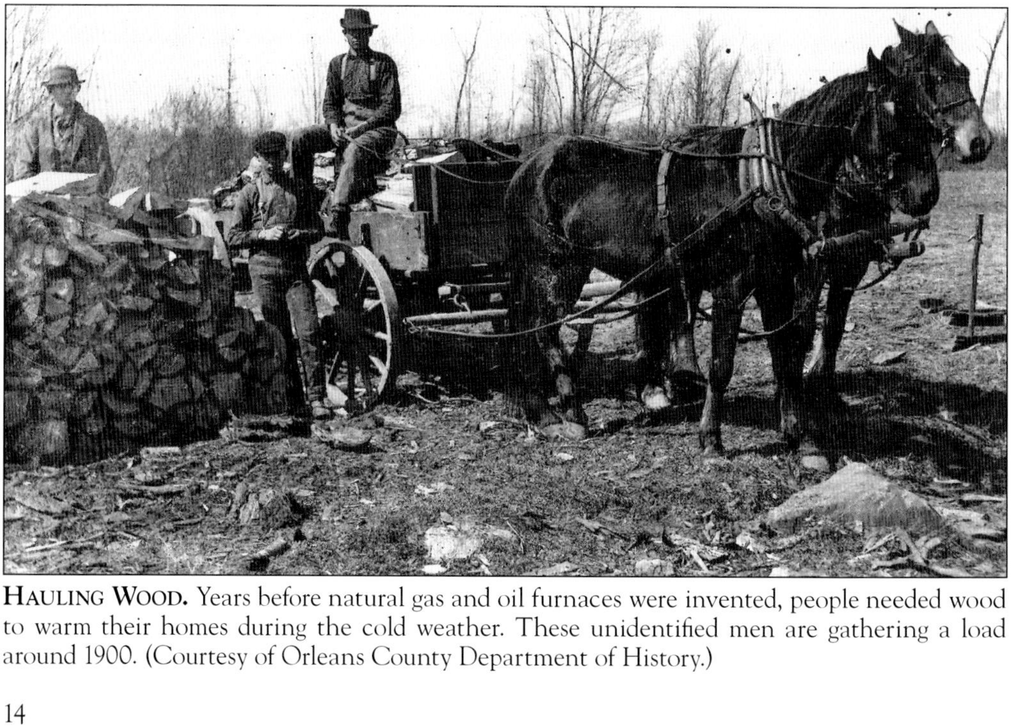

Hauling Wood. Years before natural gas and oil furnaces were invented, people needed wood to warm their homes during the cold weather. These unidentified men are gathering a load around 1900. (Courtesy of Orleans County Department of History.)

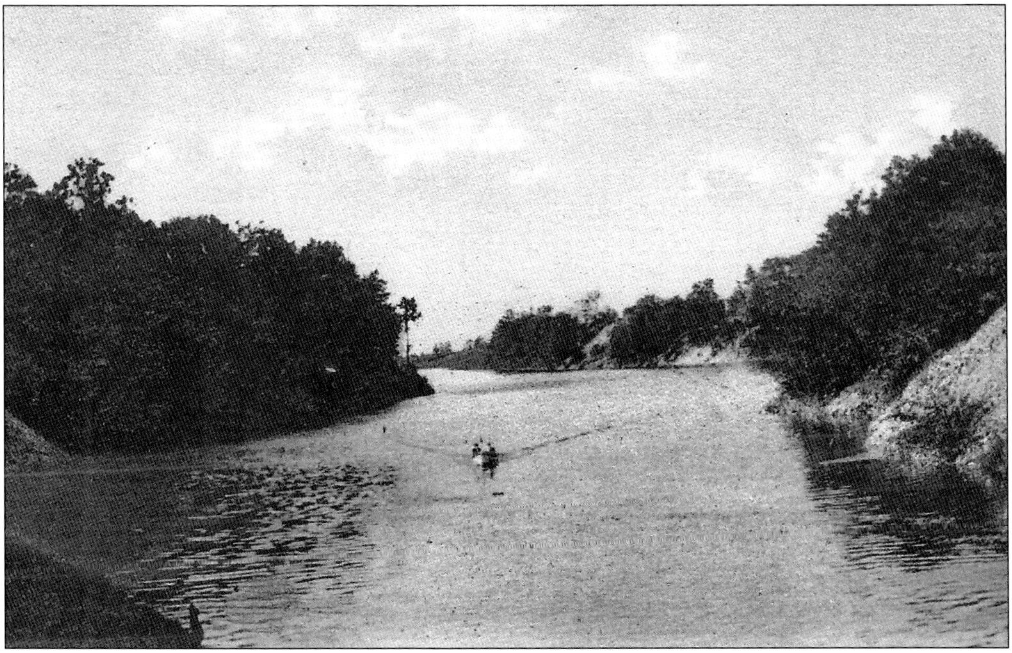

Glenwood Lake. Glenwood Lake is a lovely, serene body of water north of Medina on North Gravel Road. It has been used as a pleasure area for swimming and boating since the late 19th century. In the early 20th century, Albert Swett installed a large dam at the south end to provide power for the area. There is now a boat launch off the road, and if a sign did not tell travelers the lake was there, no one would know. (Courtesy of Grant-Pollard Insurance Office.)

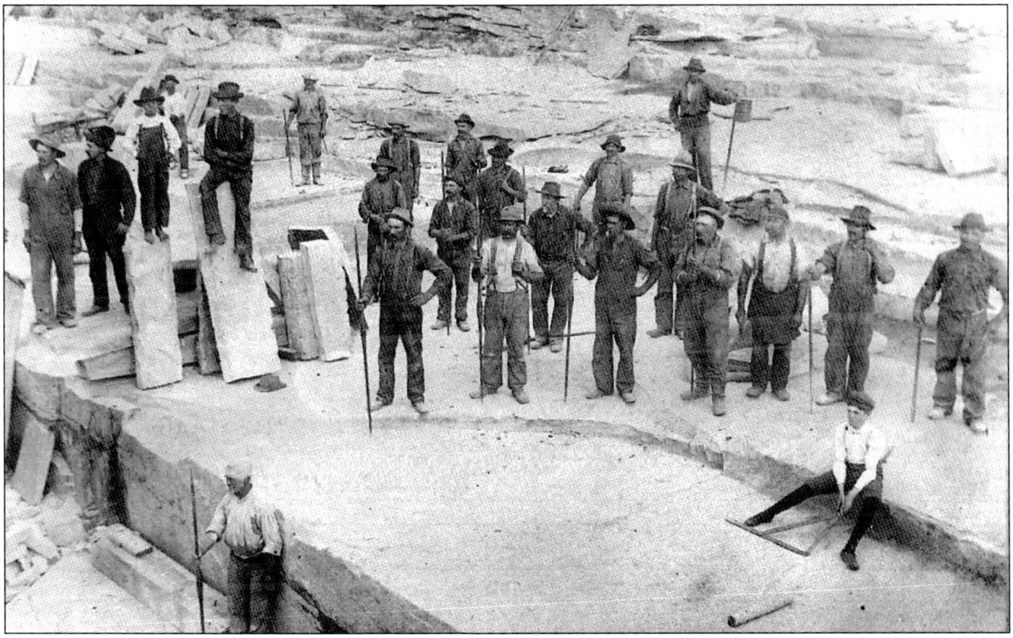

McCormick Quarry. Workers take a rest at the McCormick Sandstone Quarry around 1900. The quarry was located south of Ridgeway near Oak Orchard Creek. Note the large slabs leaning up against the quarry walls. (Courtesy of Richard Nellist.)

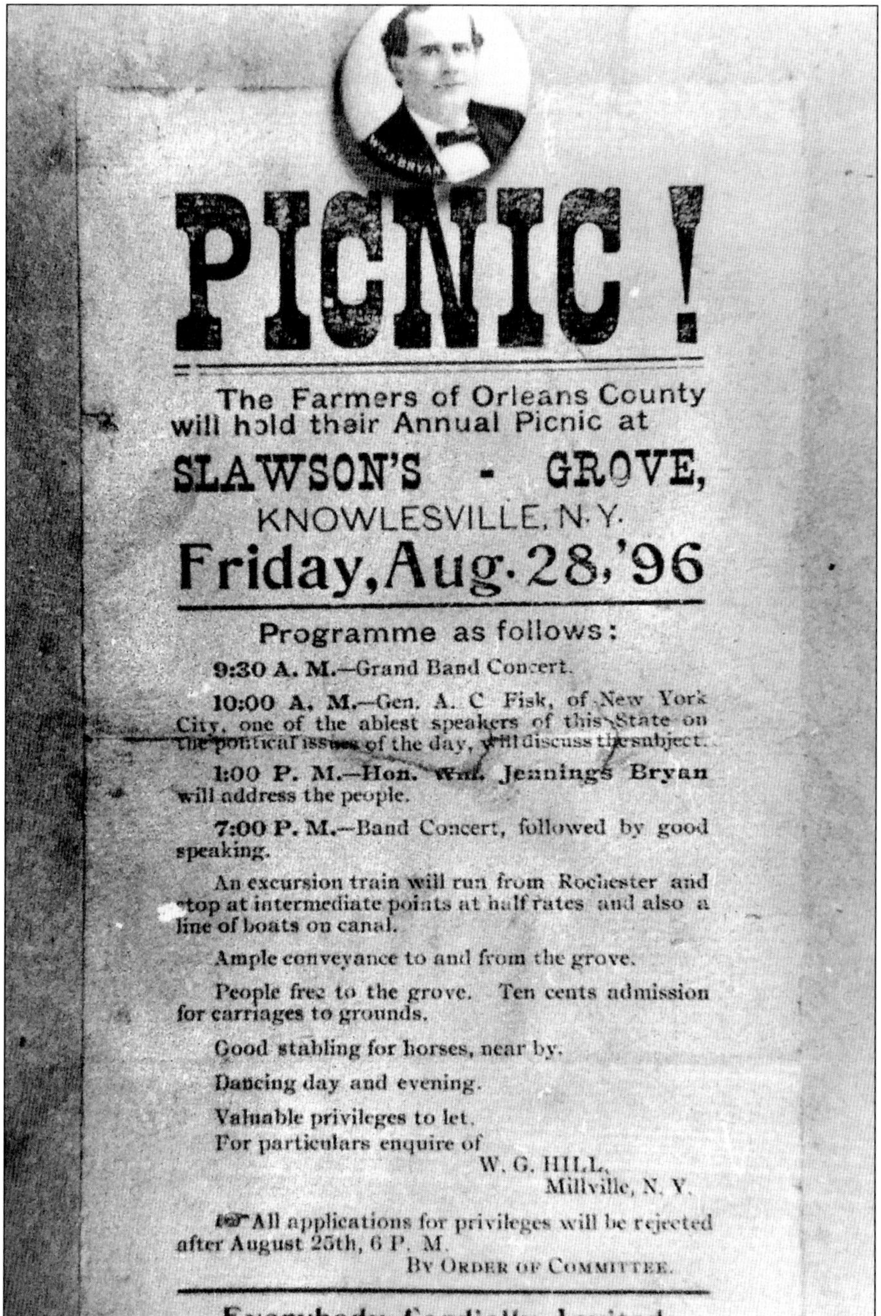

KNOWLESVILLE PICNIC POSTER. William Jennings Bryan was the featured speaker for the Orleans County farmers' annual picnic at Slawson's Grove, August 28, 1896. Band concerts opened and closed the picnic. An excursion train offered half rates for those coming from Rochester, and a line of boats would arrive via the Erie Canal. People were allowed free access to the grove, but carriages paid 10¢ to help defray costs for the good stabling for horses. There was dancing day and evening and a shuttle coach to take visitors to the grove. Gen. A. C. Fisk of New York City also spoke on the political issues of the day. (Courtesy of Richard Nellist.)

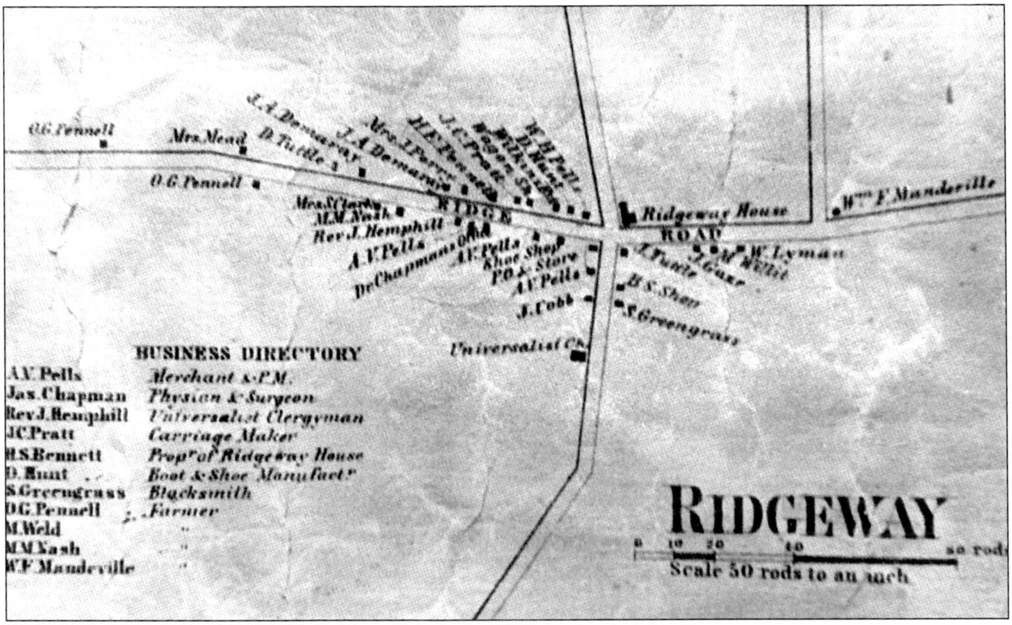

RIDGEWAY BUSINESS DIRECTORY, C. 1900. This map shows the farms and hotels on Ridge Road and North Gravel Road (Route 63). Two main features of this map are the Ridgeway House Hotel and the Universalist Church. Of the other listings on the map, there was a merchant store, physician, clergyman, carriage maker, hotel owner, boot maker, blacksmith, and farmer.

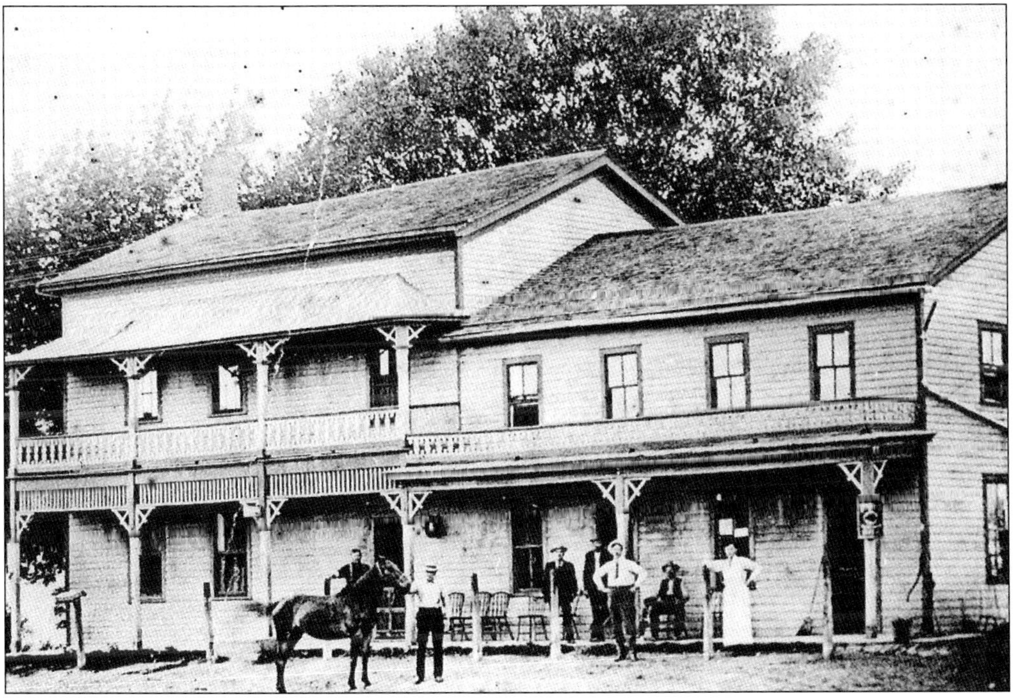

RIDGEWAY HOUSE, C. 1890. This building still stands today on the north side of Ridge Road where Route 63 turns to go to Medina. It began as a hotel, turned into a motel and tavern, and now is an apartment house. (Courtesy of Richard Nellist.)

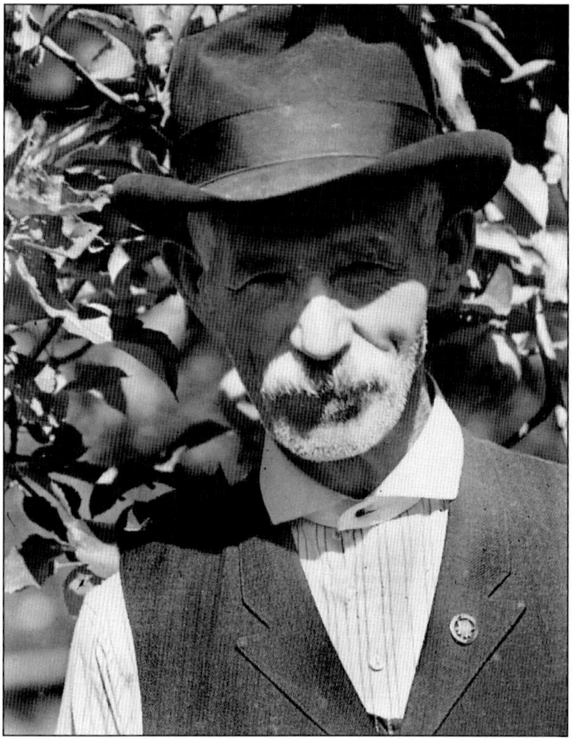

APPLE PICKER. This unidentified man seemed too well dressed for an apple picker on Joseph Prahler's farm around 1900. (Courtesy of Mrs. Elmer Chatt.)

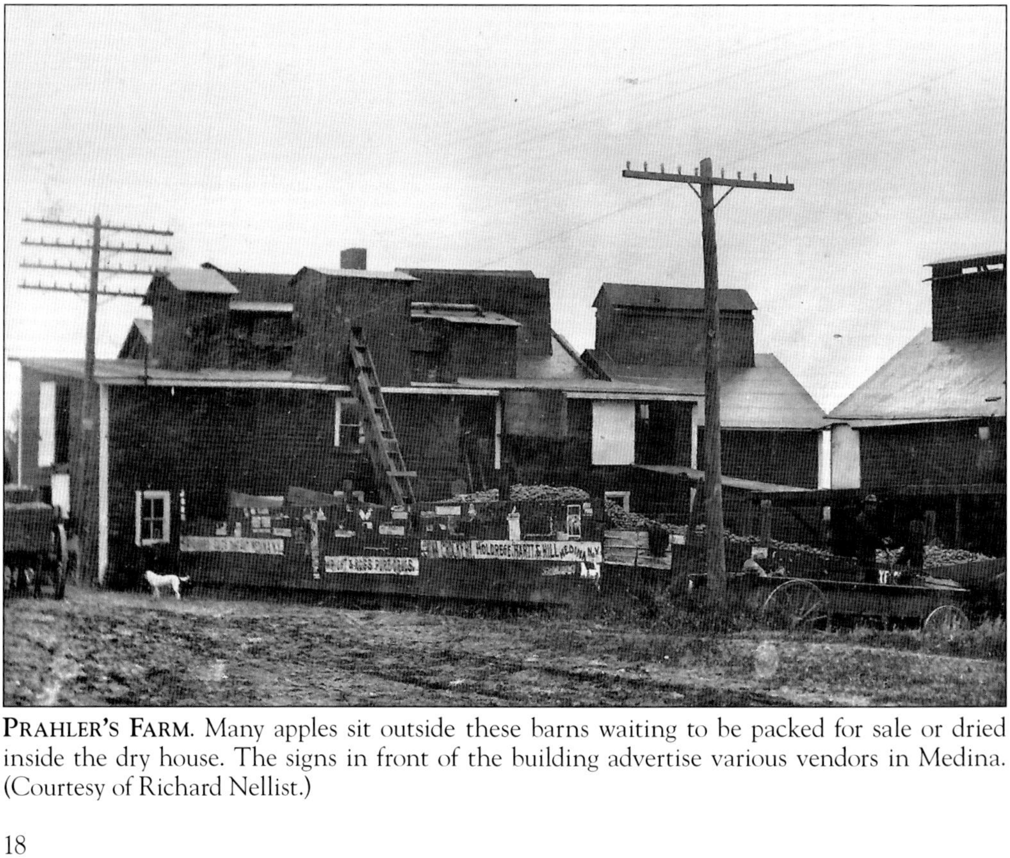

PRAHLER'S FARM. Many apples sit outside these barns waiting to be packed for sale or dried inside the dry house. The signs in front of the building advertise various vendors in Medina. (Courtesy of Richard Nellist.)

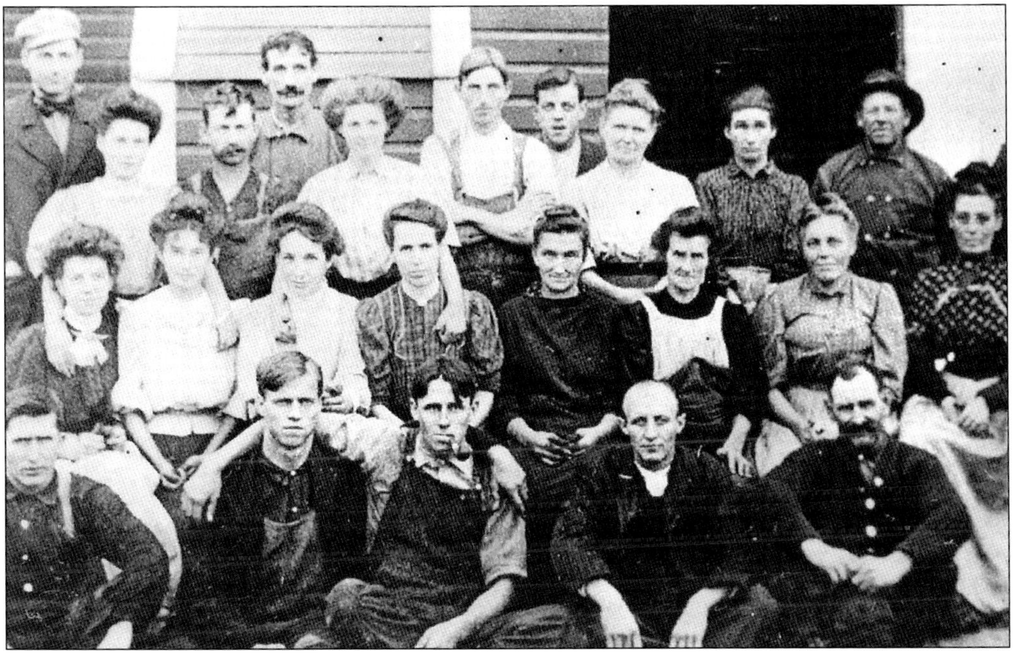

Prahler Employees. Some of the workers pose for the camera at Joseph Prahler's farm around 1900. (Courtesy of Richard Nellist.)

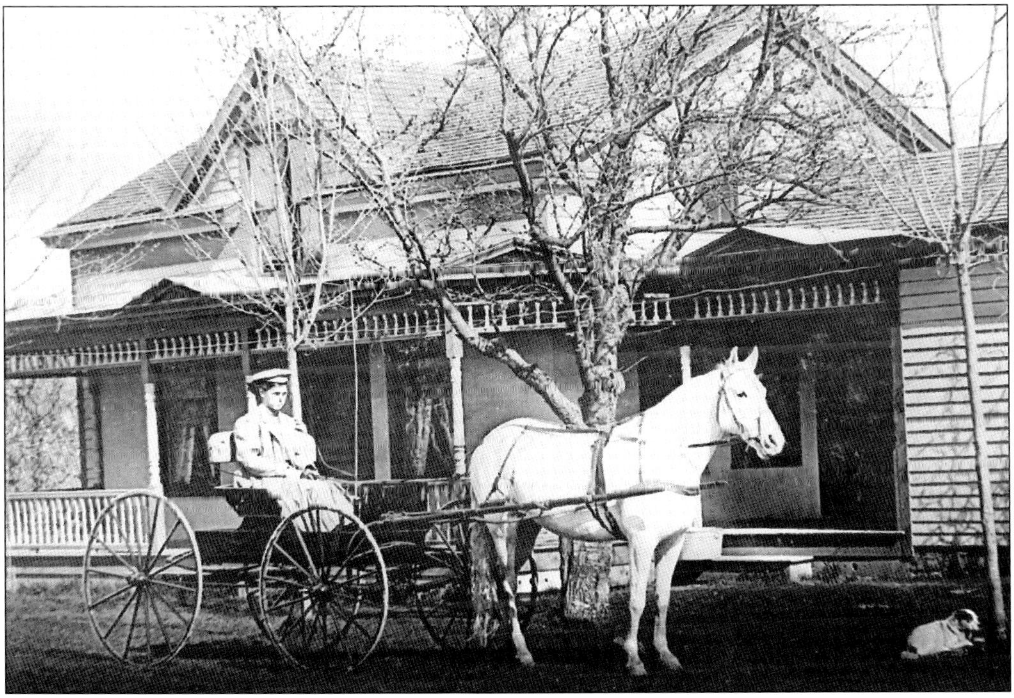

Ready to Roll. An unidentified woman poses with her horse and her dog in front of her Ridge Road home around 1900.

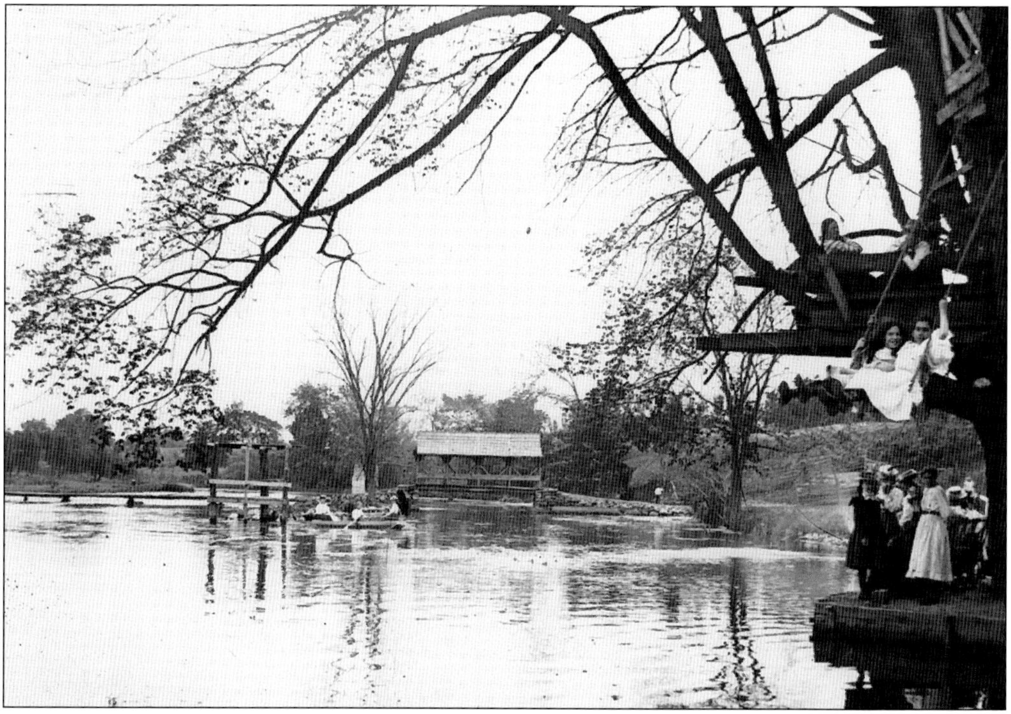

SWINGING ON GLENWOOD LAKE. Elm Park was a popular spot for folks to visit before the automobile was invented. The large elm tree at right was the focal point for children and adults, with a huge swing allowing people to swing out over Glenwood Lake. (Courtesy of Mrs. Elmer Chatt.)

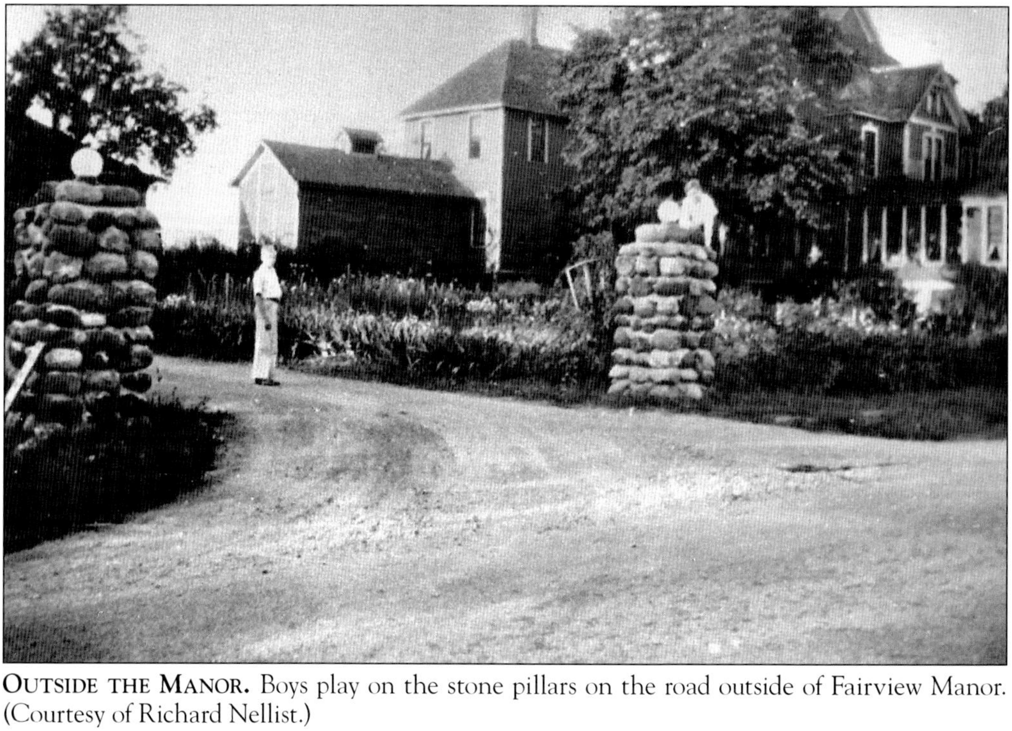

OUTSIDE THE MANOR. Boys play on the stone pillars on the road outside of Fairview Manor. (Courtesy of Richard Nellist.)

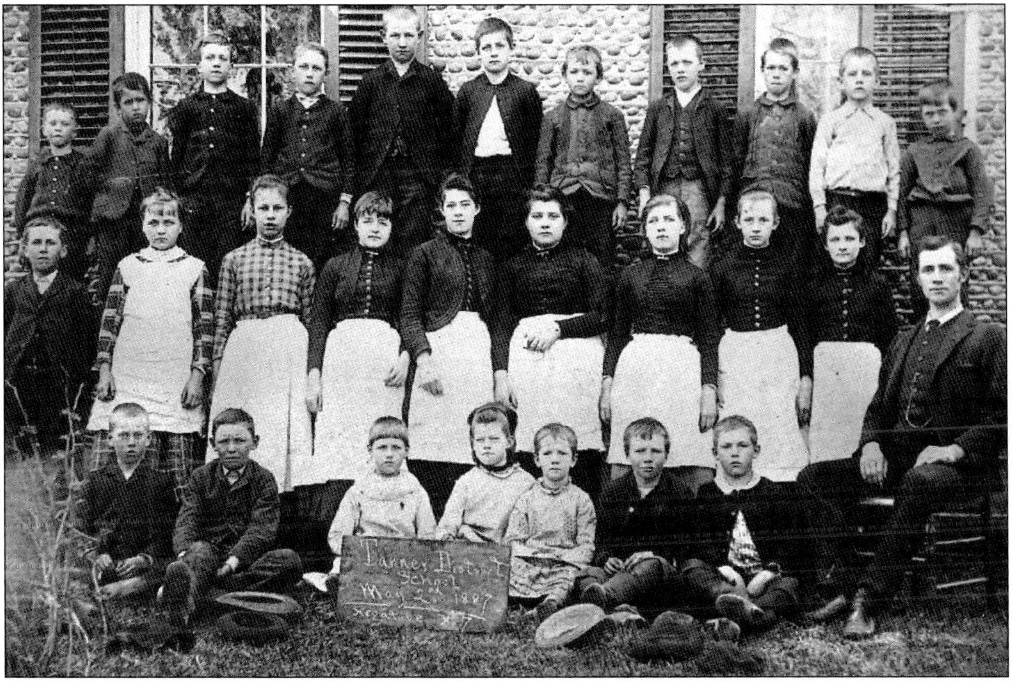

TANNER DISTRICT STUDENTS. The Tanner District was in the area of what is now Route 31 and Culvert Road. One of Medina's first settlers was named Tanner, and when his wife died, he built a cemetery in the same area. Tanner Cemetery is filled with most of the descendents of this man. Unfortunately no names were supplied with this photograph, taken May 2, 1887.

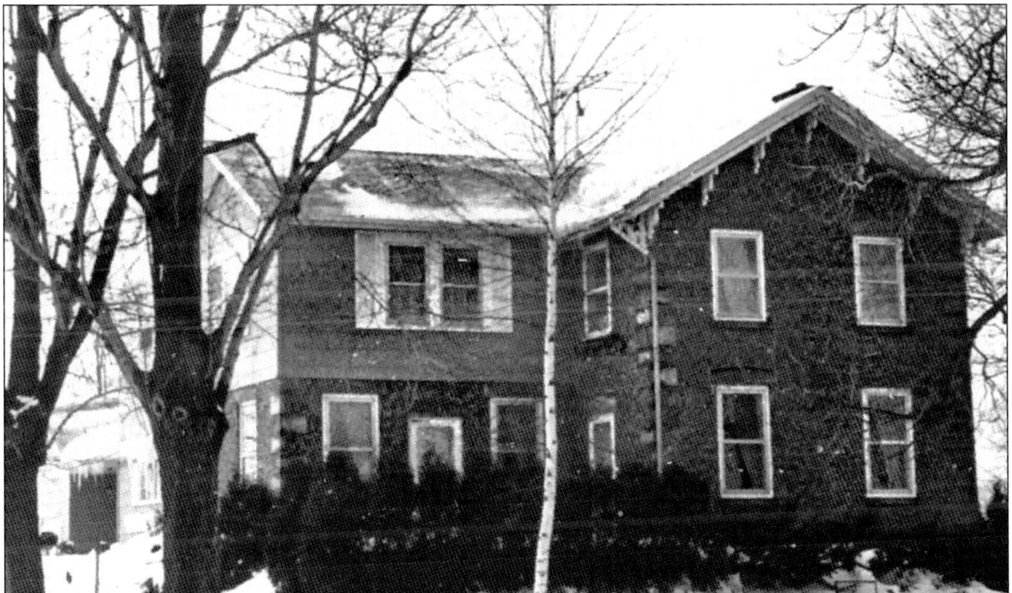

TANNER HOMESTEAD. This is the original home of the Tanner family and is located on the corner of Culvert Road and Route 31.

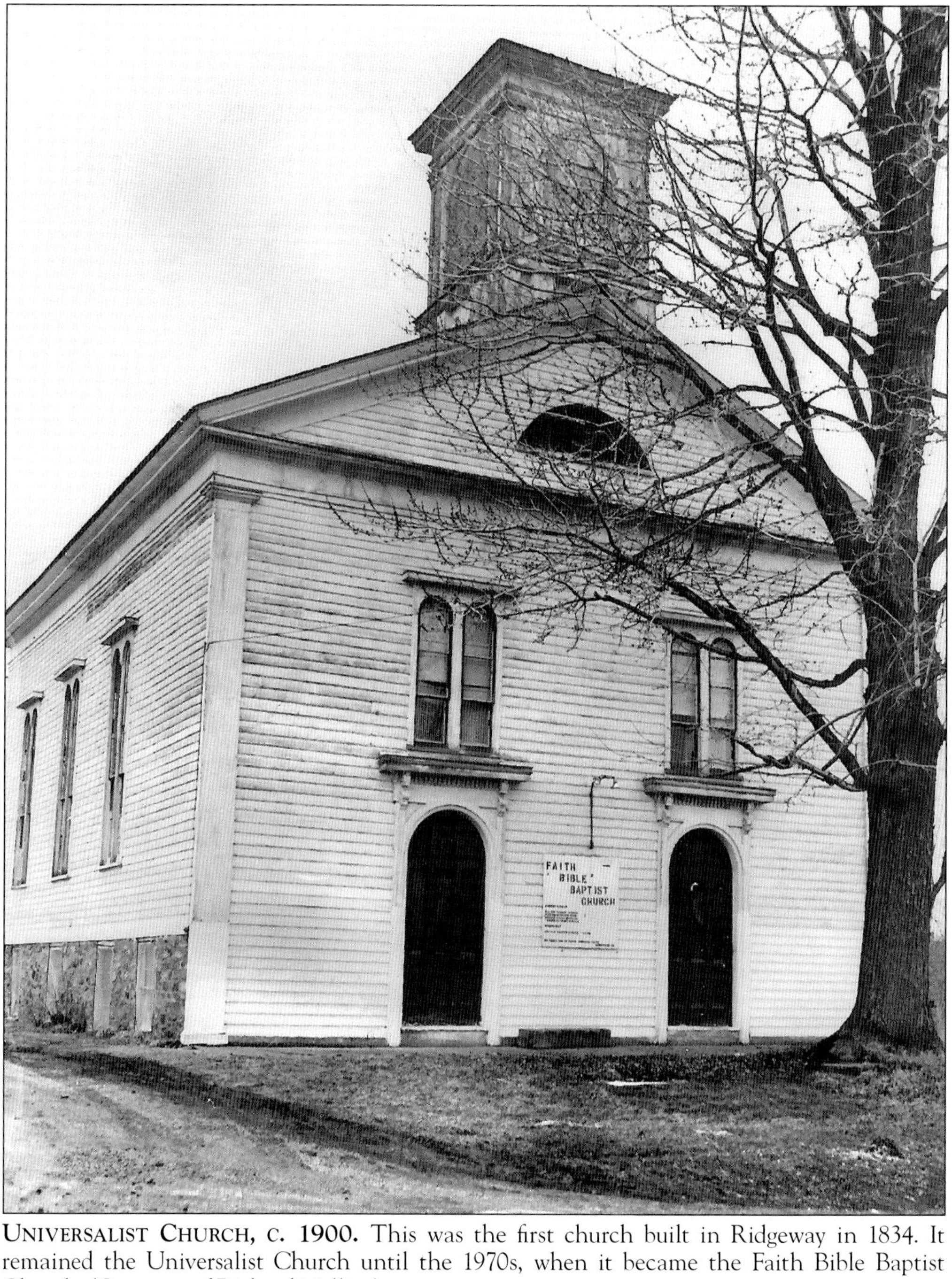

UNIVERSALIST CHURCH, C. 1900. This was the first church built in Ridgeway in 1834. It remained the Universalist Church until the 1970s, when it became the Faith Bible Baptist Church. (Courtesy of Richard Nellist.)

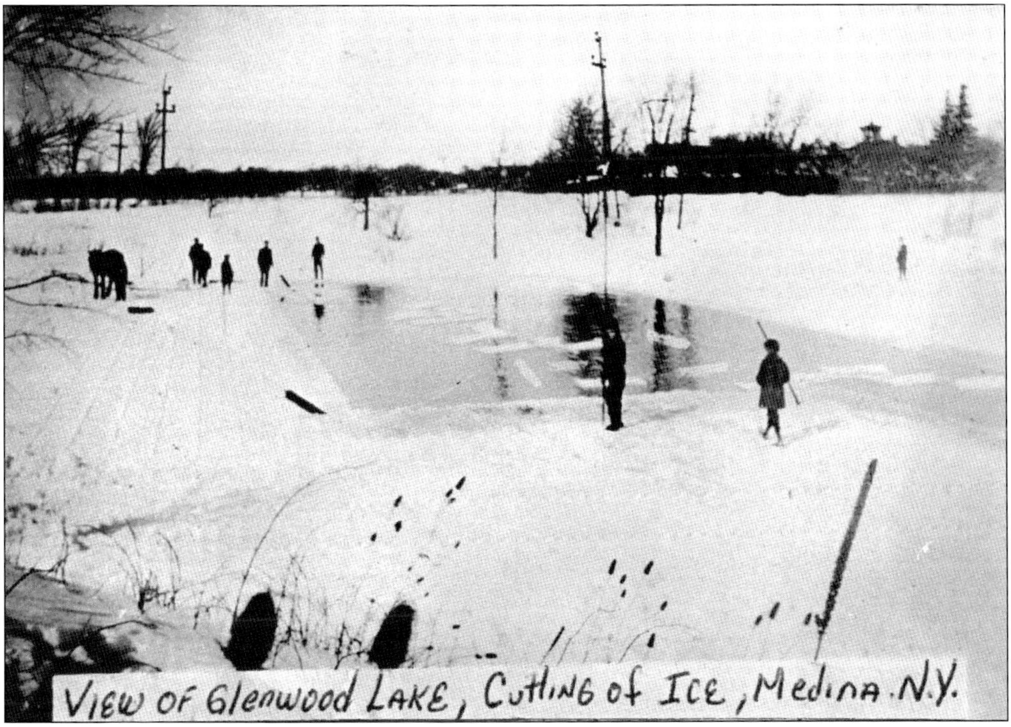

CUTTING ICE, C. 1900. Ice blocks were cut from Glenwood Lake to store in icehouses for residents' use when warm weather came. (Courtesy of Richard Nellist.)

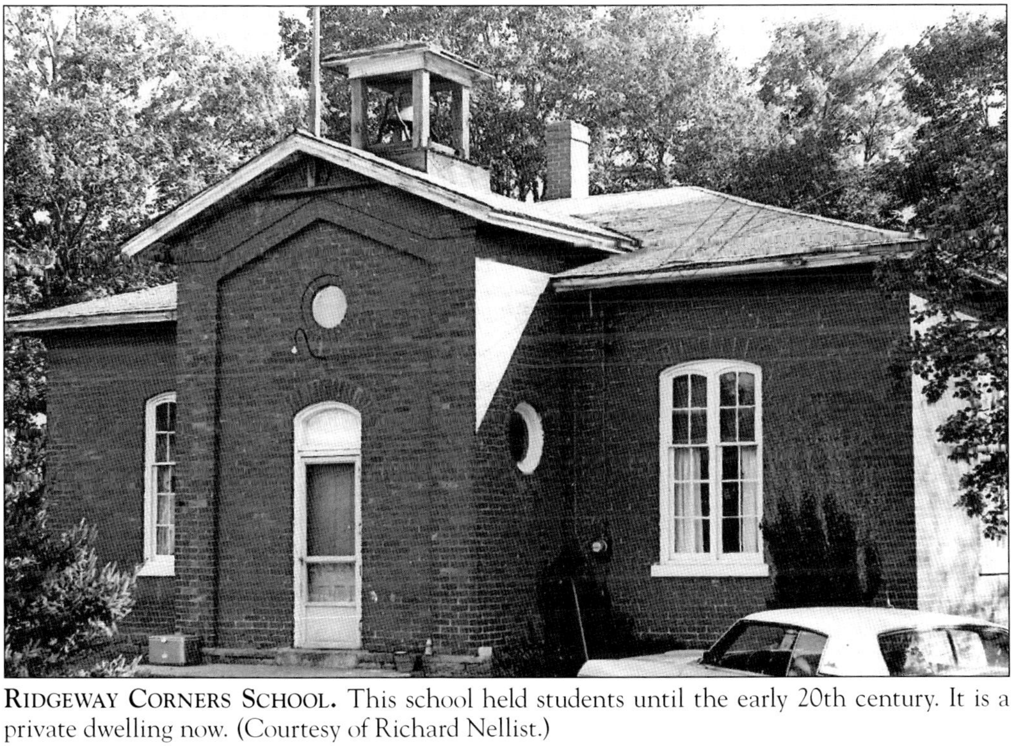

RIDGEWAY CORNERS SCHOOL. This school held students until the early 20th century. It is a private dwelling now. (Courtesy of Richard Nellist.)

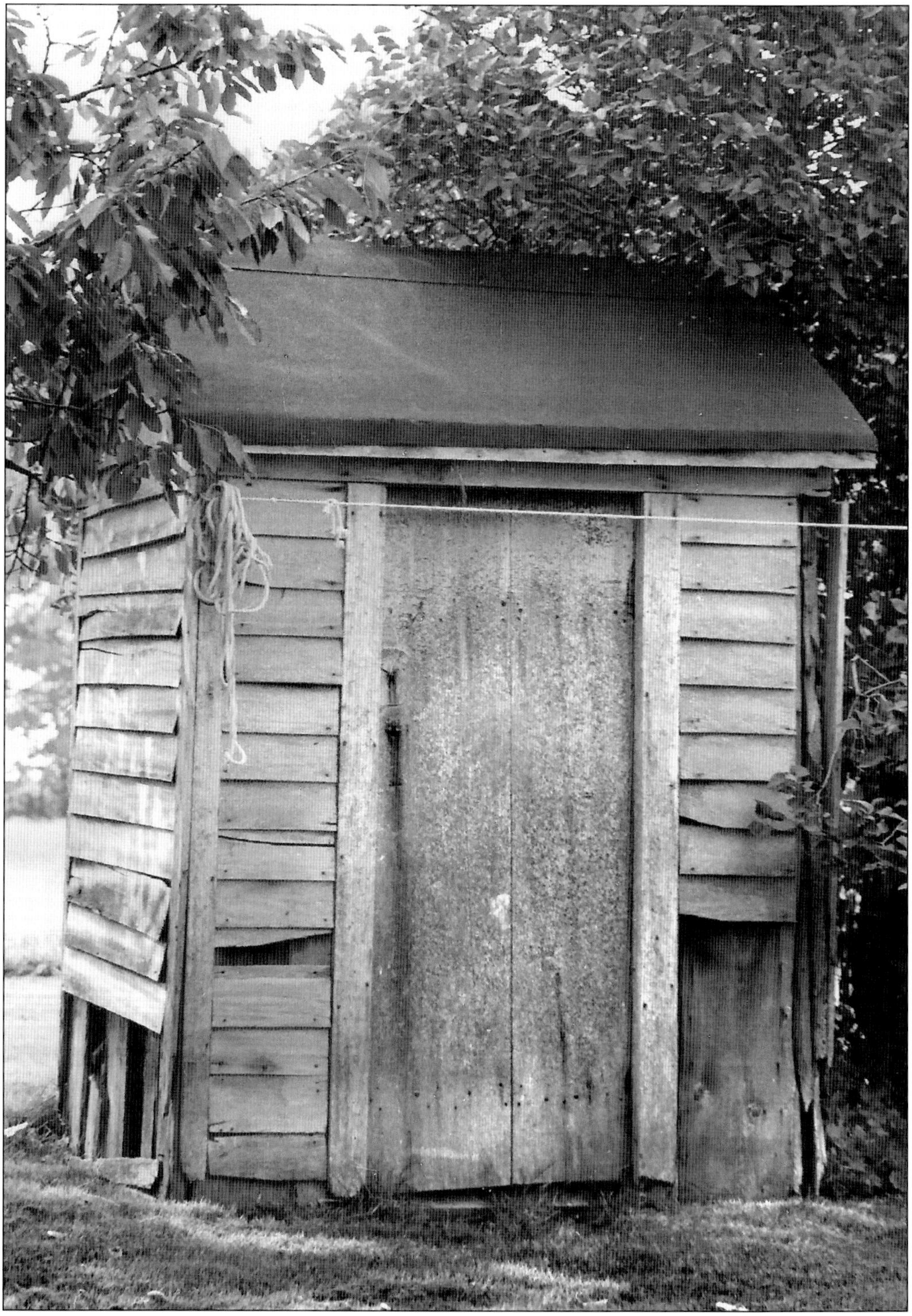

COMFORT STATION, C. 1930. This outhouse was on the Morganberger homestead on Horan Road. Note the convenience of the clothesline attached to the corner of the outhouse, which was said to have been a two-seater. (Courtesy of Richard Nellist.)

Two

AGRICULTURE

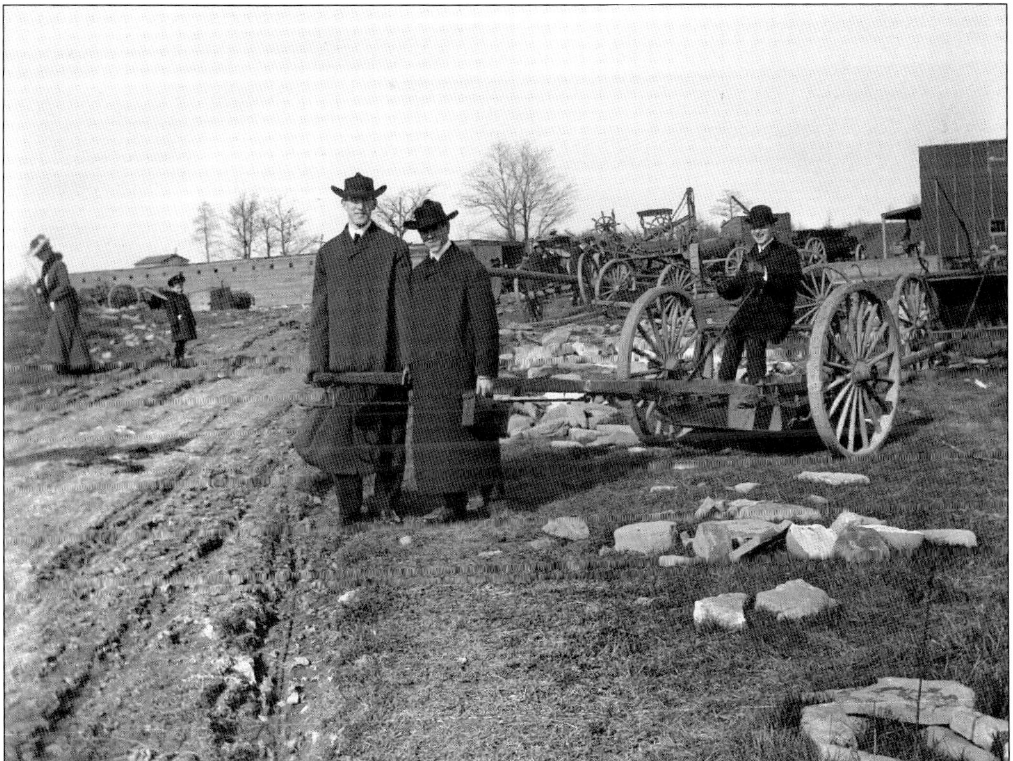

IN THEIR SUNDAY BEST. This unidentified family hams it up for the camera outside a quarry on North Gravel Road about 1910. (Courtesy of Mrs. Elmer Chatt.)

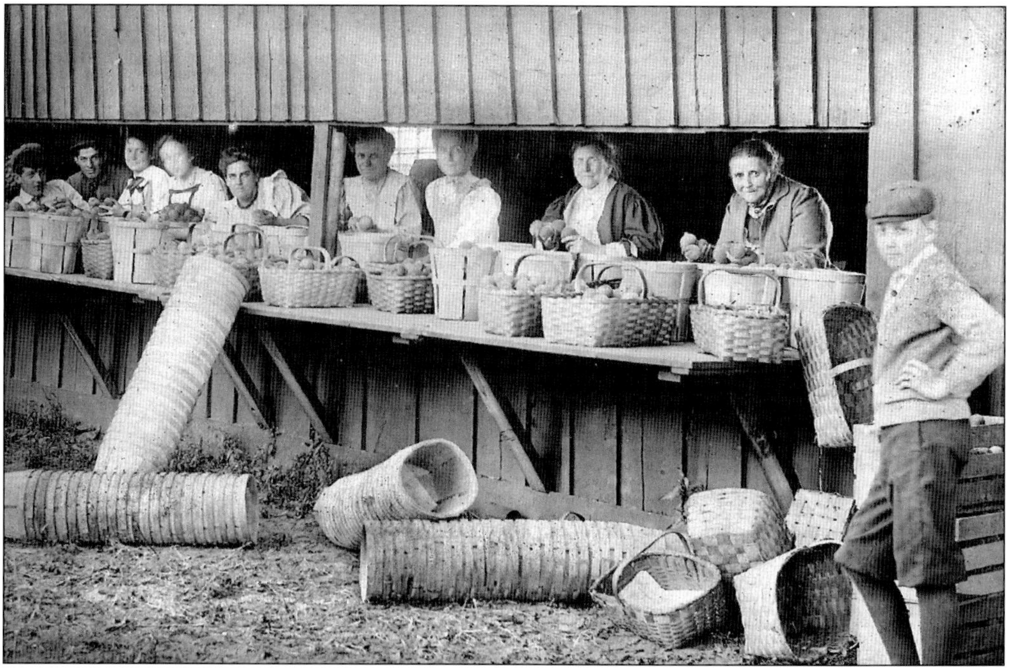

SMILING WORKERS. Peeking through the opening are the workers at Prudom's Fruit Farm in Ridgeway around 1908. (Courtesy of Bill Henderson.)

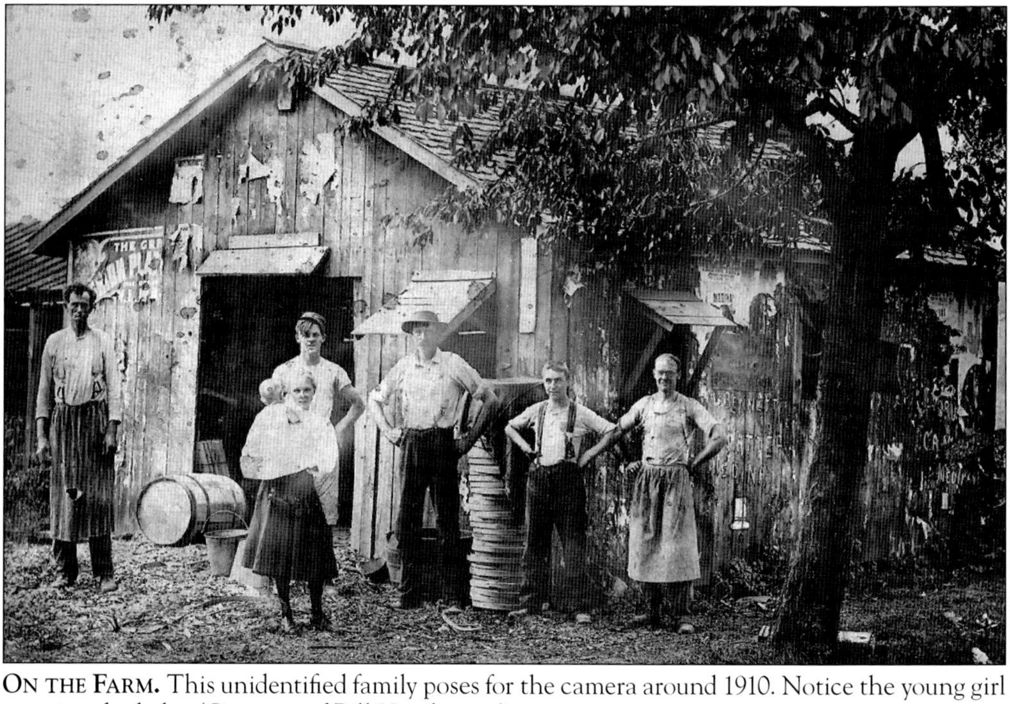

ON THE FARM. This unidentified family poses for the camera around 1910. Notice the young girl carrying the baby. (Courtesy of Bill Henderson.)

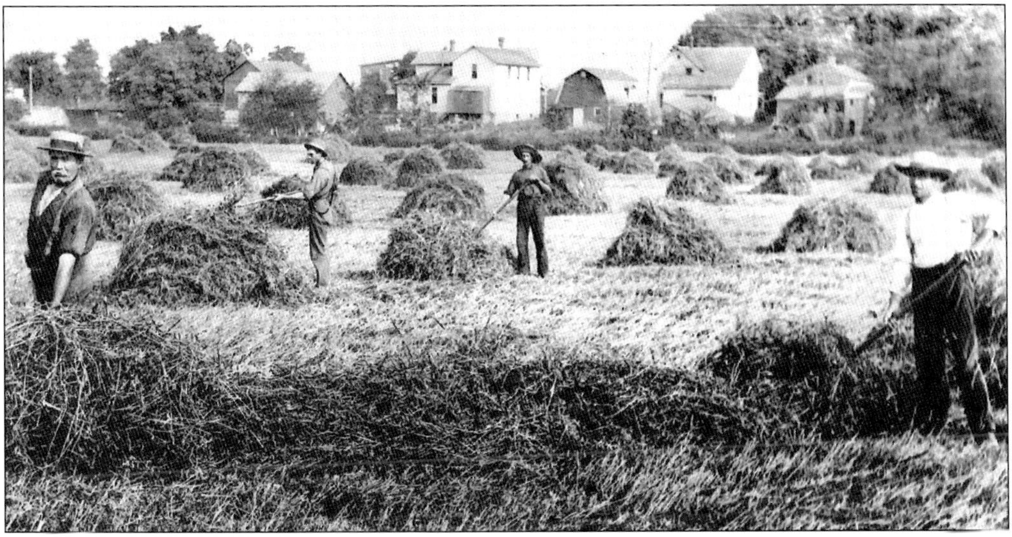

Medina Pea Pickers. These men are harvesting peas on the south side of Ridge Road outside of Jeddo. From left to right are Henry Bateman, Emory Breitsman, Charles Hooker, and Frank Bayne. (Courtesy of Claire Waterson, daughter of Frank Bayne.)

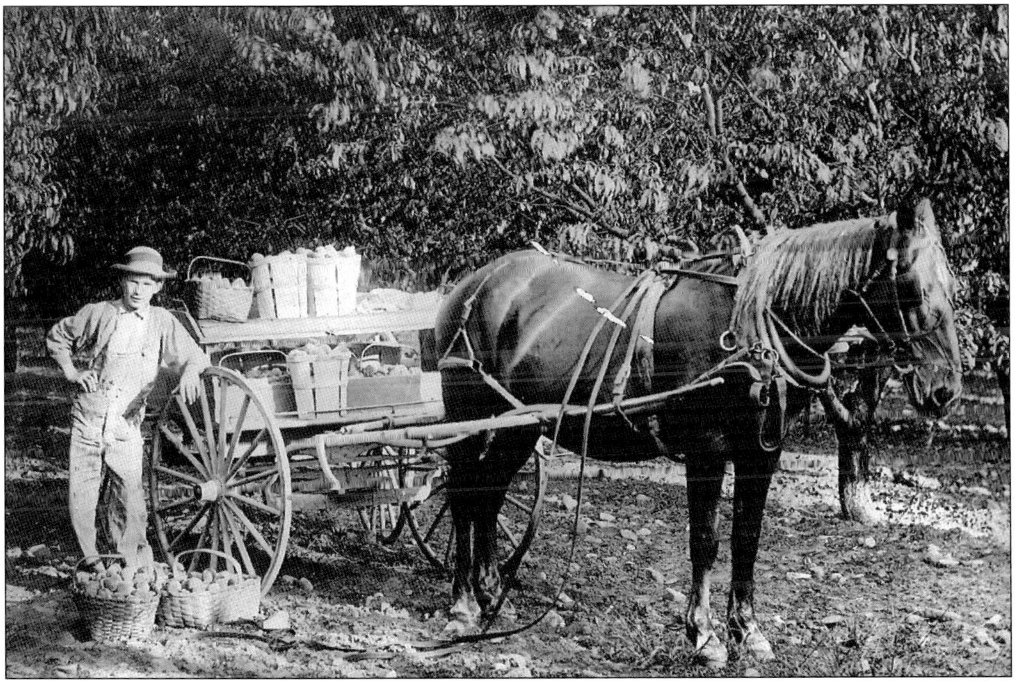

Peach Boy. Willie Pritchard leans on his wagon after picking several baskets of peaches in Jeddo around 1909. (Courtesy of Bill Henderson.)

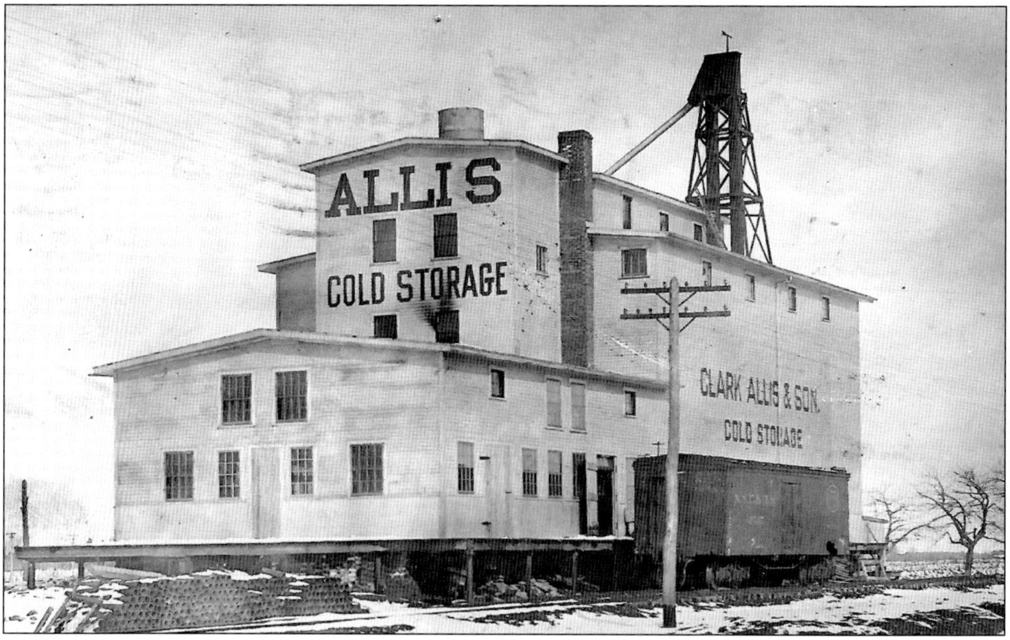

ALLIS COLD STORAGE. Clark Allis and his sons ran this company in the early 20th century. There is an Allis Road in Medina, which is named after this family. Clark was known as the Apple King; Jay Allis was known as the Peach King. (Courtesy of Bill Henderson.)

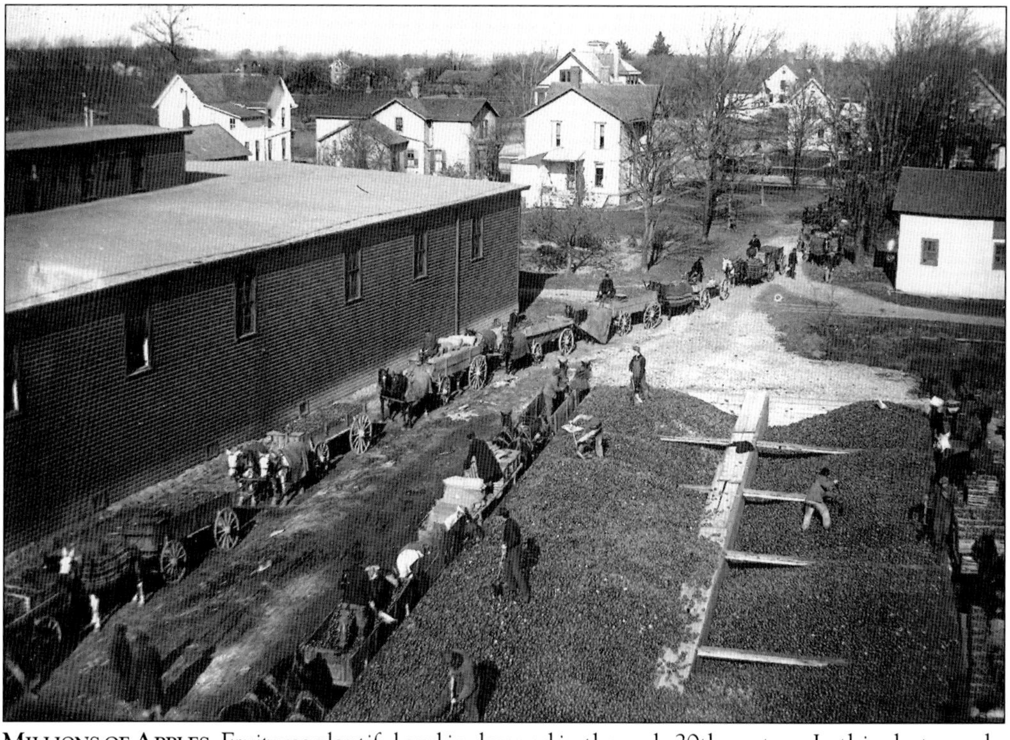

MILLIONS OF APPLES. Fruit was plentiful and in demand in the early 20th century. In this photograph, people are unloading apples at the vinegar works plant. (Courtesy of Mrs. Elmer Chatt.)

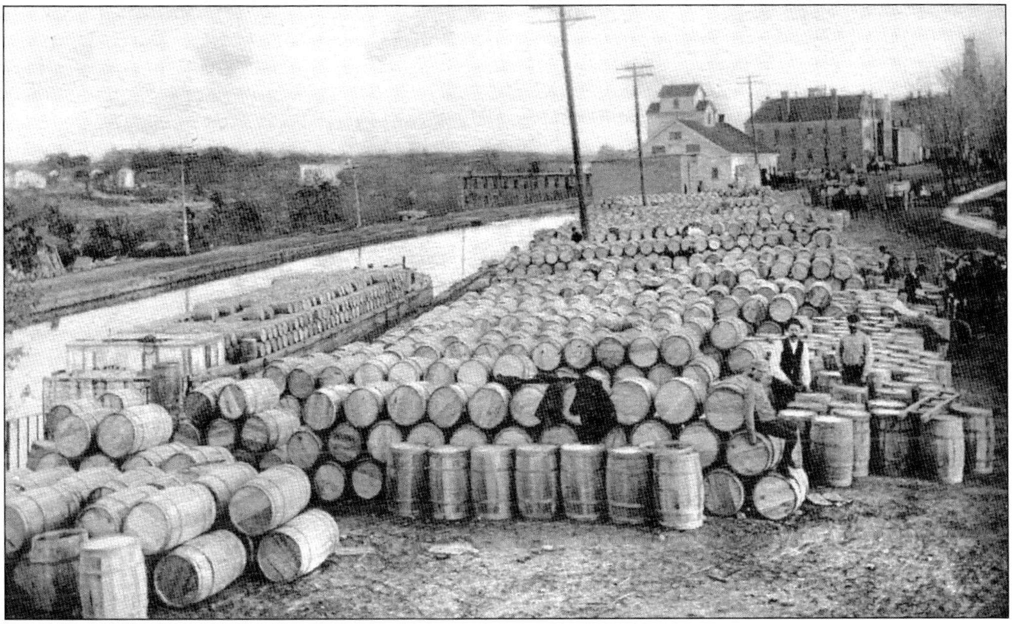

APPLE YARD, C. 1910. This is one of many apple yards along the canal outside of Medina. Apples were packed in barrels. (Courtesy of Bill Henderson.)

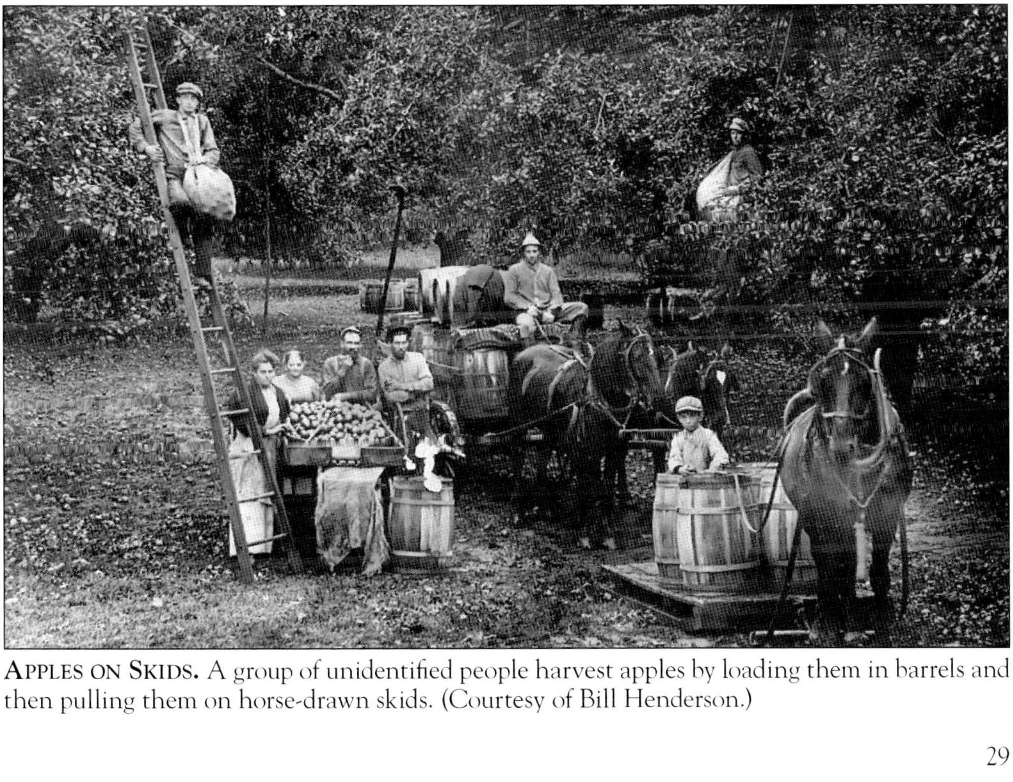

APPLES ON SKIDS. A group of unidentified people harvest apples by loading them in barrels and then pulling them on horse-drawn skids. (Courtesy of Bill Henderson.)

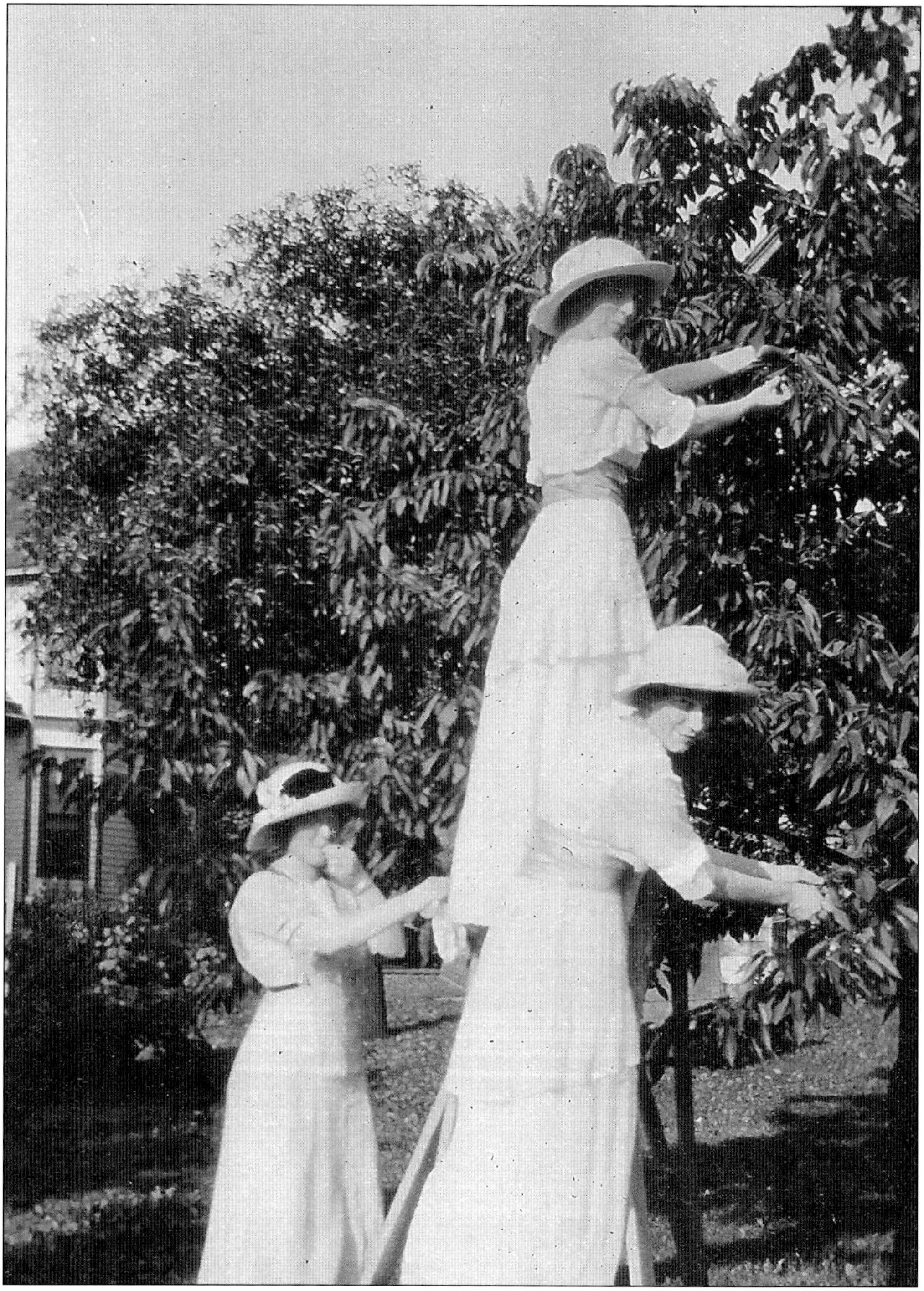

CHERRY PICKERS. Dressed in their Sunday finery, June Bailey, left, Addis Hartt, top, and Janet Bailey enjoy picking cherries on a June afternoon in 1914.

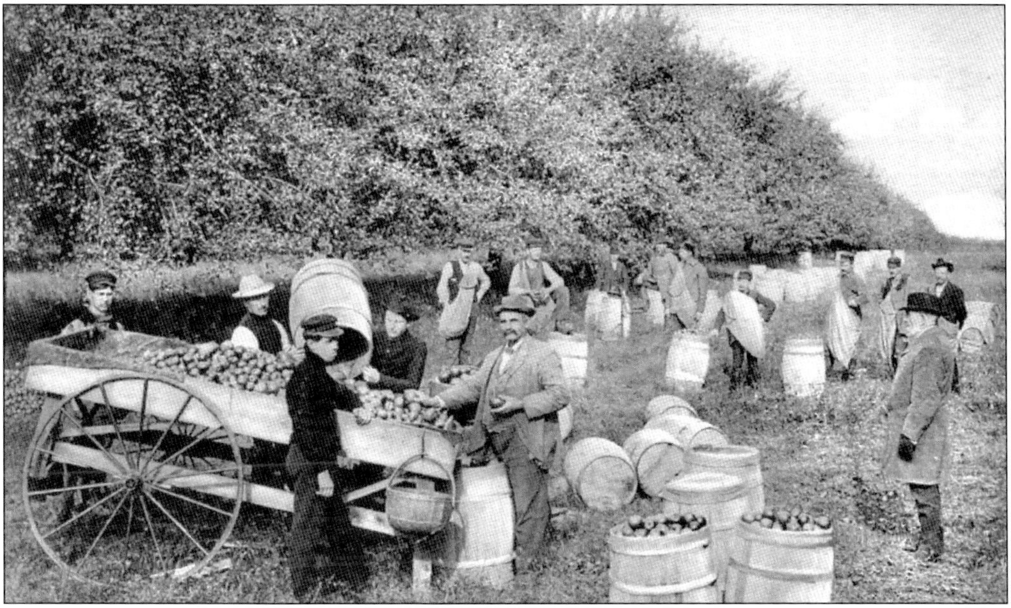

CLARK ALLIS'S ORCHARDS, 1920. Clark Allis, the Apple King, oversaw the harvesting of thousands of acres of apples. (Courtesy of Bill Henderson.)

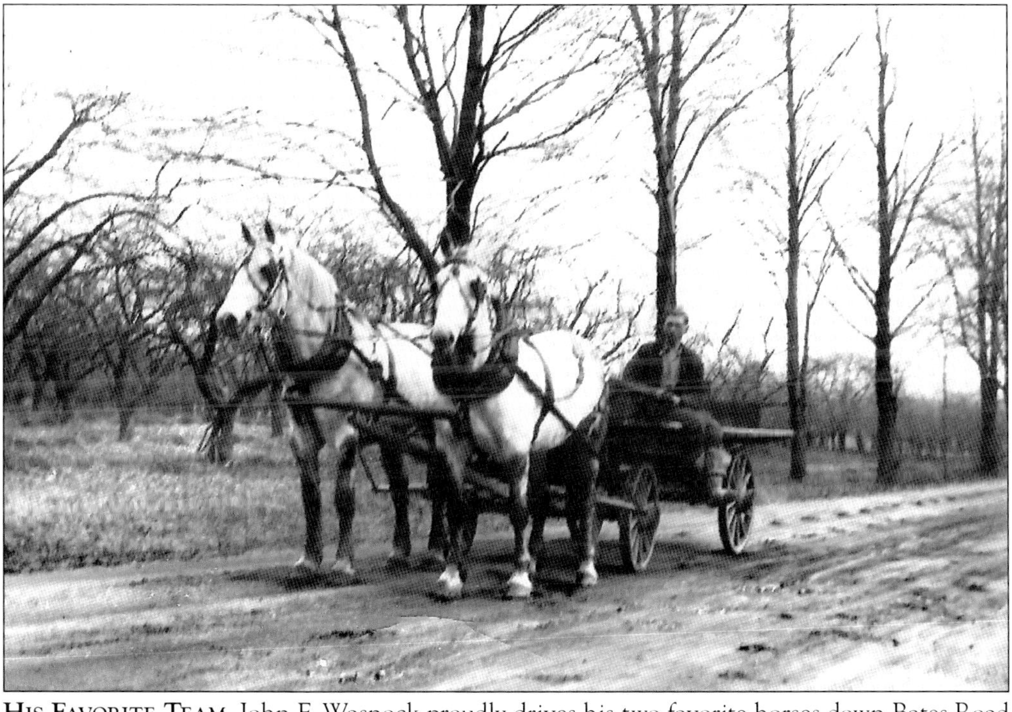

HIS FAVORITE TEAM. John F. Wasnock proudly drives his two favorite horses down Bates Road around 1928, long before it was paved.

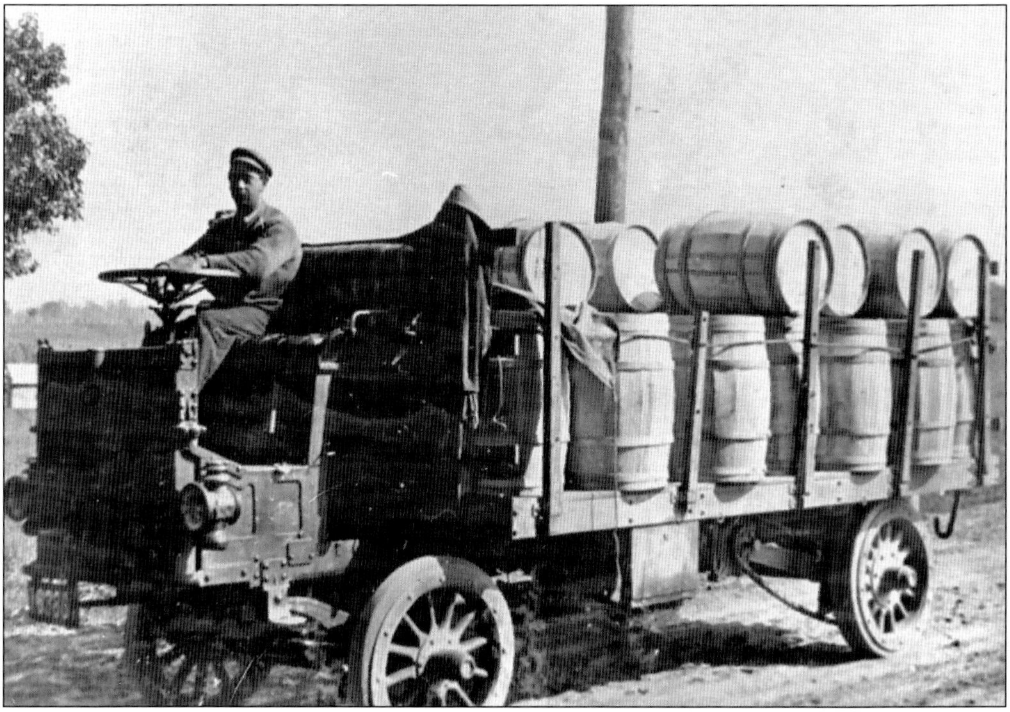

Apples to Market by Truck. An unidentified worker drives apples to market in this unique farm truck about 1913. (Courtesy of Richard Nellist.)

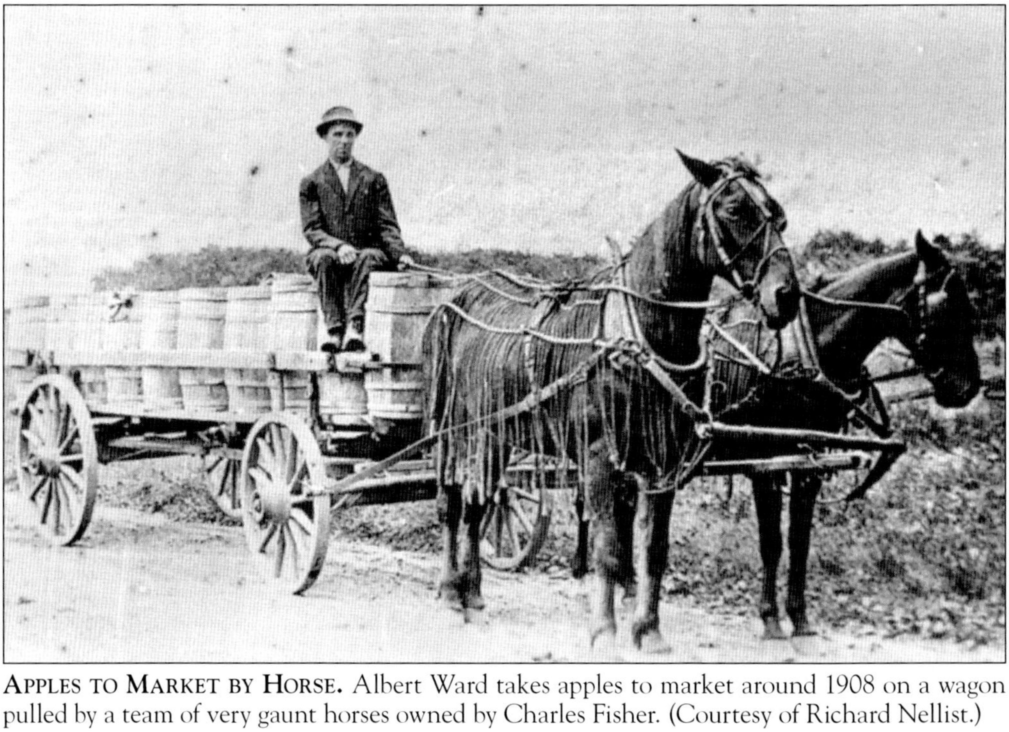

Apples to Market by Horse. Albert Ward takes apples to market around 1908 on a wagon pulled by a team of very gaunt horses owned by Charles Fisher. (Courtesy of Richard Nellist.)

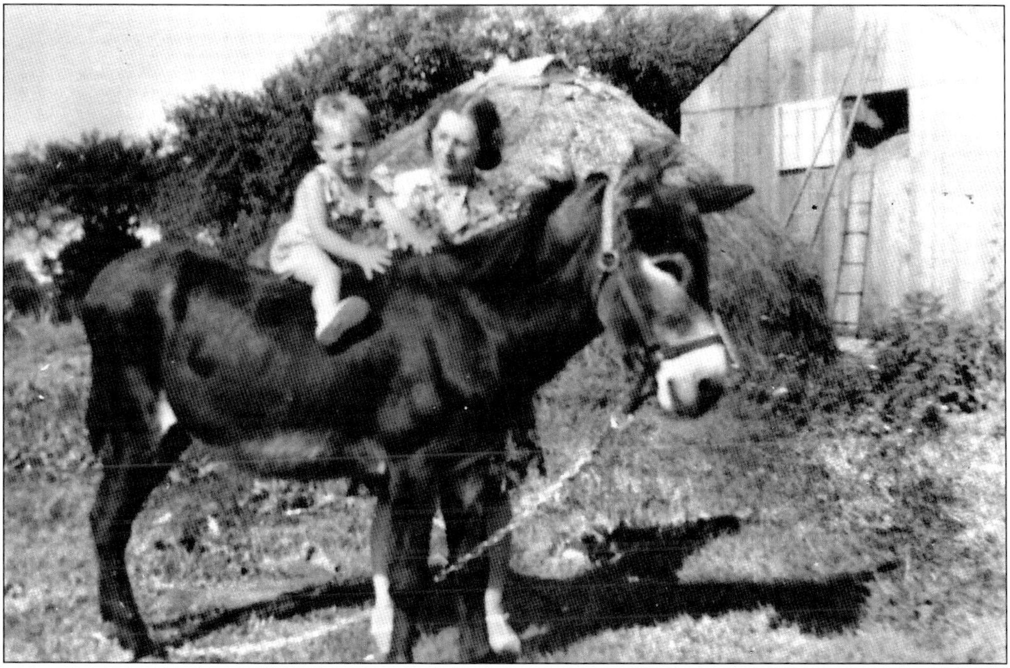

JACK RIDING JACK. A young Jack Wasnock gets help from his mother, Emma King Wasnock, as he takes a ride on Jack the donkey around 1940. The donkey belonged to Jack Wasnock's grandparents Peter and Grace King. Peter built the barn in the background, located on Postle Road. (Courtesy of John Wasnock.)

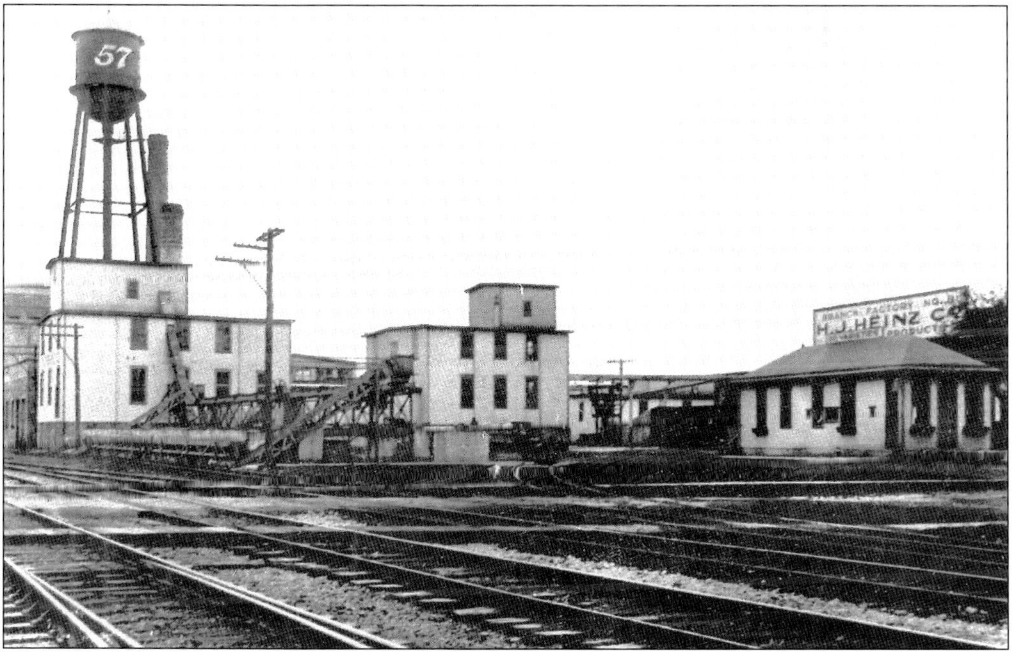

H. J. HEINZ COMPANY. This was a longtime canning/bottling business in Medina, lasting until the 1950s. The building was taken over by the Fisher Price Company, which was a major employer of Medina residents until the 1990s. (Courtesy of Richard Nellist.)

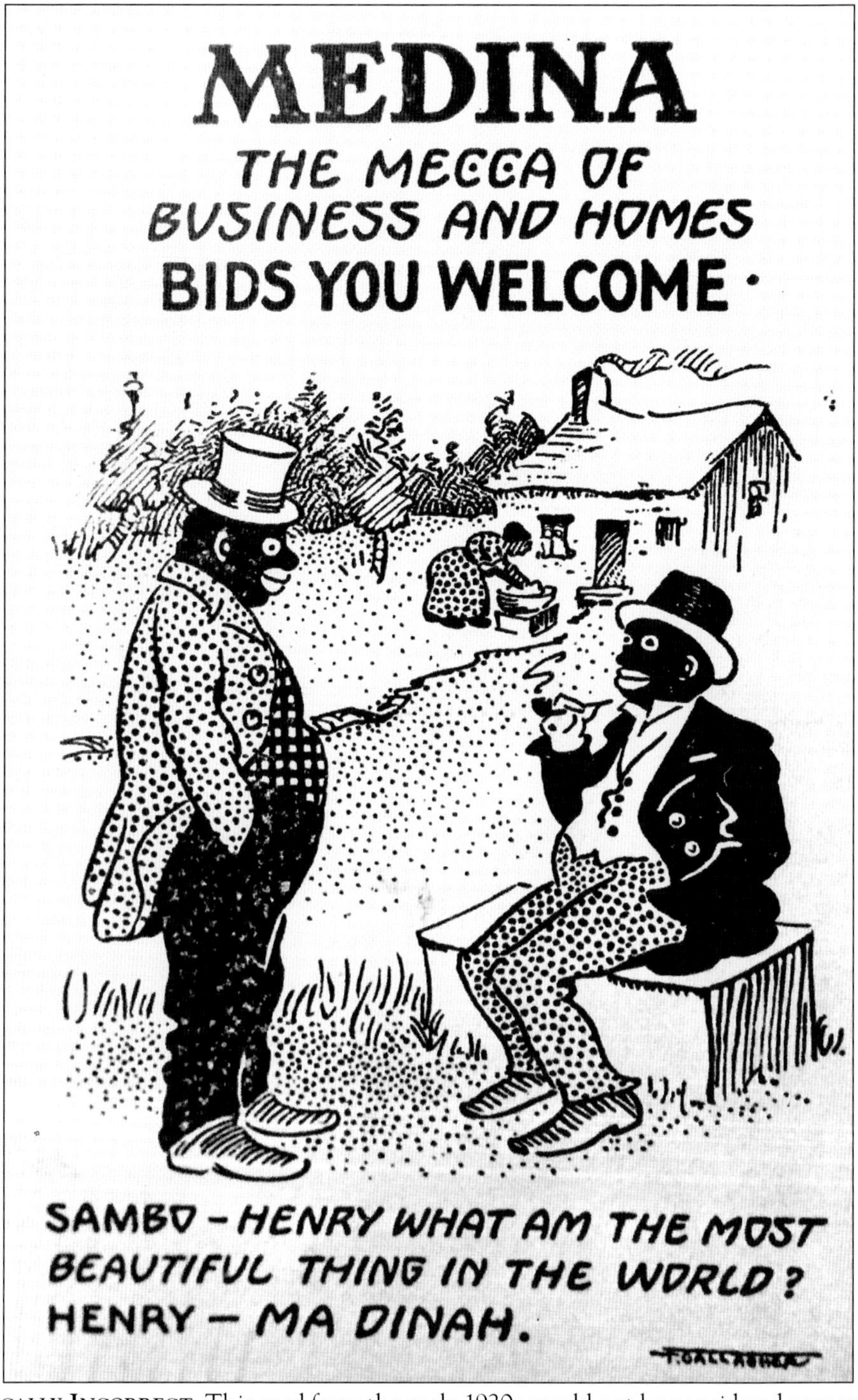

POLITICALLY INCORRECT. This card from the early 1920s would not be considered proper today, but it was accepted after the beginning of the 20th century. It states, "Medina the Mecca of Business and Homes Bids You Welcome." Sambo says, "Henry what am the most beautiful thing in the world?" Henry answers, "Ma Dinah." It was a false rumor that the joke gave Medina its name. In fact, no one knows who named it. (Courtesy of Richard Nellist.)

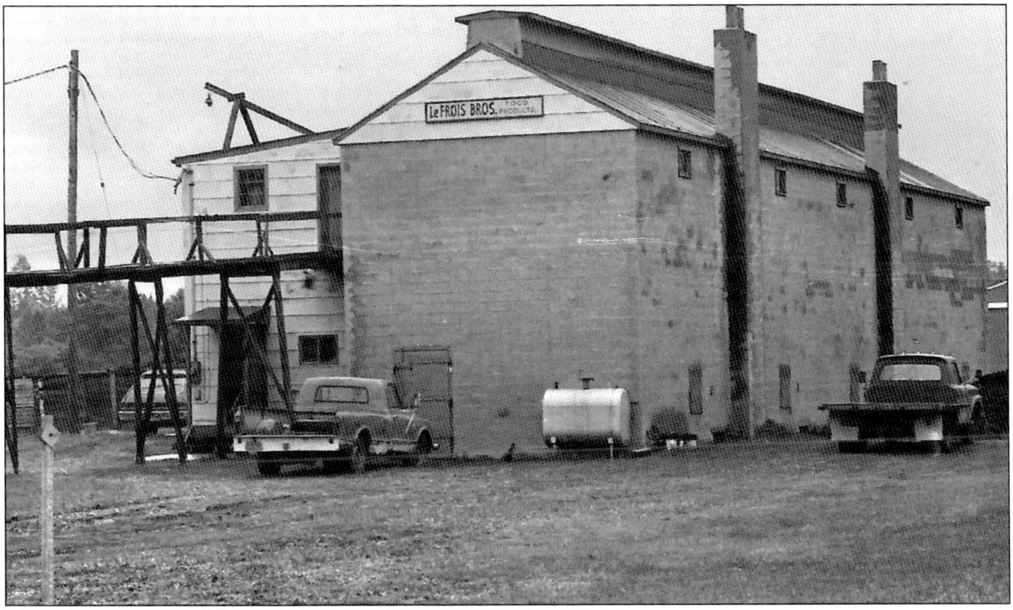

DRY HOUSE AT MILLERS. Dry houses were common in the late 19th and early 20th centuries. People took their fruits and vegetables there for drying, selling much of the finished product. This photograph was taken in the 1970s. The building is now used as a food processing plant. (Courtesy of Richard Nellist.)

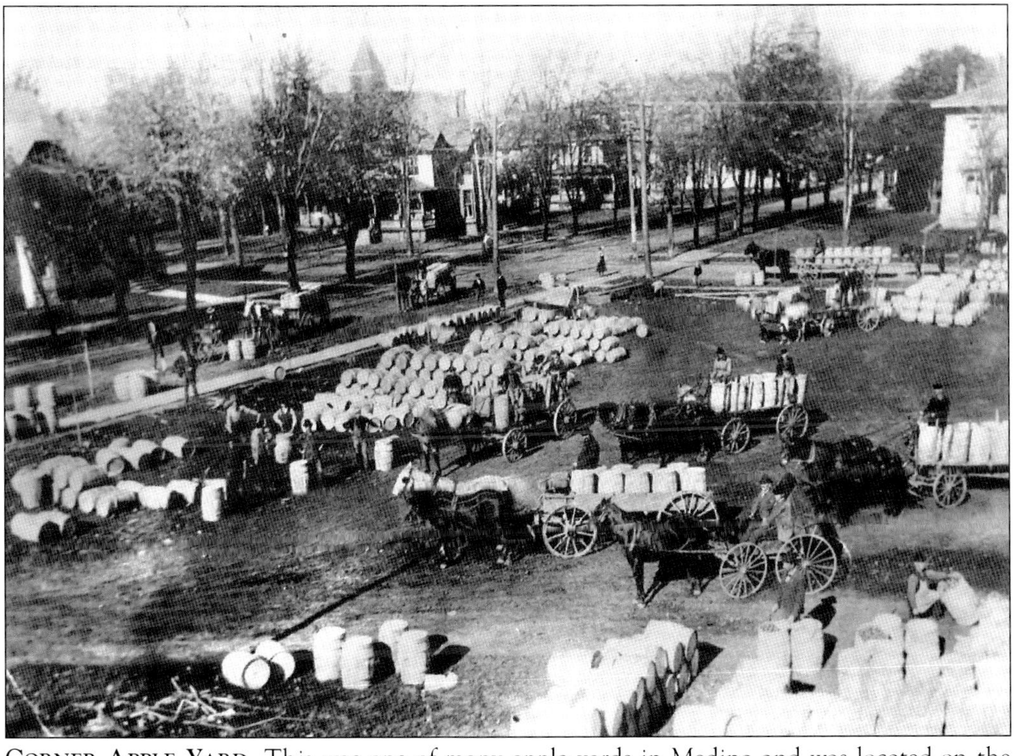

CORNER APPLE YARD. This was one of many apple yards in Medina and was located on the corner of Park and West Avenues around 1900. (Courtesy of Richard Nellist.)

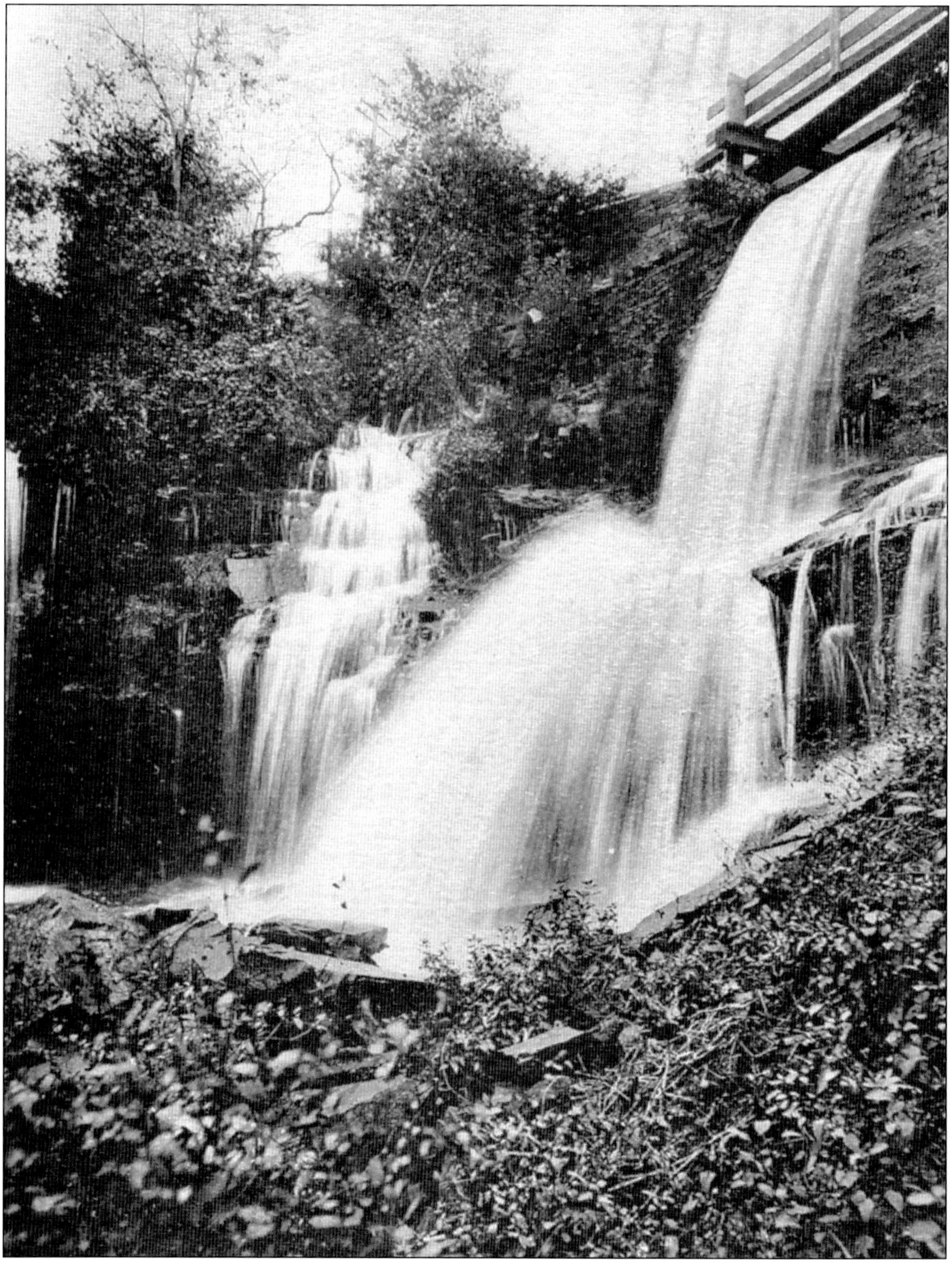

RAINBOW FALLS, 1909. One of the many falls, Rainbow Falls was majestic and breathtaking. (Courtesy of Bill Henderson.)

Three

WATERWAYS

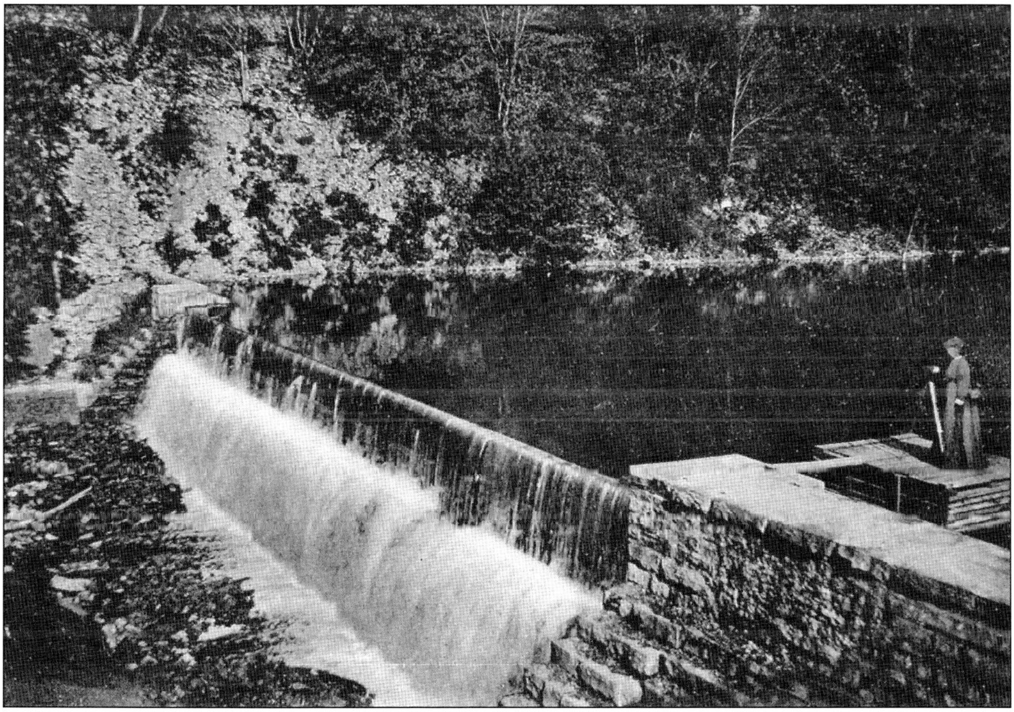

THE OLD DAM, 1909. A solitary woman stands on the edge of the dam over Oak Orchard Creek. This dam was part of the A. L. Swett Iron Works, created in April 1896. The spillway was 110 feet wide. (Courtesy of Bill Henderson.)

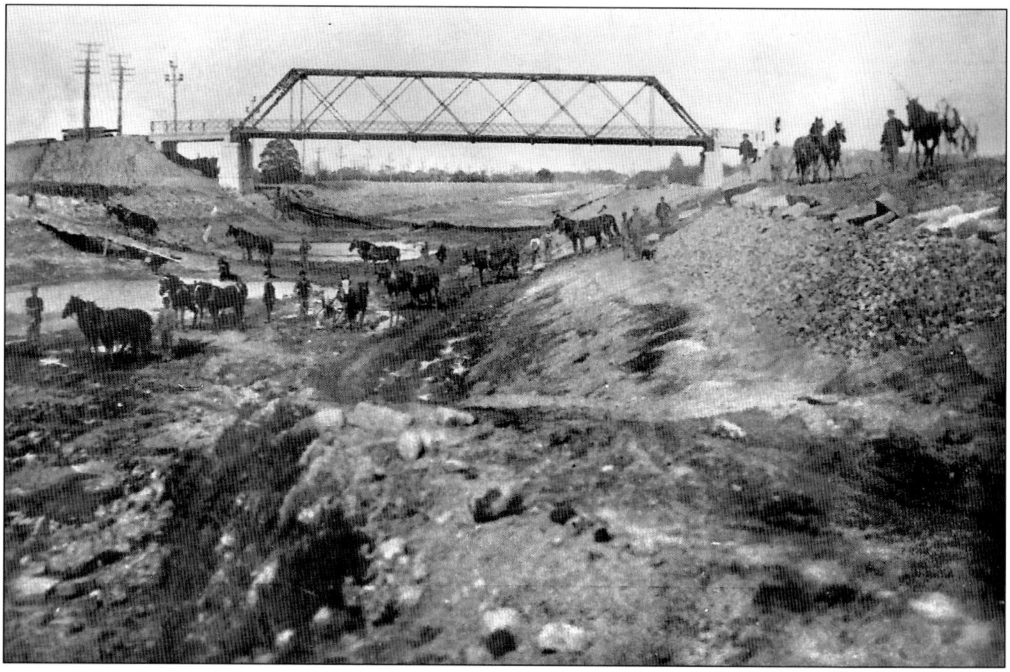

CANAL WORK. Men and teams of horses were busy on canal reconstruction at Beale Road when the water was drained for winter around 1900. Even now the water is drained from the canal each winter about December 1, and it is refilled in the spring. (Courtesy of Richard Nellist.)

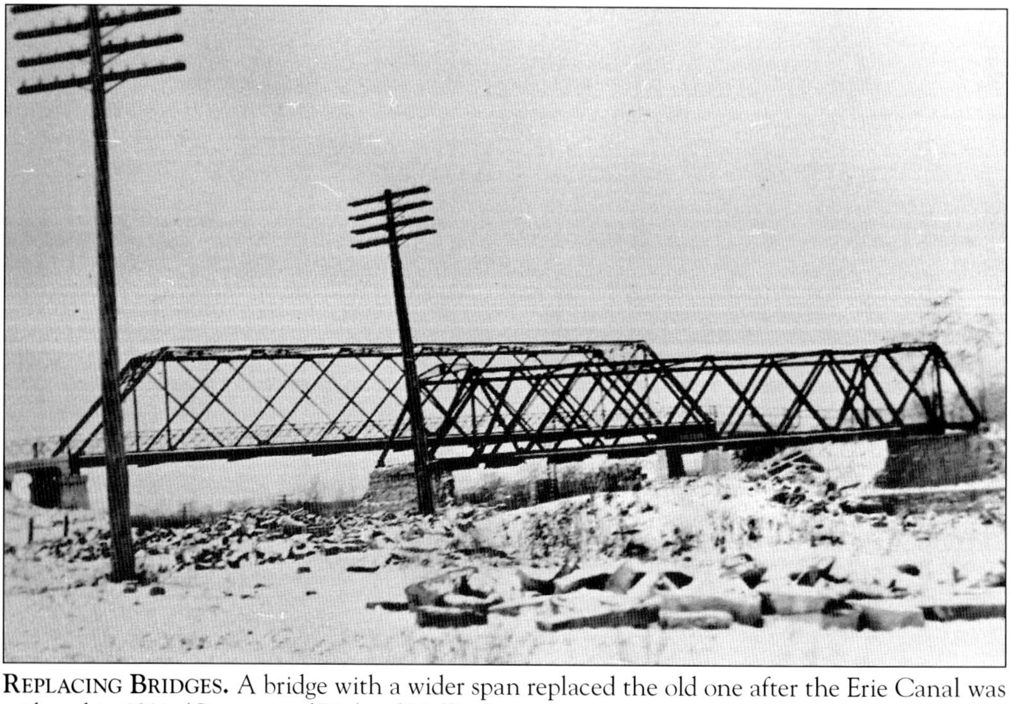

REPLACING BRIDGES. A bridge with a wider span replaced the old one after the Erie Canal was widened in 1911. (Courtesy of Richard Nellist.)

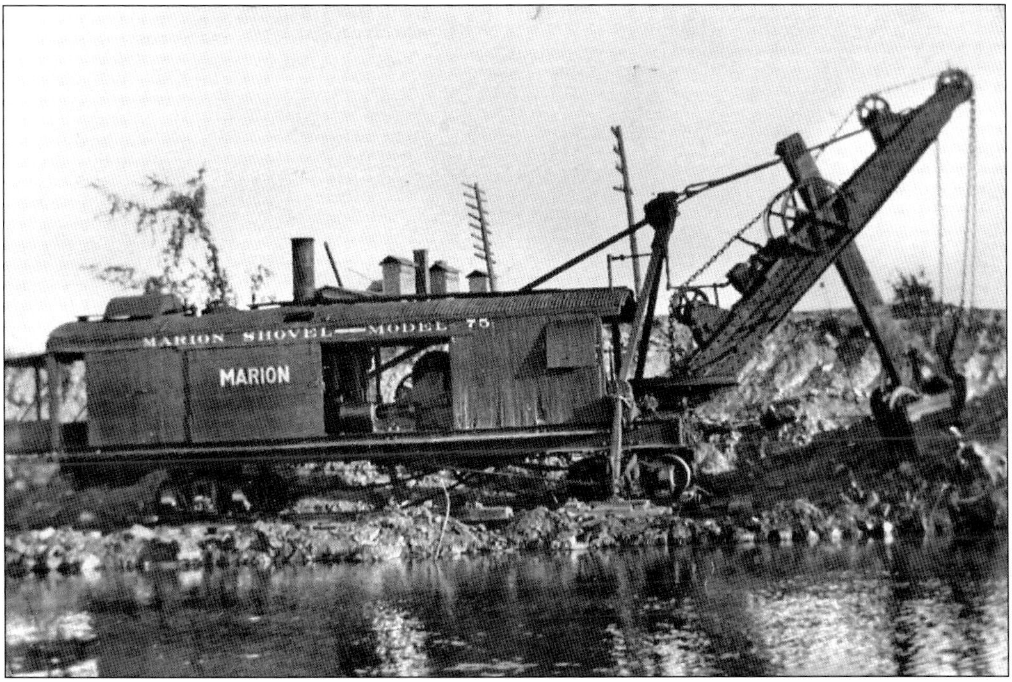

WORKING ON THE CANAL. This steam shovel chugged away, digging out the Erie Canal to make it deeper in 1902. Behind it are the cupolas of a dry house on State Street. (Courtesy of Richard Nellist.)

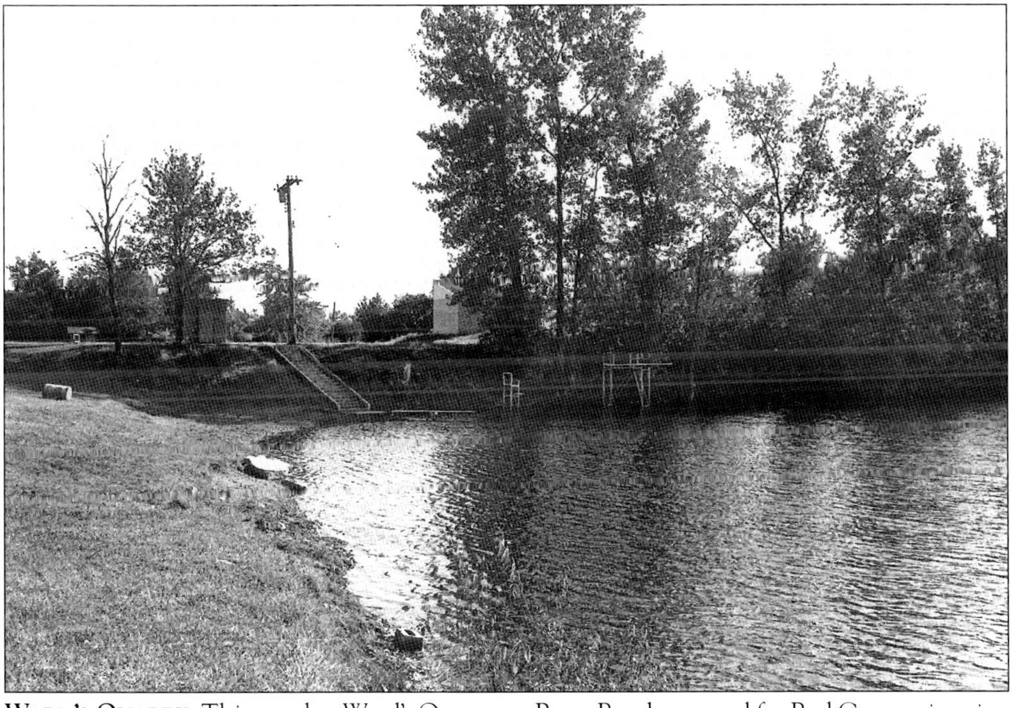

WARD'S QUARRY. This pond at Ward's Quarry on Bates Road was used for Red Cross swimming classes in the 1940s after the quarrying business waned. (Courtesy of Richard Nellist.)

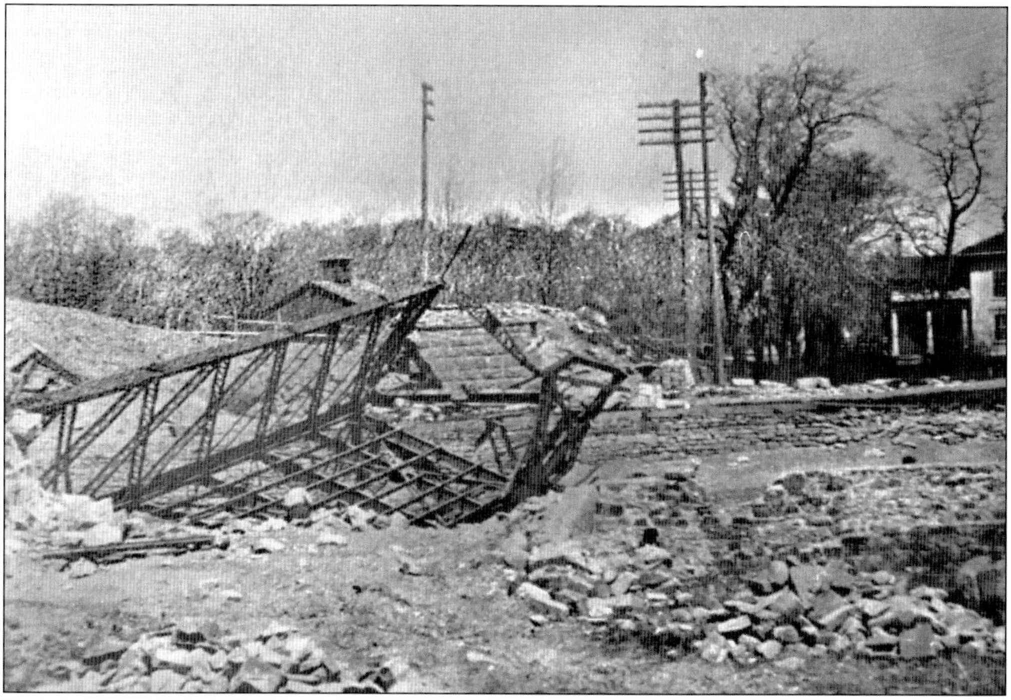

Bridge Collapse. The bridge on Fruit Avenue did not withstand the wrath of the winter of 1912 and had to be replaced. (Courtesy of Richard Nellist.)

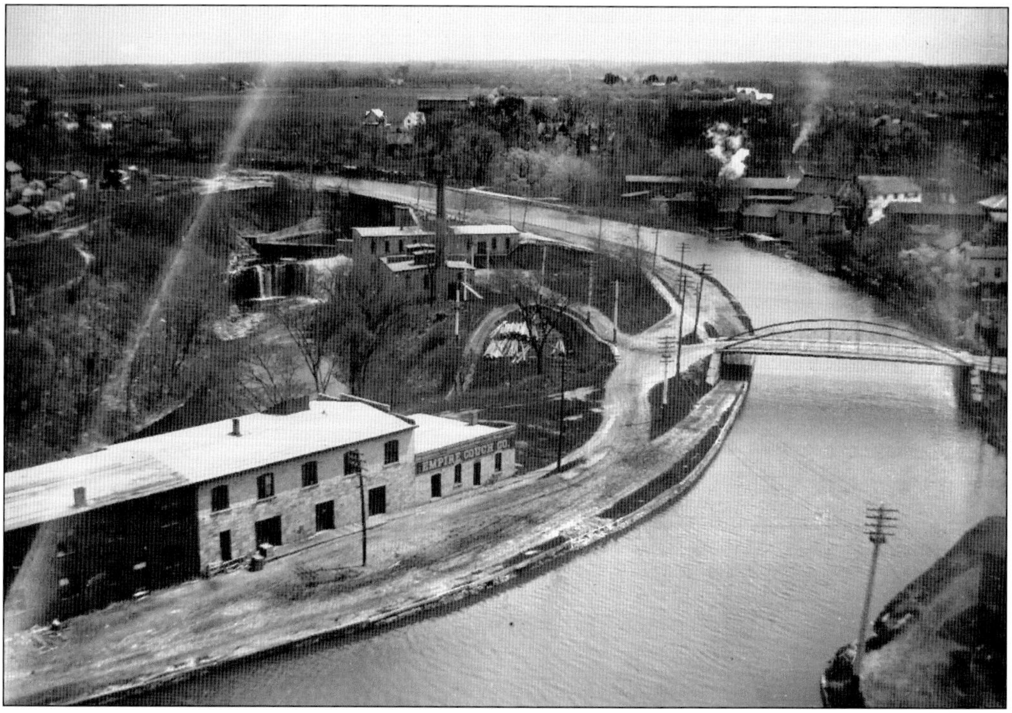

Church Street Bridge. The Erie Canal curves like a swan around Medina's Church Street about 1890. (Courtesy of Frank Berger.)

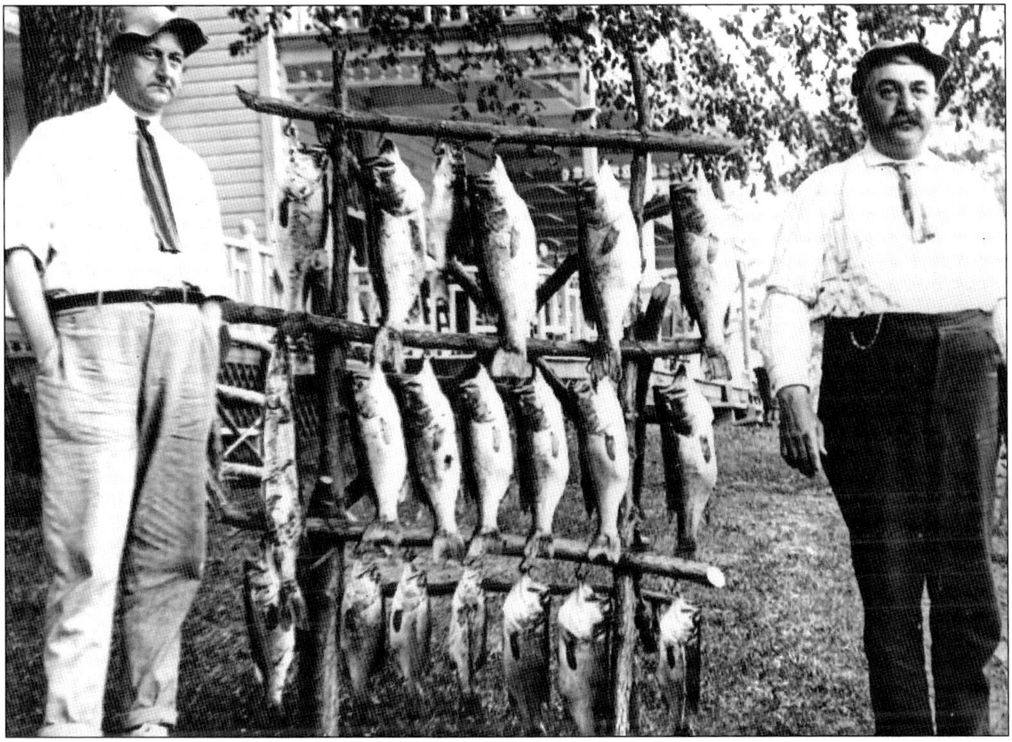

Fish in a Frame. Harry Spencer (left) and Bruce Baldwin pose with their catch from Oak Orchard Creek around 1910. (Courtesy of Tillman's Village Inn.)

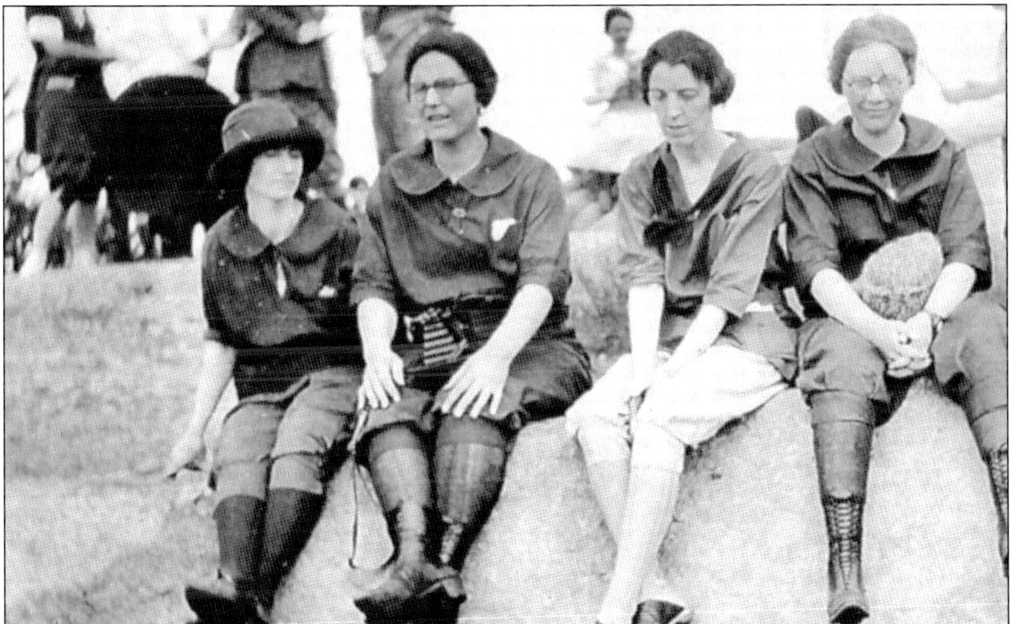

Sunning on a Rock. From left to right, Elaine Hartt, June Bailey, Addis Hartt, and Alice Bailey enjoy sunning themselves on a rock near Oak Orchard Creek around 1914. (Courtesy of the A. Hartt estate.)

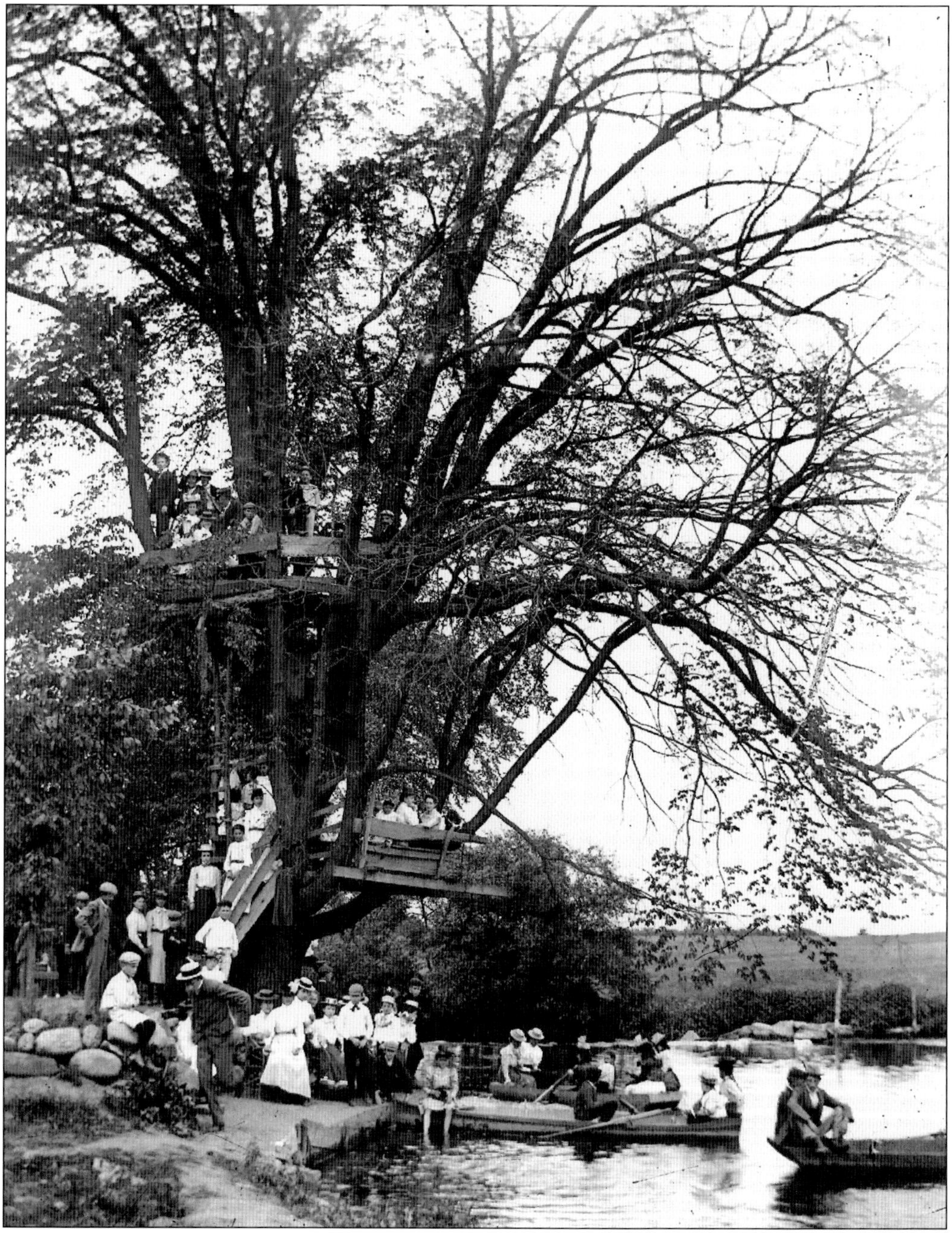

PLAYING ON THE ELM TREE. Elm Park got its name for the huge elm tree located on the banks of Glenwood Lake. The tree was so large that residents made a playground out of it, as seen here. There was a large swing that accommodated two people on the seat, great for lovers, as long as they had a proper chaperone. The park closed about 1930. (Courtesy of Mrs. Elmer Chatt.)

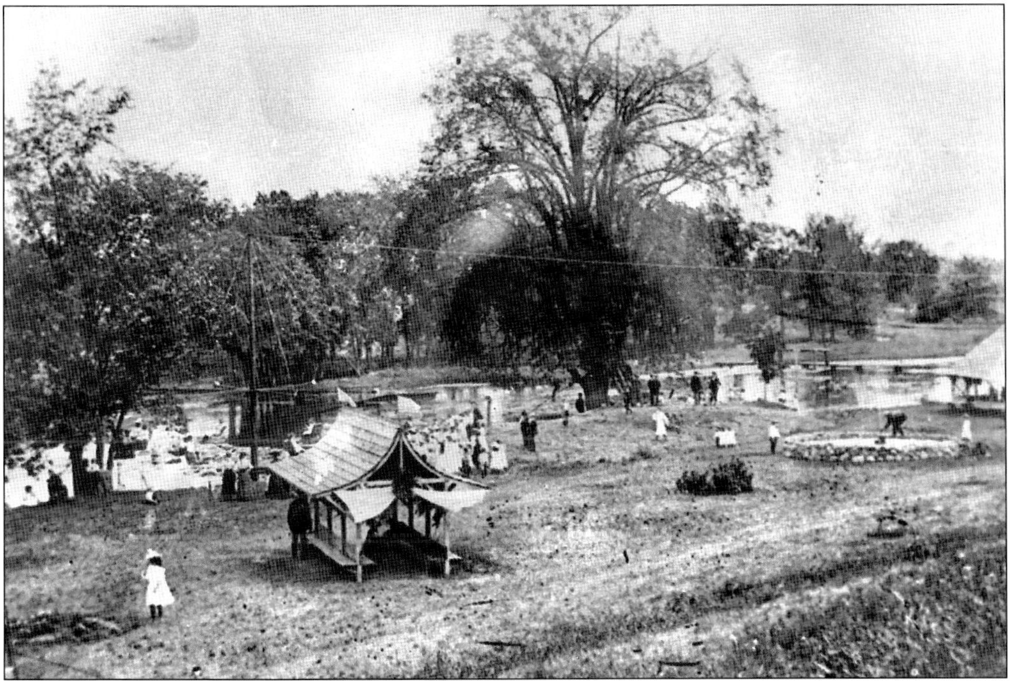

ELM PARK, C. 1905. The park was only about a mile north of Medina's business district and was the local pleasure resort for residents before automobiles made travel to other areas possible. (Courtesy of Richard Nellist.)

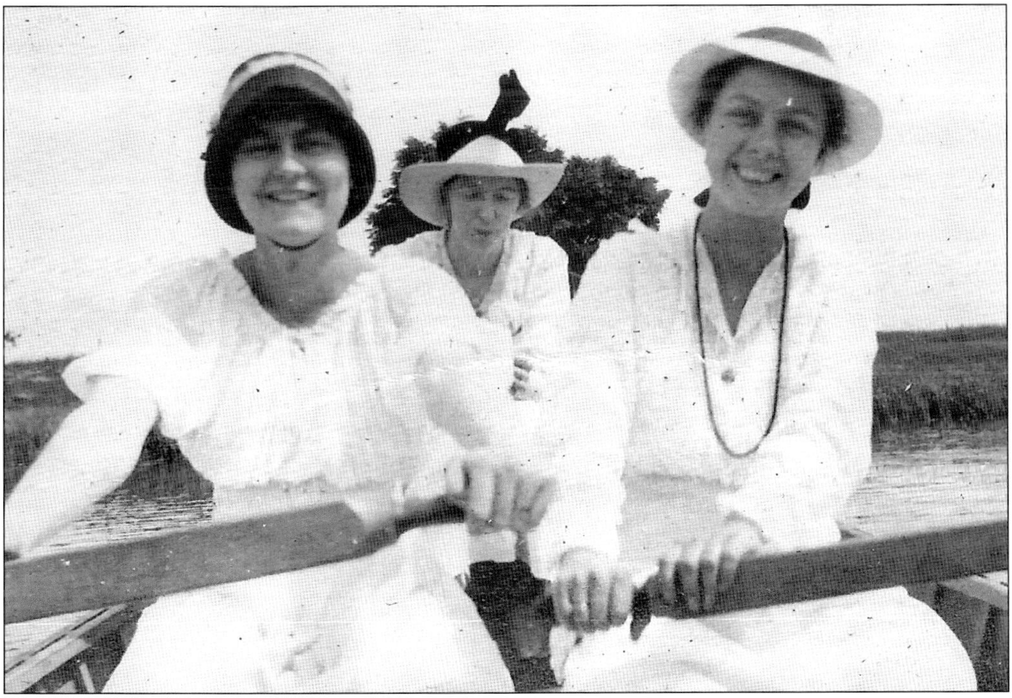

MEDINA ROWERS. From left to right, June Bailey, Addis Hartt, and Alice Bailey had fun rowing across Glenwood Lake in their white dresses around 1915. (Courtesy of the A. Hartt estate.)

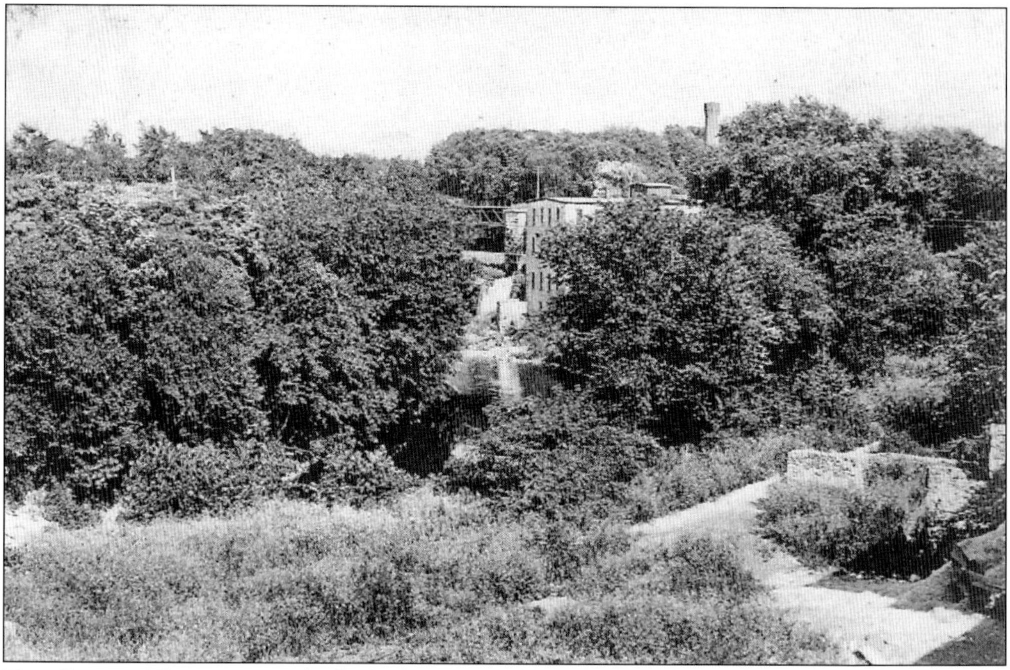

THE GORGE. The gorge overlooked a large waterfall used for one of the first mills, just north of Medina on Oak Orchard Creek. (Courtesy of Grant-Pollard Insurance Office.)

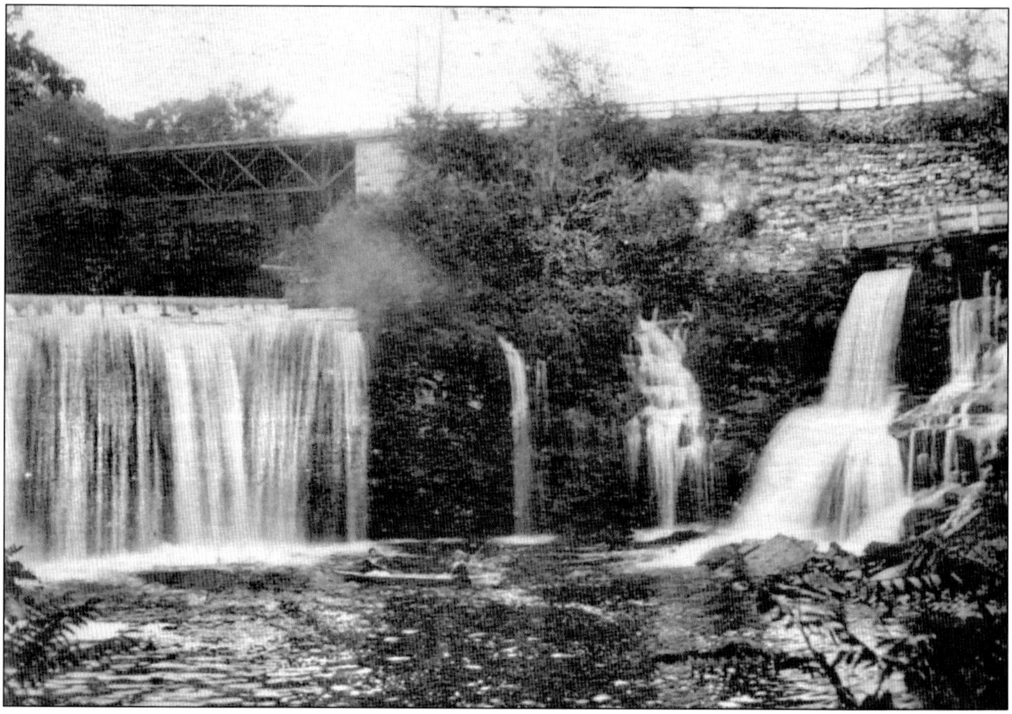

MANY FALLS. Before Oak Orchard Creek and the Erie Canal were diverted to create power, there were numerous falls on Oak Orchard Creek. This is how they looked before they were channeled into other outlets. (Courtesy of the Charles Rand Penney Collection.)

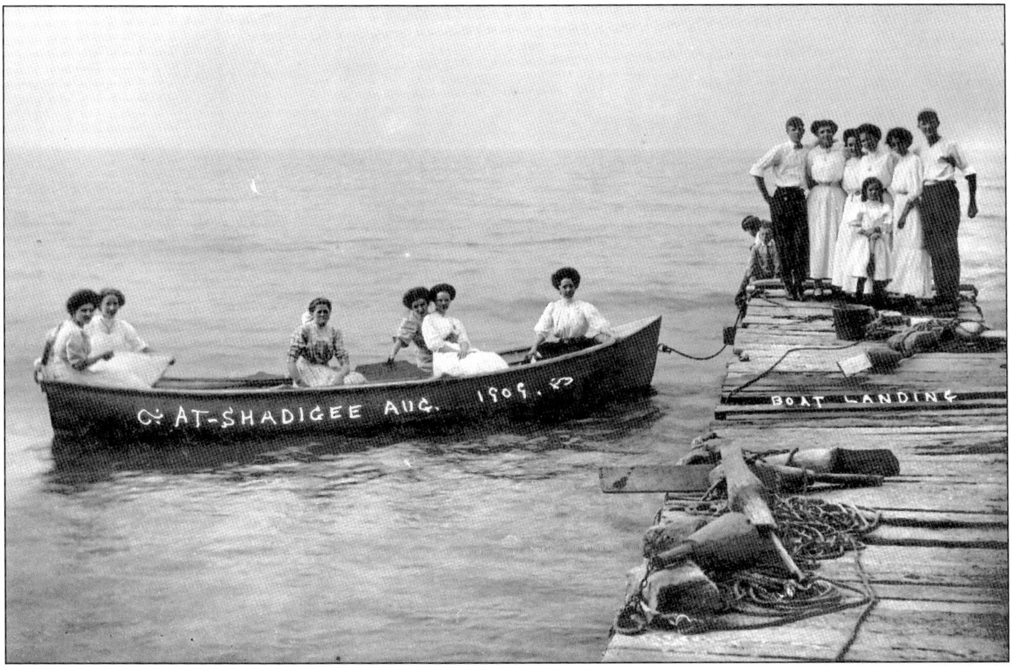

BOATING ON THE LAKE. A youthful church group took an excursion to Lake Ontario in 1909. The unidentified people wrote on the photograph that they were going to Shadigee. (Courtesy of the Charles Rand Penney Collection.)

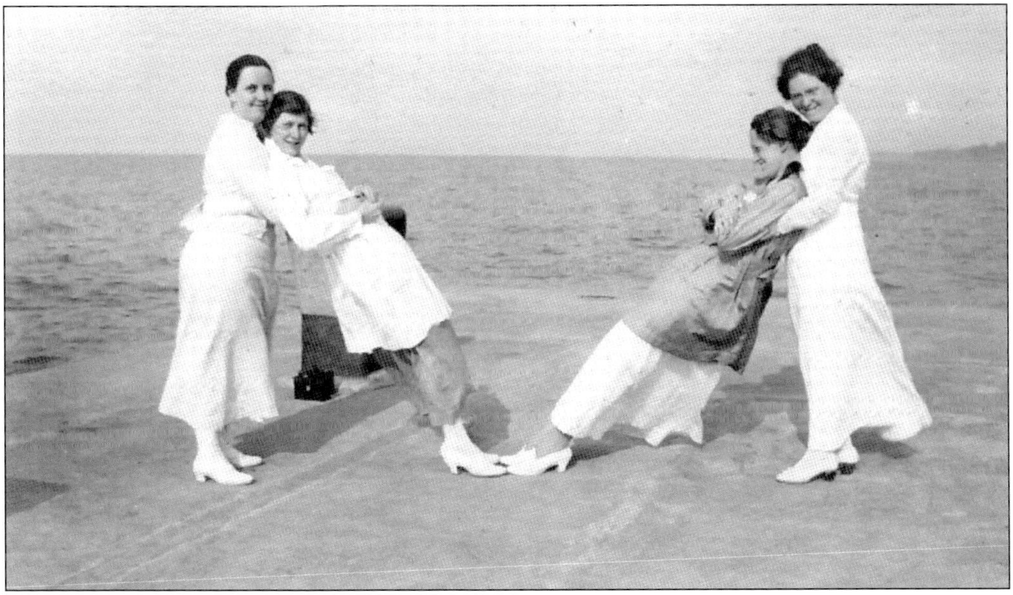

M IS FOR MEDINA. From left to right, Ellie Snell, Alice Bailey, and Addis and Elaine Hartt form the letter M as they stand on a pier overlooking Lake Ontario around 1910. In her photo album, Addis wrote "M is for Medina."

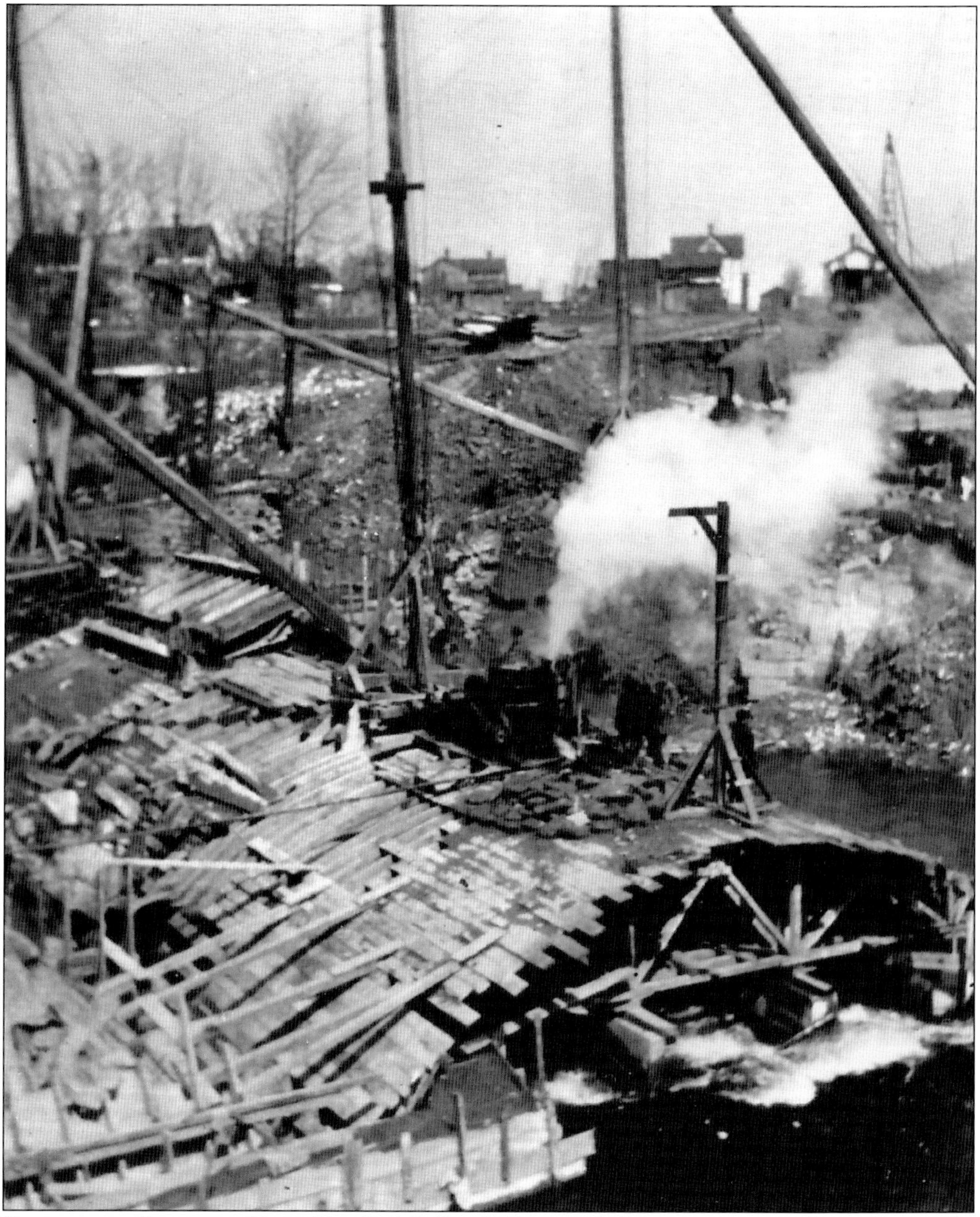

BUILDING A RACEWAY DAM. Nearby Medina Falls provided power to gristmills and sawmills, with races diverting the water from the falls to various businesses in Medina. This is the dam southeast of the canal, where water was diverted to run a sawmill behind the Walsh Hotel. Parts of the waterwheel can still be found in that area. (Courtesy of Richard Nellist.)

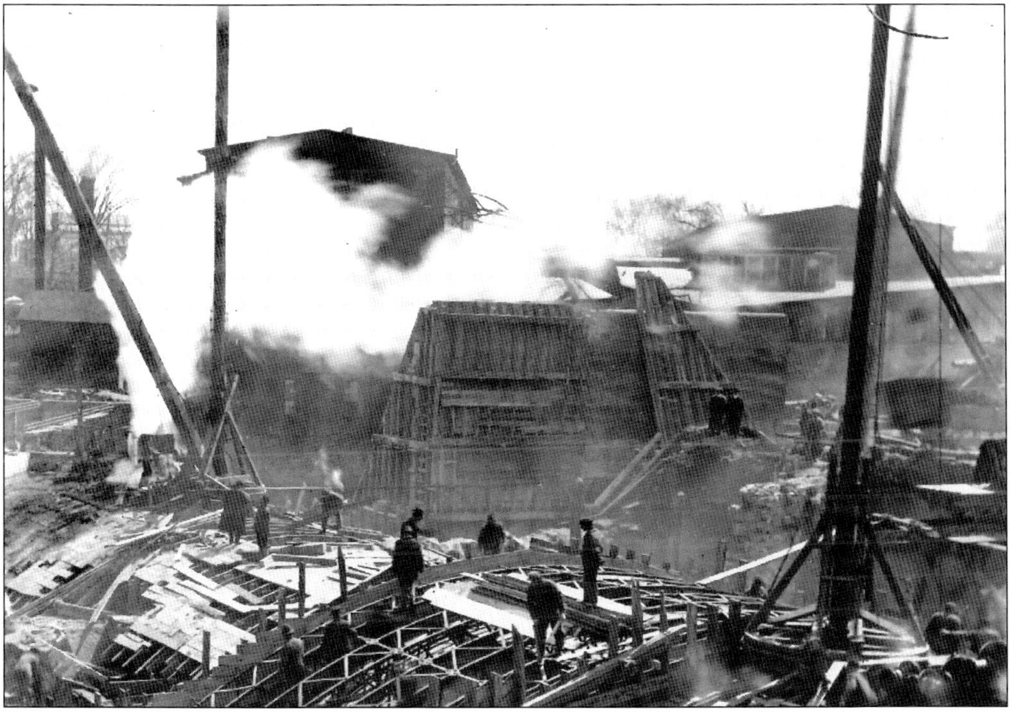

PREPARING THE FORMS. Steam rises as workers construct the huge forms that will hold the concrete for the power dam. (Courtesy of Richard Nellist.)

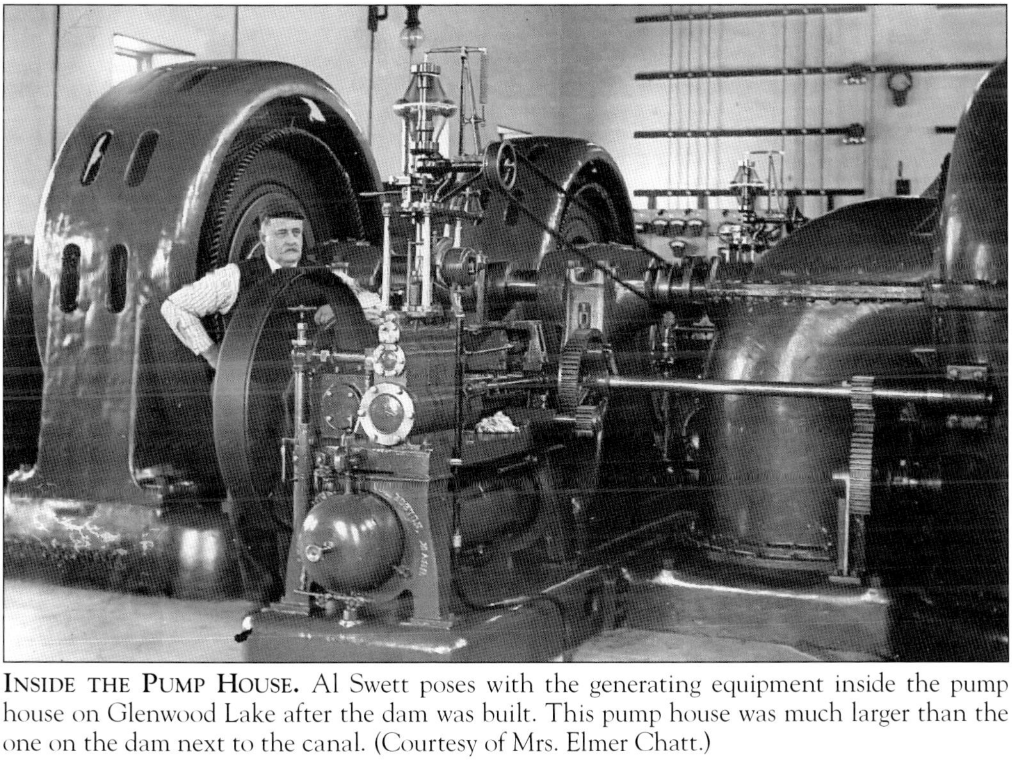

INSIDE THE PUMP HOUSE. Al Swett poses with the generating equipment inside the pump house on Glenwood Lake after the dam was built. This pump house was much larger than the one on the dam next to the canal. (Courtesy of Mrs. Elmer Chatt.)

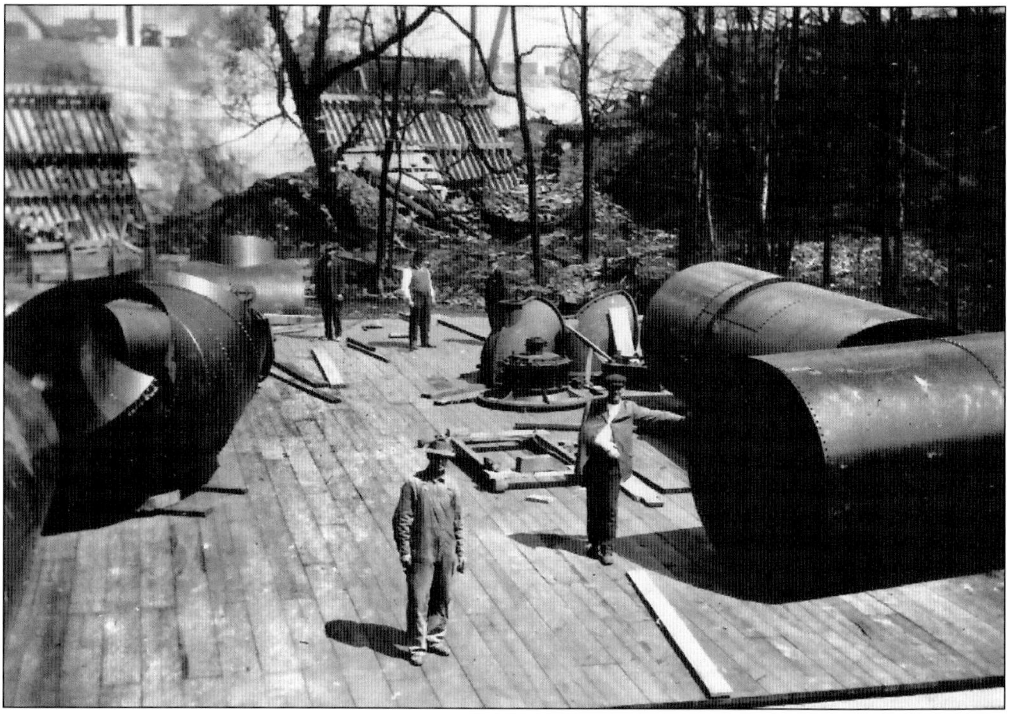

HUGE CULVERTS. Workmen stand by the large culverts that will be used in conjunction with the dam, which looms large in the background. (Courtesy of Richard Nellist.)

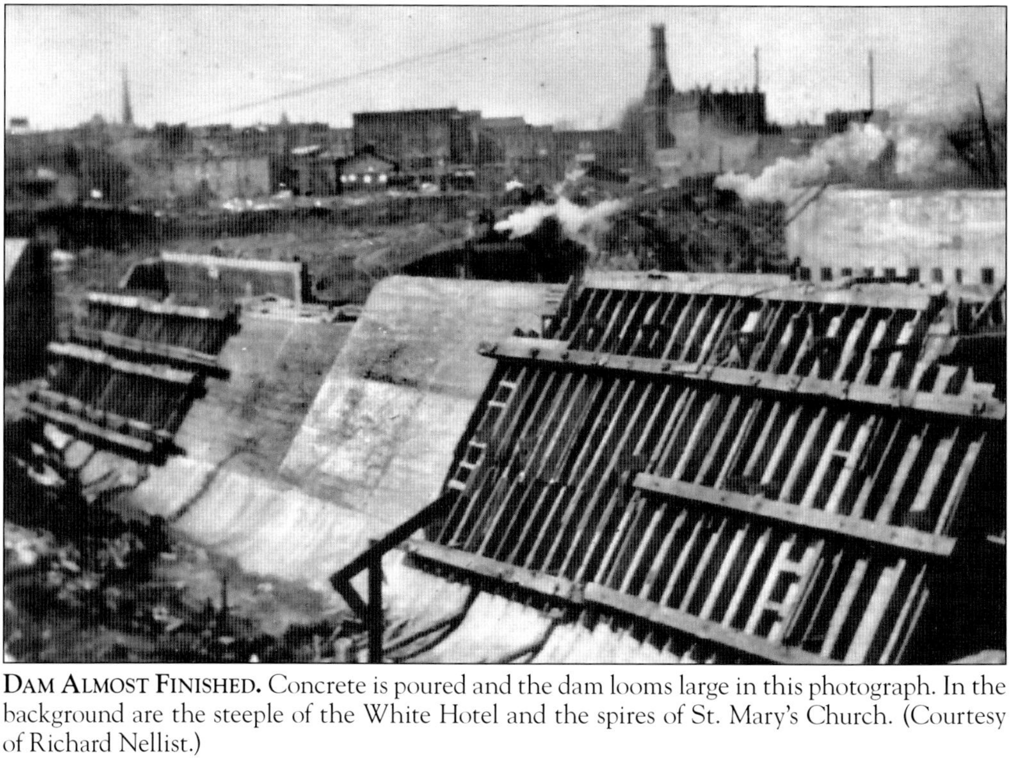

DAM ALMOST FINISHED. Concrete is poured and the dam looms large in this photograph. In the background are the steeple of the White Hotel and the spires of St. Mary's Church. (Courtesy of Richard Nellist.)

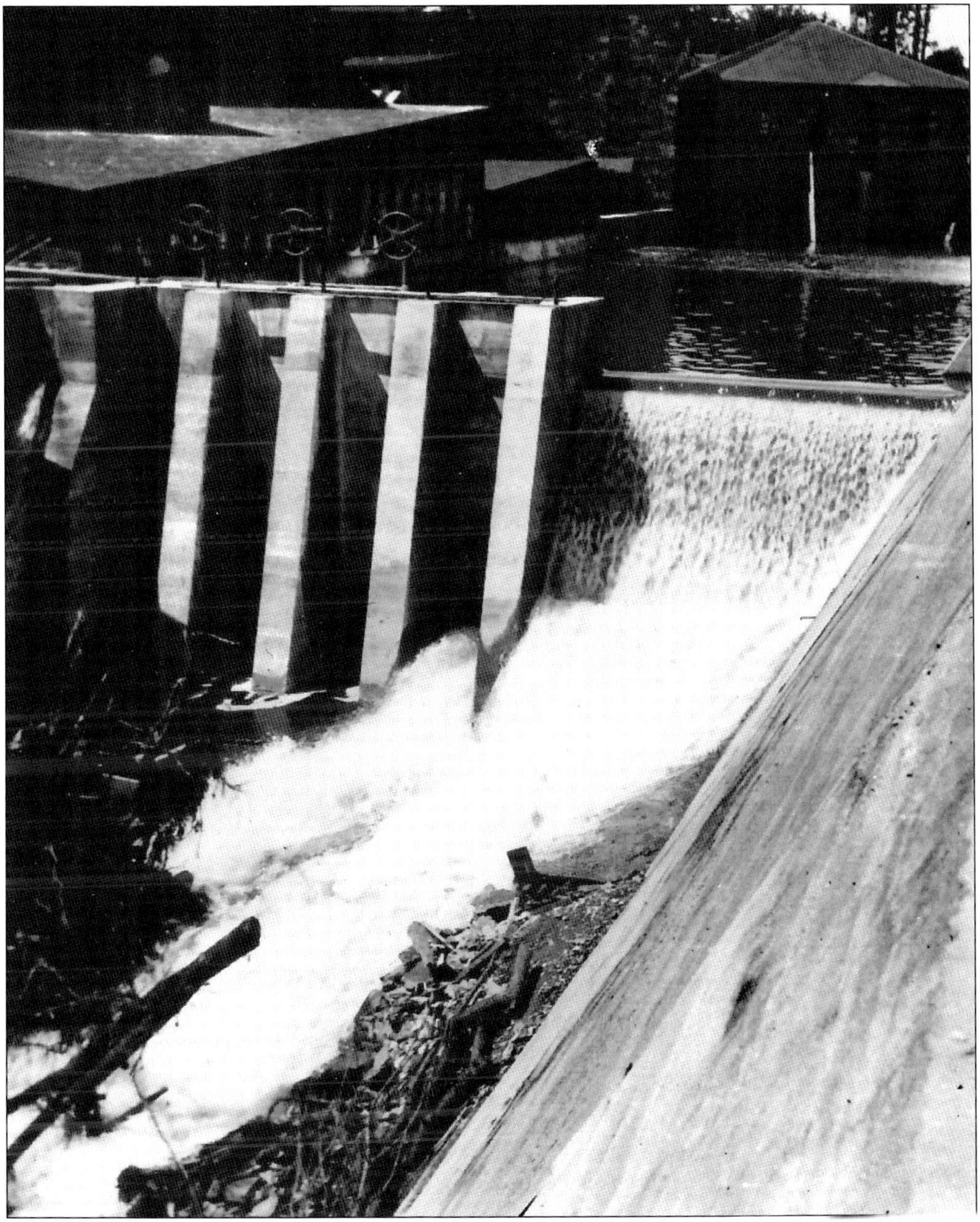

WATER DIVERTED. The raceway is completed, and the water rushes over the dam, diverted from the canal to other areas. Today it is difficult to observe this dam, though if one is standing in State Street Park or on the adjacent one-lane bridge over the canal, one can get a peek at it and hear the raging water. The underbrush in the area surrounding the dam has become so thick, it is only possible to glimpse this scenic wonder in the winter or spring when the temperature is not below freezing. (Courtesy of Richard Nellist.)

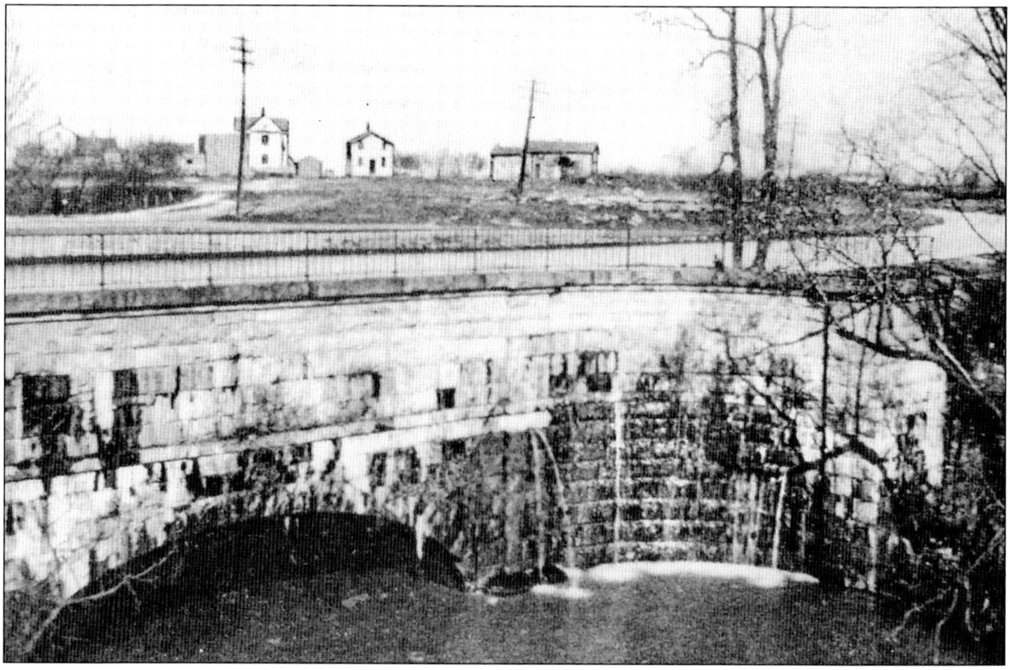

THE AQUEDUCT. Artemas Allen came to Medina in 1822, named master mason, building the aqueduct for the Erie Canal on Oak Orchard Creek. The canal travels over the creek just east of Medina's current business district via this aqueduct. This now is obscured from view because of new roads, many houses, growth of surrounding underbrush and trees, and new businesses.

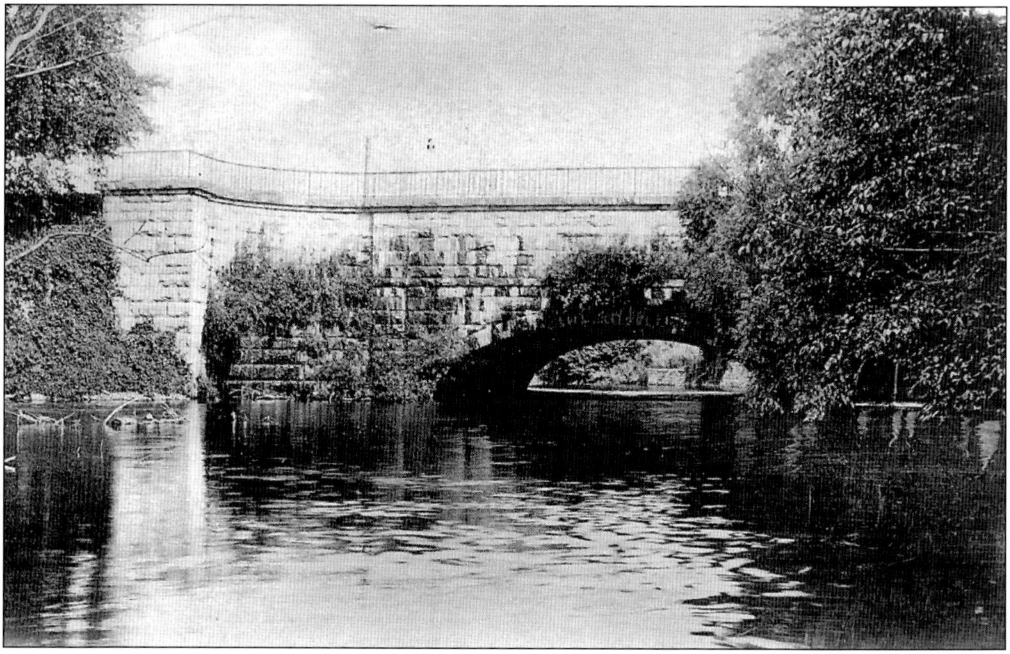

THE AQUEDUCT FROM THE CREEK. This c. 1905 photograph shows a view of the aqueduct from Oak Orchard Creek. The creek was high when this photograph was taken. Sometimes the water is very shallow.

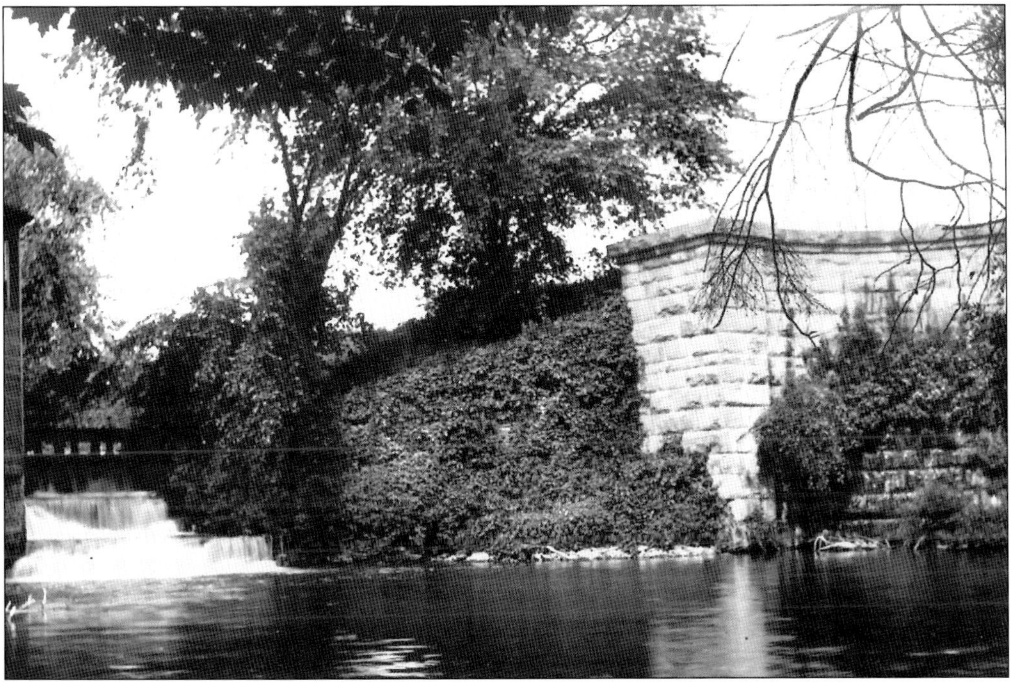

FALLS BY THE AQUEDUCT. Next to the aqueduct is one of Medina's many falls. This photograph was taken about 1910. The canal is at the top of the hill and flows above the creek.

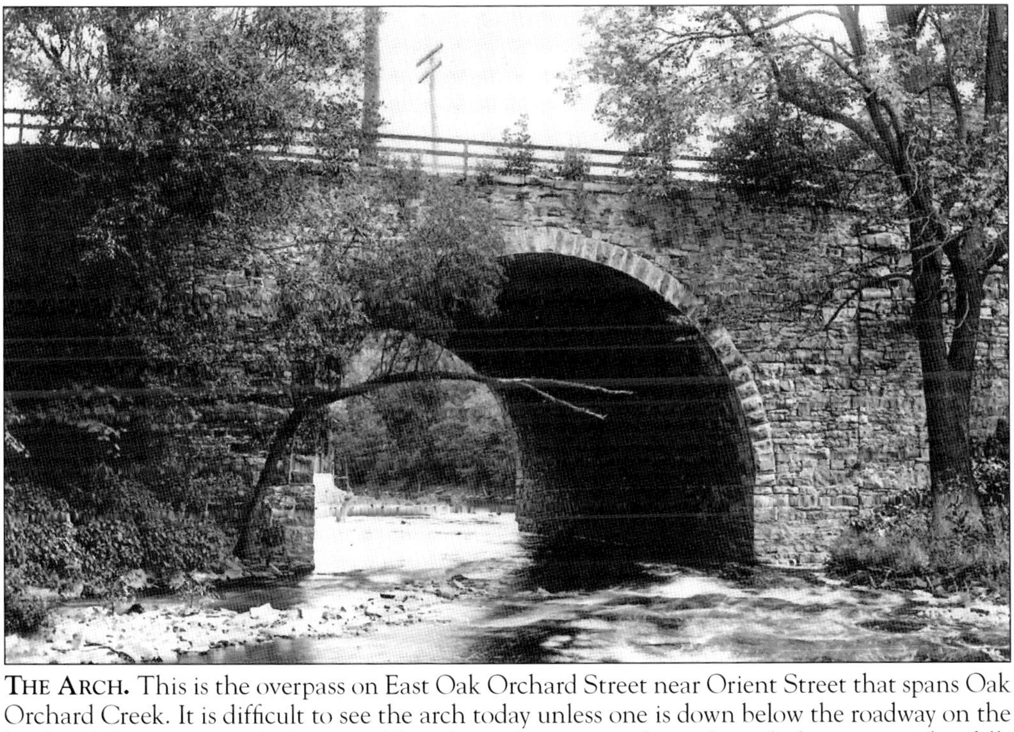

THE ARCH. This is the overpass on East Oak Orchard Street near Orient Street that spans Oak Orchard Creek. It is difficult to see the arch today unless one is down below the roadway on the banks of the raging creek. It is possible to hear the water rushing through, however, with a falls under the road and the water frothing out of the opening on the north side of the roadway.

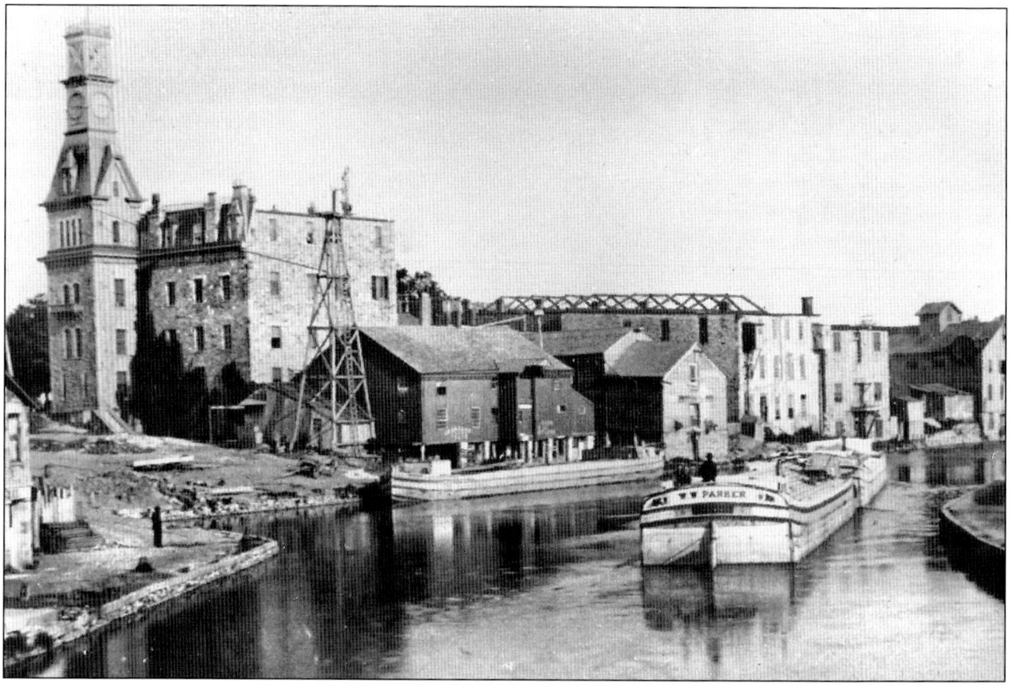

CRUISING THE CANAL. A packet boat winds its way through the curve of the Erie Canal after leaving the wide-water area, not seen at the right of this picture. The White Hotel looms large at the left of the photograph. (Courtesy of Mrs. Elmer Chatt.)

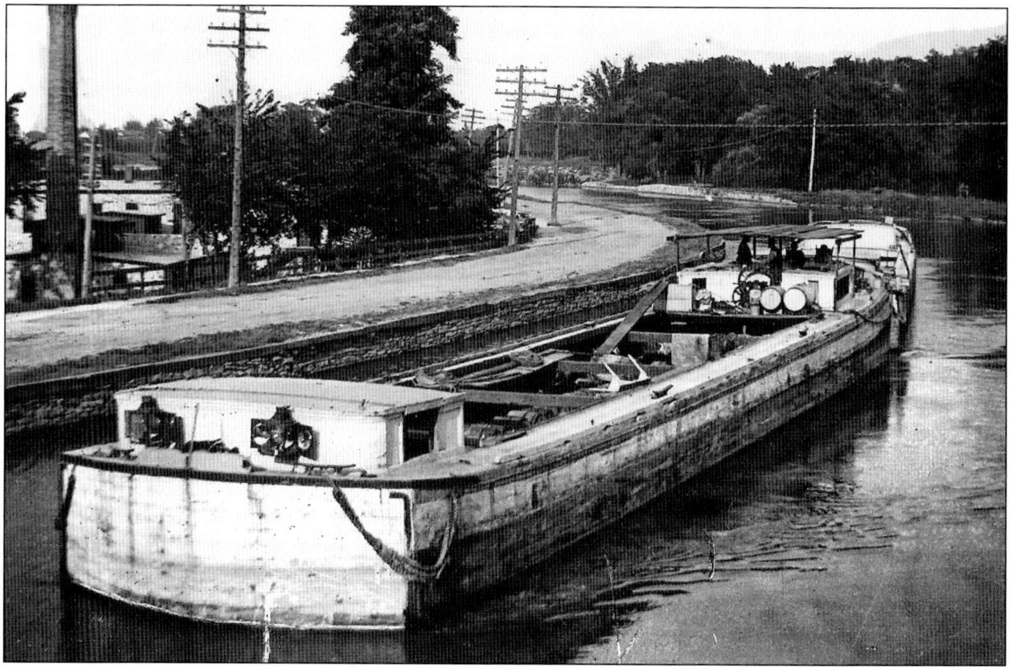

PACKET BOAT. This is one of the many boats that traveled the Erie Canal around 1860. The enclosed area at the back held crude beds for sleeping. The planks on the sides of the boat are used by the people to walk from the boat to the bank. (Courtesy of Mrs. Elmer Chatt.)

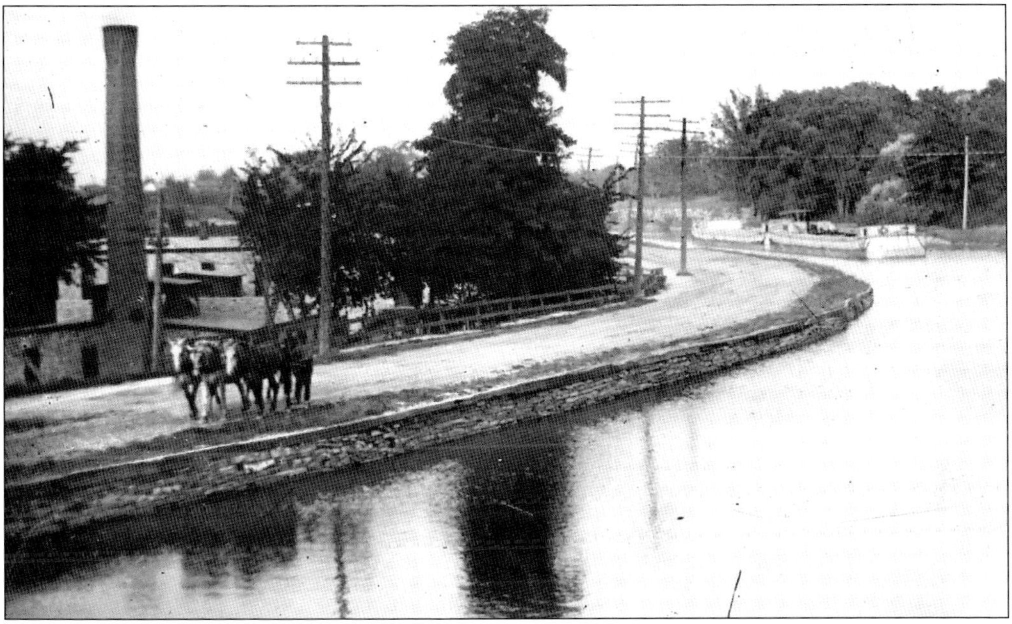

READY TO TOW. Men prepare a team of horses for their jobs pulling the packet boat. They could be waiting for the boat in the background. Tow ropes were thrown from the bank to the boat, tied to the boat's hull, and the horses or mules pulled the boats along. There were large stalls on some of the more expensive boats for the horses to rest when not being used. (Courtesy of Mrs. Elmer Chatt.)

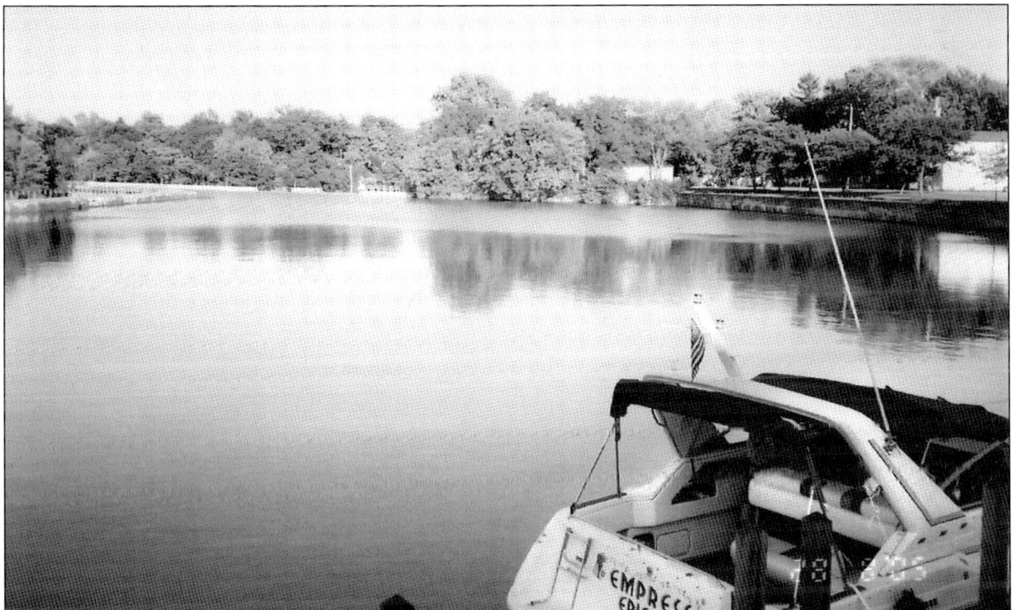

CANAL TODAY. A solitary boat from Pennsylvania docks at the large canal turnaround at Medina's Canal Port. Note how the water ripples farther away from the dock. This is because the dam is pulling water to flow over its walls just left of the large tree in the center of the photograph. The canal veers left, following the tree line.

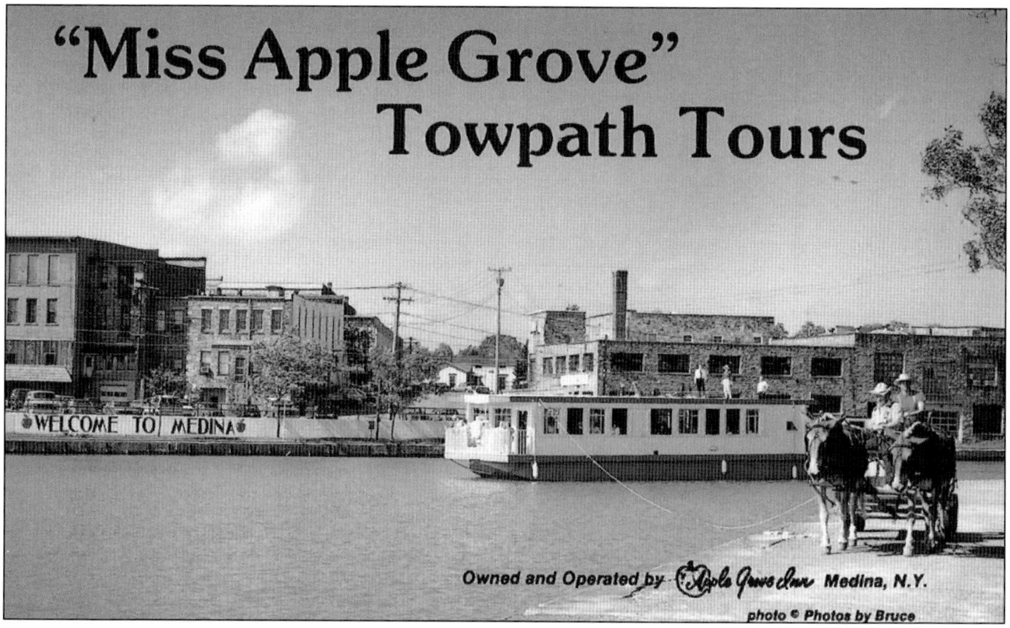

PACKET BOAT RIDE. In the 1980s, the Apple Grove Restaurant brought back history when it offered packet boat rides on the canal. The ride began at the entrance near the Apple Grove and went into Medina, docked at the falls, and returned. Mules pulled the boat and Muleskinner Dave told the history of the packet boat and sang songs. The restaurant burned and is under new management now. (Courtesy of Bill Henderson.)

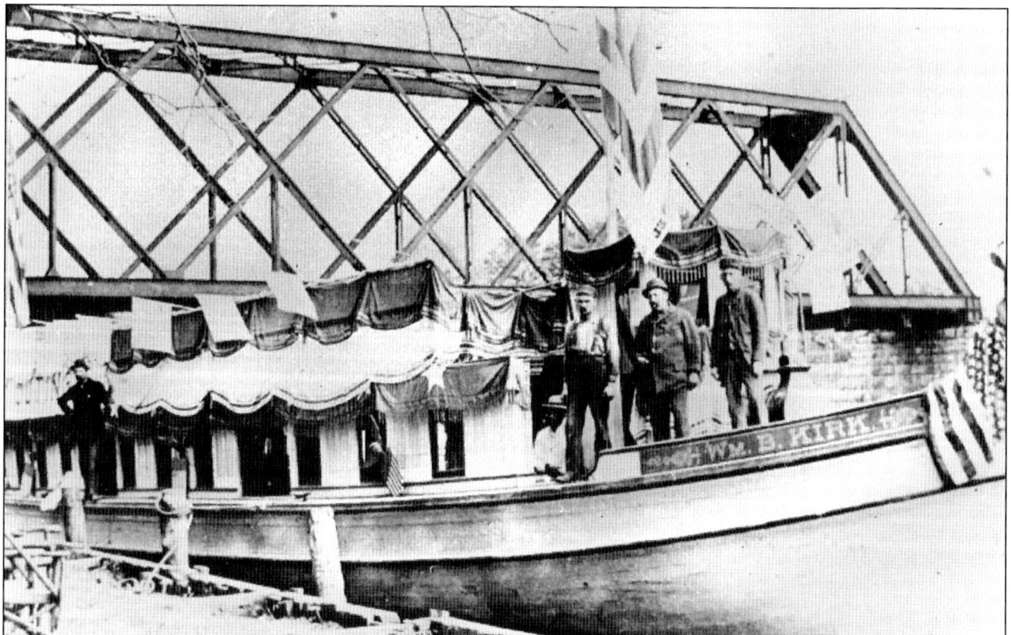

CANAL BARGERS. This photograph, taken prior to 1900, shows a group of men lined up on the deck of the canal boat the *Wm. B. Kirk*. The boat was decked out in flags and bunting and was probably celebrating July Fourth. (Courtesy of Mrs. Elmer Chatt.)

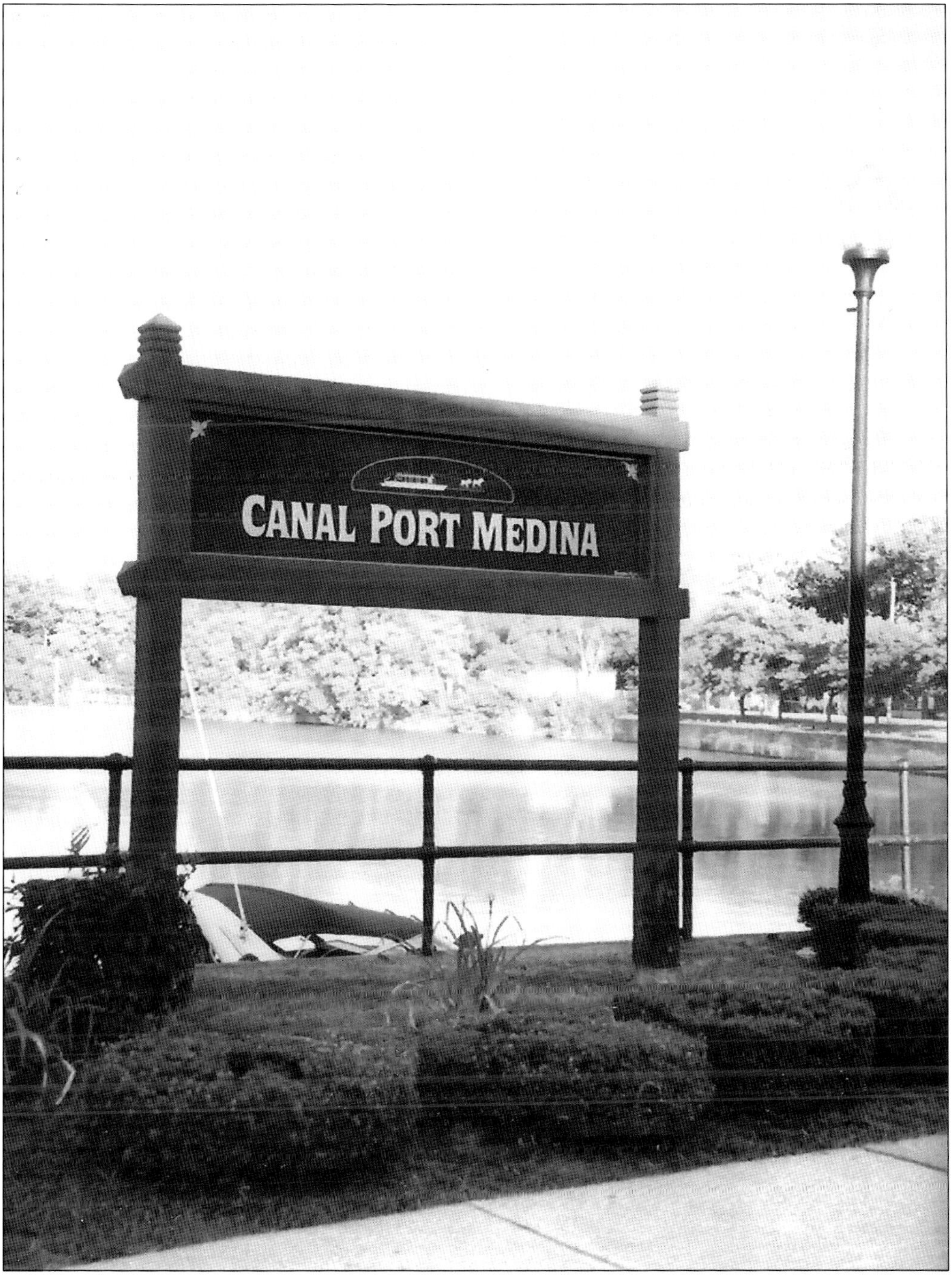

HARBOR TODAY. Boats still dock at the natural harbor near Medina's Main Street, with a welcoming sign that says Canal Port Medina. They can tie their boats, walk up several stairways, and shop or eat at many of the establishments on and off of Main Street. The picture above the wording depicts a packet boat being towed by horses.

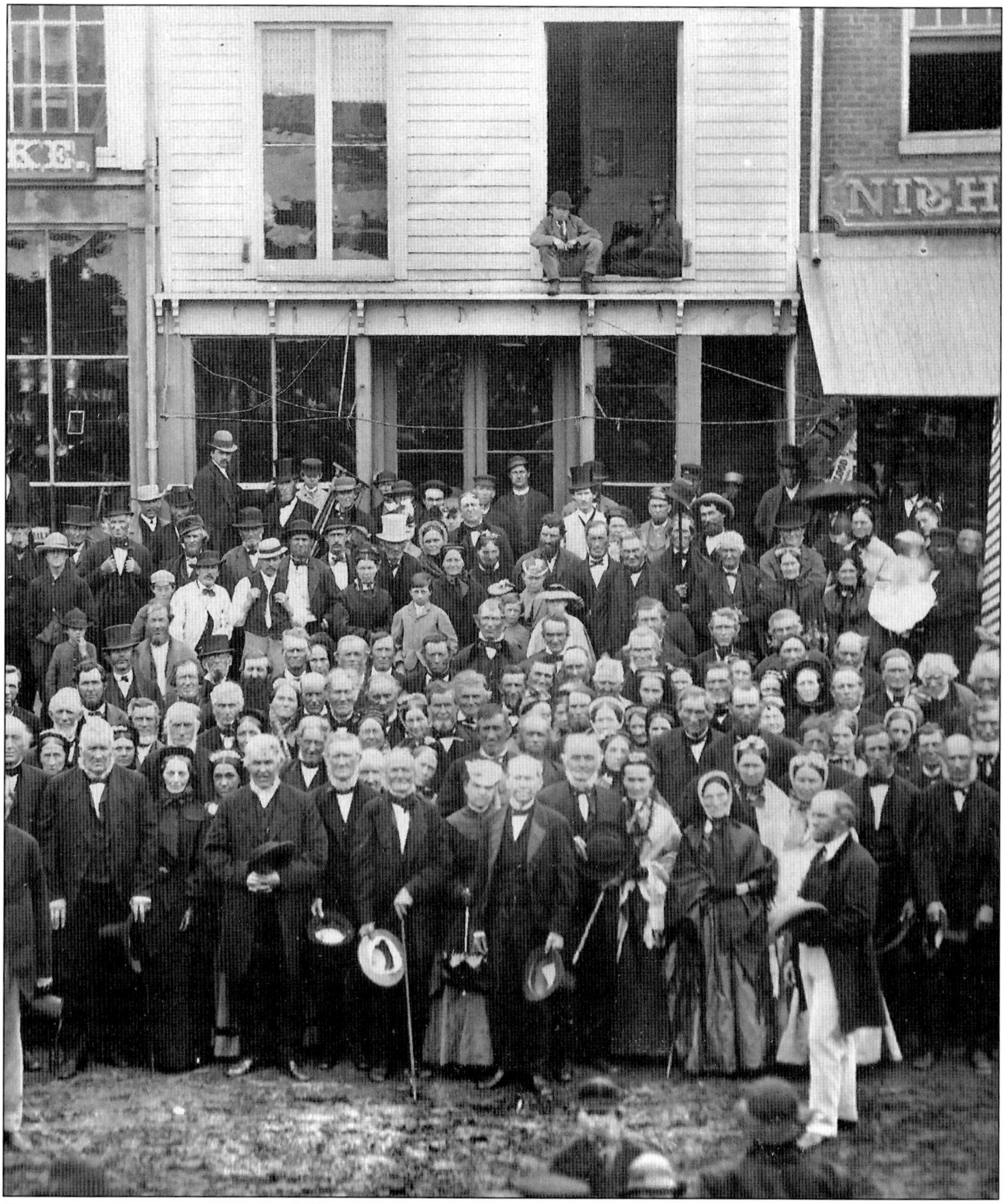

ORIGINAL FOUNDERS. The folks who settled in Medina and the surrounding region got together for a group photograph on Main Street in 1906 for Old Homecoming Week. (Courtesy of Orleans County Department of History.)

Four

Busy Streets

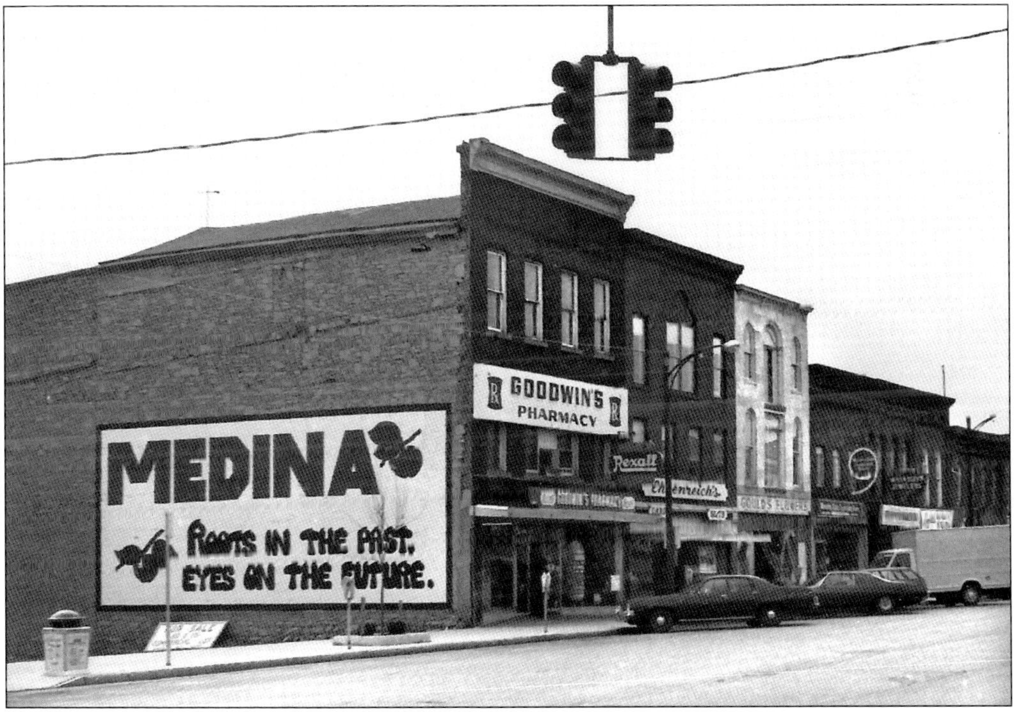

Main Street Looking South. This is the east side of Main Street around 1970. The sign on the pharmacy tells Medina's story—"Roots in the Past, Eyes on the Future." (Courtesy of Richard Nellist.)

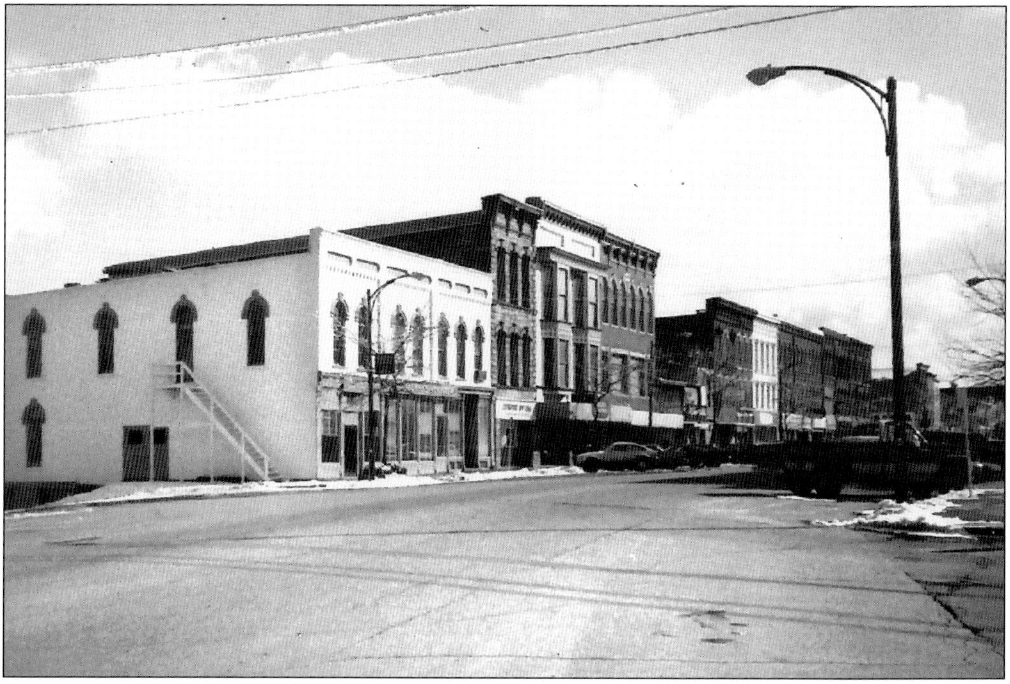

Entering Town. The *Medina Journal Register* newspaper office is at the left as one crosses the bridge and enters town from the south. Although this scene is from the 1970s, one can see that the buildings still reflect a century of history. (Courtesy of Bill Henderson.)

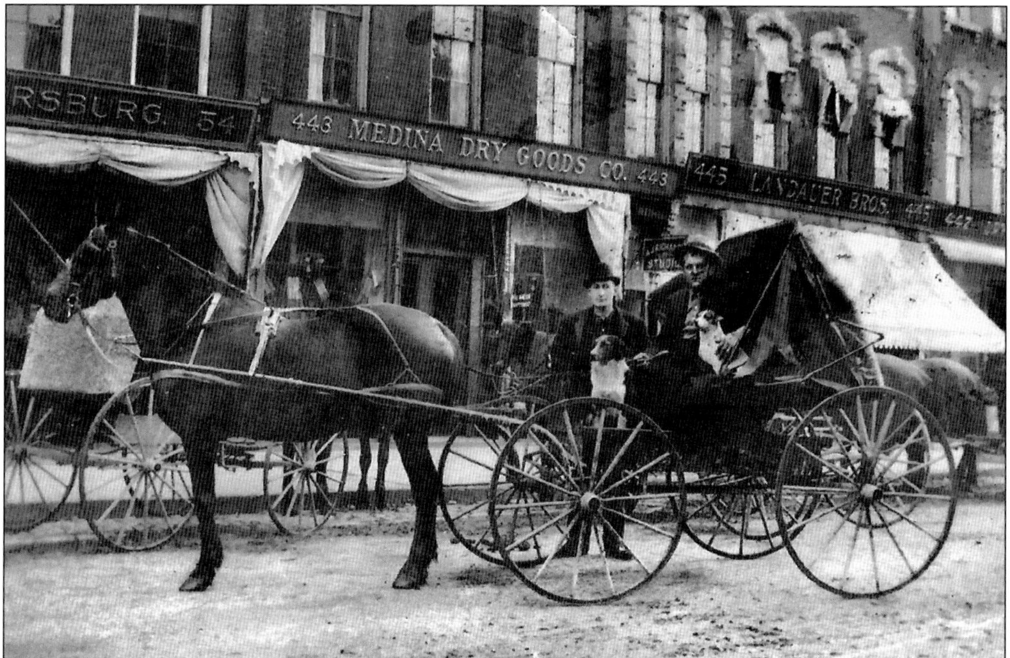

Outside the Dry Goods Store. A solitary horse and driver prepare to park in front of the dry goods store on Main Street around 1901. (Courtesy of Bill Henderson.)

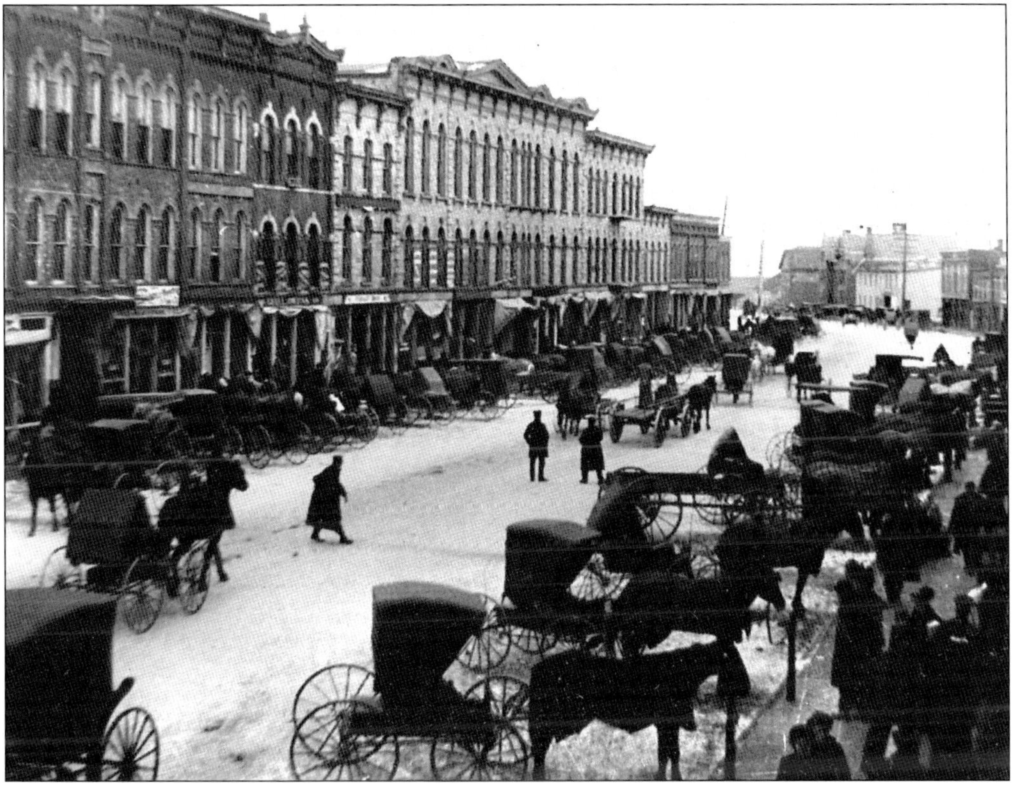

MAIN STREET LOOKING NORTH, C. 1907. Horses and buggies line the streets on the south end of Main Street looking toward the Erie Canal. (Courtesy of Frank Berger.)

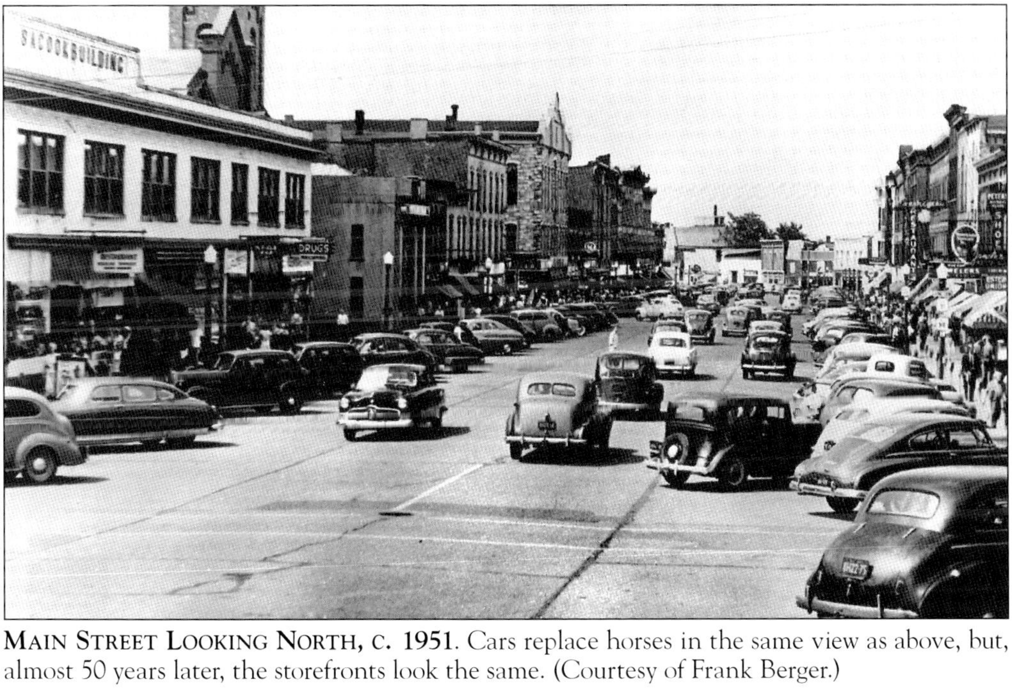

MAIN STREET LOOKING NORTH, C. 1951. Cars replace horses in the same view as above, but, almost 50 years later, the storefronts look the same. (Courtesy of Frank Berger.)

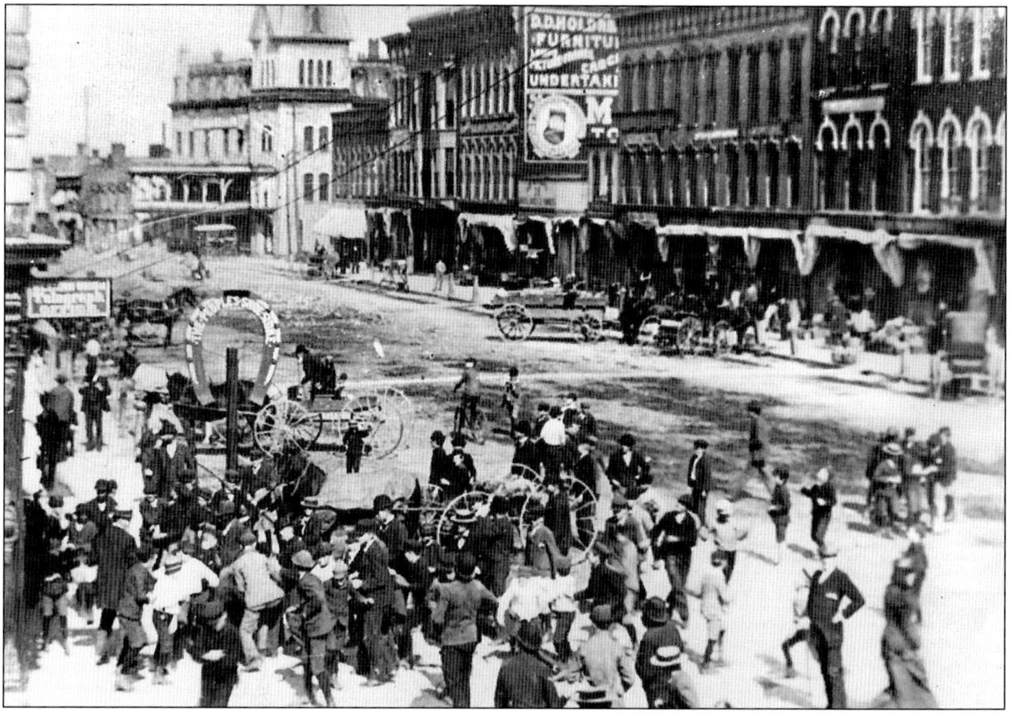

MAIN STREET, 1882. Folks line up in their finery for a day's shopping on Main Street. (Courtesy of Frank Berger.)

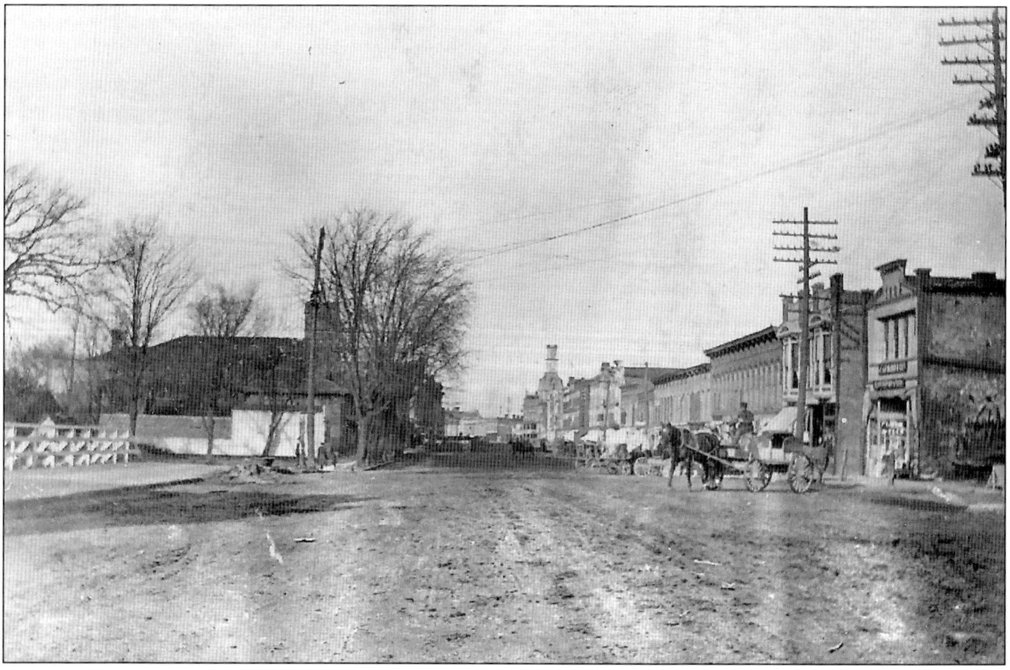

MAIN STREET FROM THE SOUTH. This photograph was taken from the south end of Main Street around 1901. The streets were wide, allowing room for horses and carriages to turn around if they needed to. (Courtesy of Bill Henderson.)

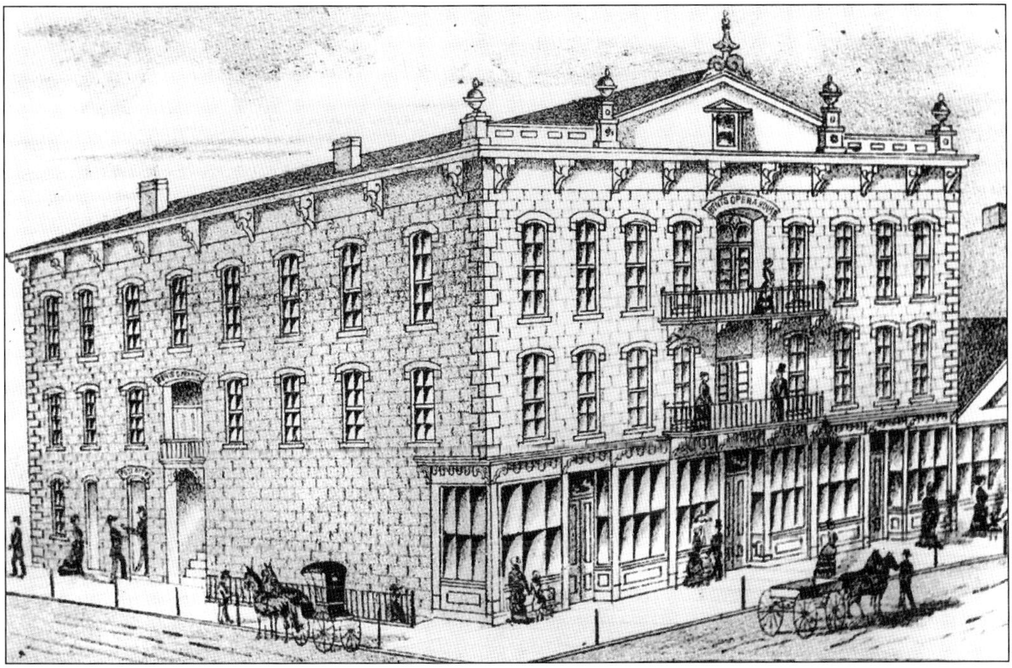

BENT'S OPERA HOUSE. This is a lovely sketch of the opera house, which had its glory years in the late 19th century. (Courtesy of Frank Berger.)

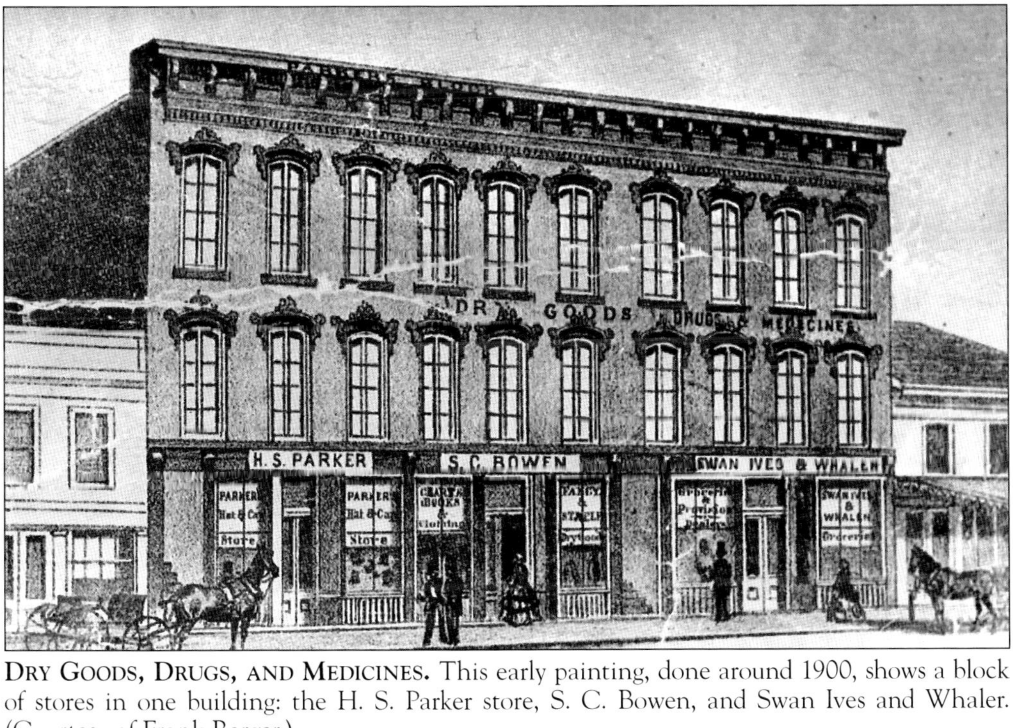

DRY GOODS, DRUGS, AND MEDICINES. This early painting, done around 1900, shows a block of stores in one building: the H. S. Parker store, S. C. Bowen, and Swan Ives and Whaler. (Courtesy of Frank Berger.)

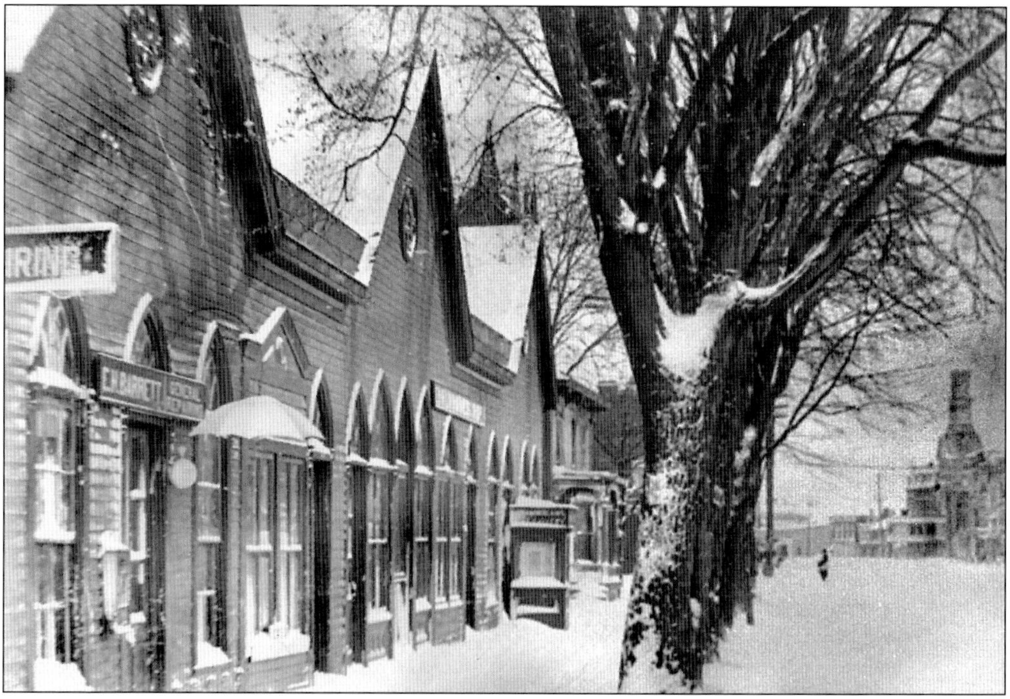

BEFORE THE FIRE. These quaint buildings stood on the west side of Main Street where the Cook building stands today. When a fire broke out in 1909 destroying the entire block, it was decreed that any future building on Main Street would be of brick and/or mortar, with no more wooden buildings offering a fire hazard. (Courtesy of Richard Nellist.)

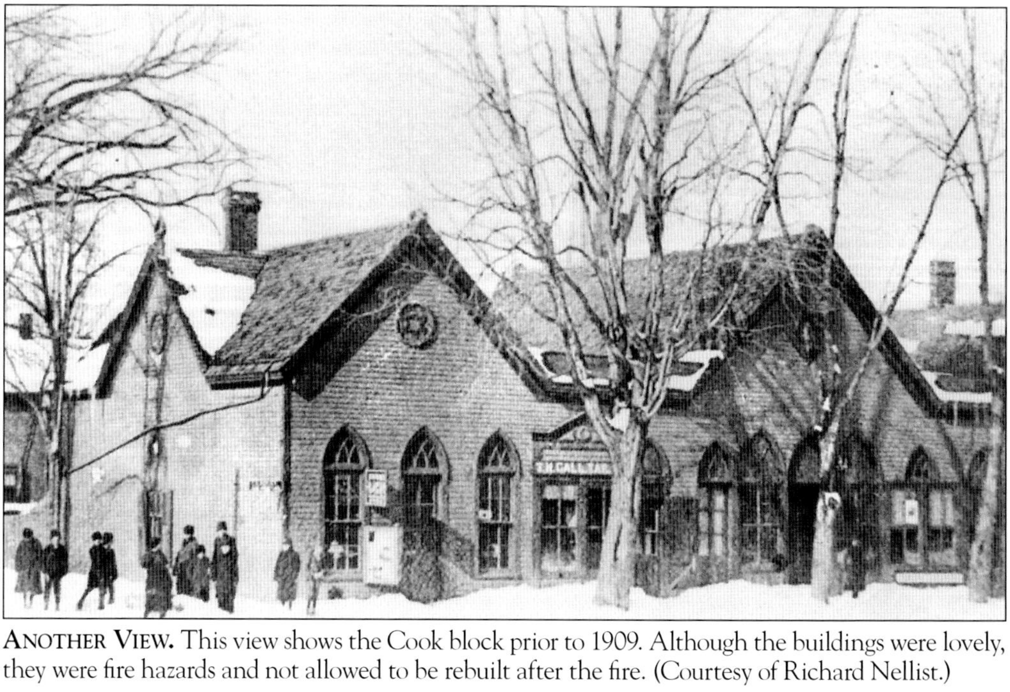

ANOTHER VIEW. This view shows the Cook block prior to 1909. Although the buildings were lovely, they were fire hazards and not allowed to be rebuilt after the fire. (Courtesy of Richard Nellist.)

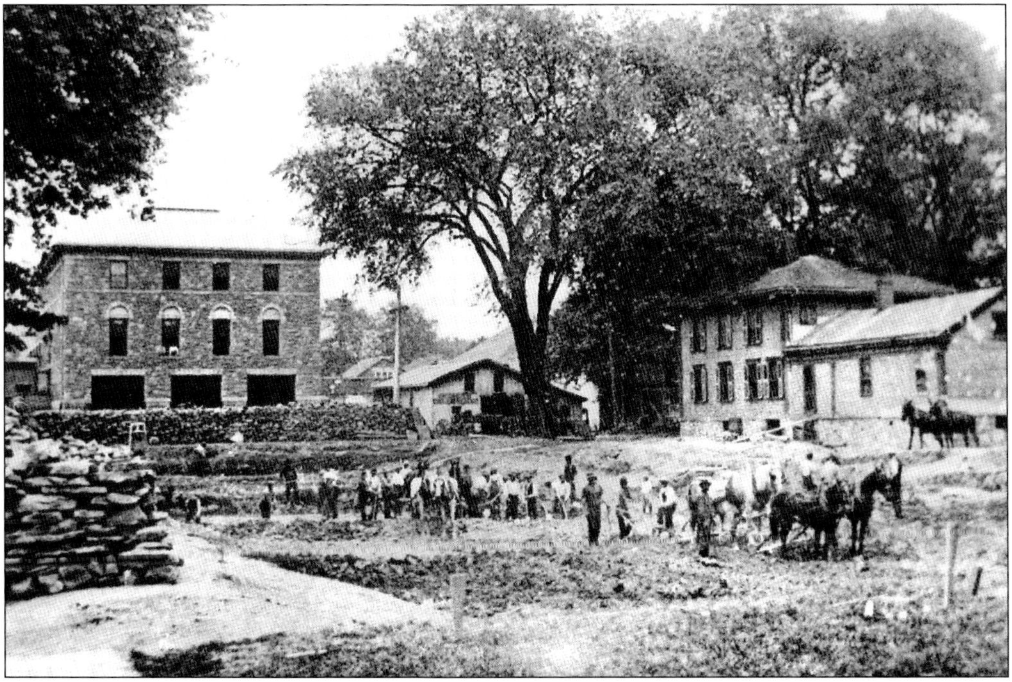

Rebuilding the Cook Block, August 10, 1910. After the fire destroyed the original buildings, the debris was cleared by the summer of 1910, and reconstruction started on the new Cook building. The new City Hall can be seen across the street from the workers. The three big doors housed the fire vehicles. (Courtesy of Richard Nellist.)

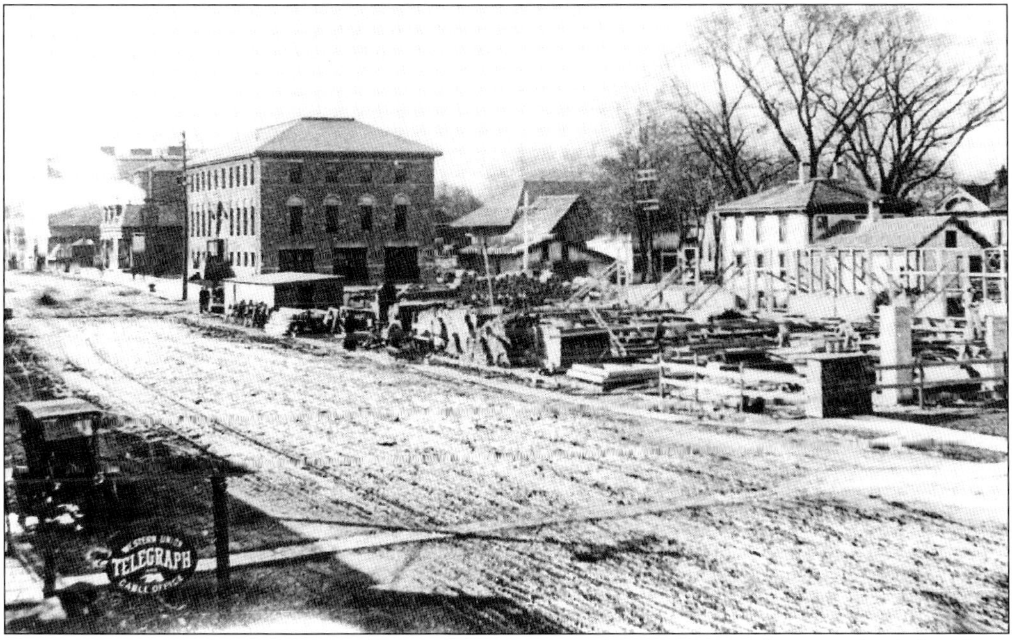

Rebuilding the Cook Block, September 1910. Rafters go up on the new Cook building. Note the Model T parked behind the telegraph sign. Medina had all the modern conveniences of the day. (Courtesy of Richard Nellist.)

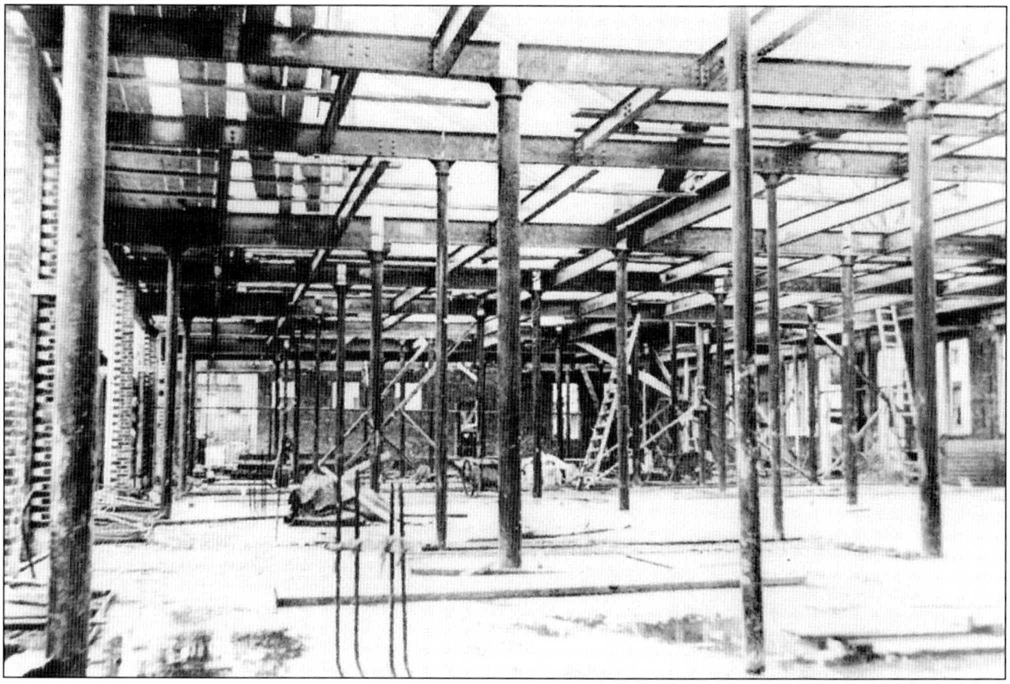

BUILDING PROGRESSES. By November 1910, the steel poles and girders were up, the foundation for the new S. A. Cook Building. With a brick façade and steel foundation, it will be difficult for the new building to be a fire hazard. (Courtesy of Richard Nellist.)

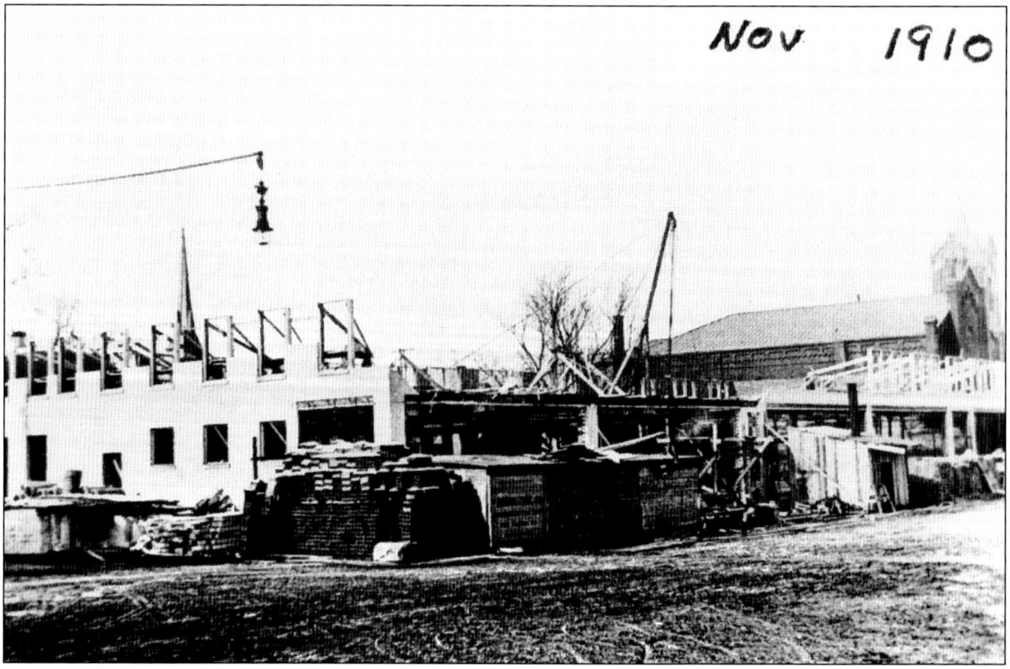

LAYING THE BRICKS. The brick exterior begins to go up in November 1910 at the new S. A. Cook Building. S. A. Cook started its roots in Medina and is now a national furniture company with offices all over. (Courtesy of Richard Nellist.)

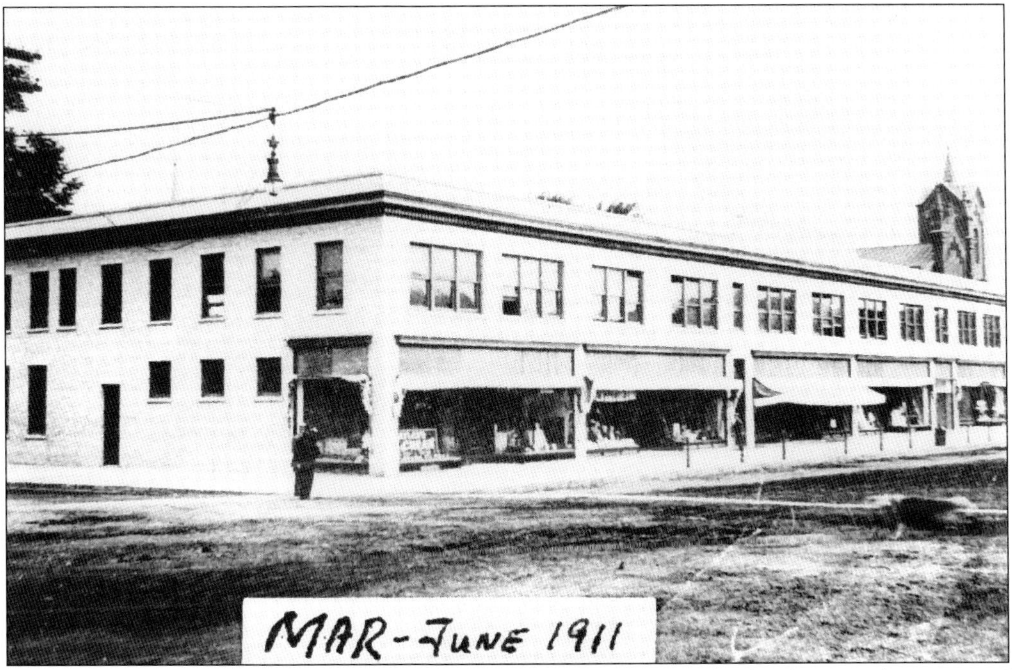

FINISHED BLOCK. By April 1911, the S. A. Cook Building was finished, taking up the corner of Main and Park Streets. The streetlight still hangs over the corner. (Courtesy of Richard Nellist.)

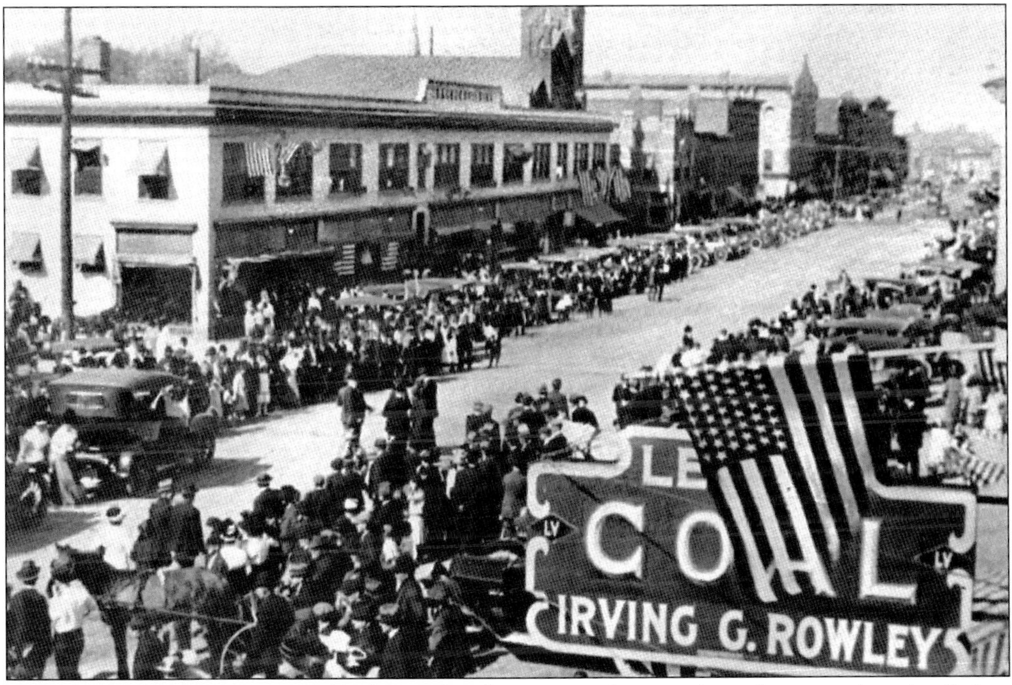

TEN YEARS LATER. The Cook block stands tall as citizens line up along the entire length of Main Street, waiting for a parade. Parades and celebrations were popular in Medina from the late 19th century through the 1950s. The wide streets made it convenient to park the car and still get a great glimpse of the festivities, leaving ample space for marching. (Courtesy of Richard Nellist.)

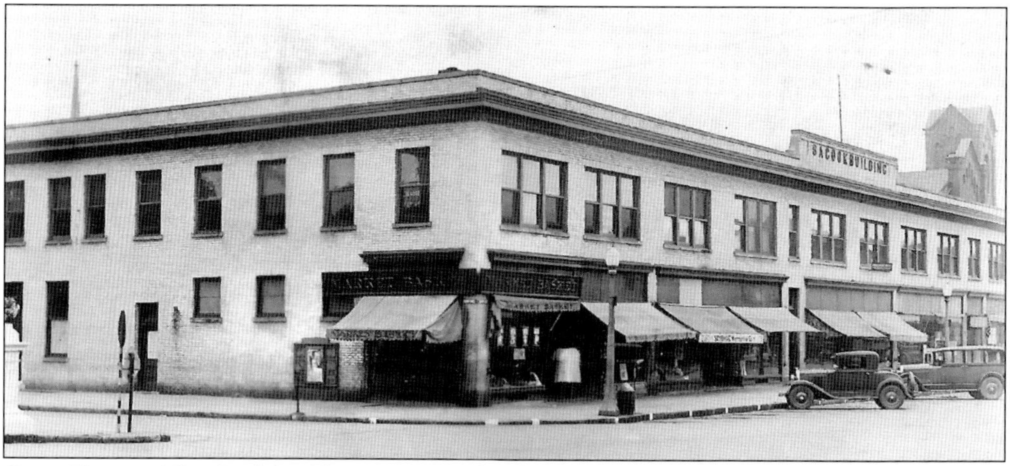

Cook Block. The Cook building was considered the "big business block" in Medina almost as soon as the building was finished. The flower urn at the left of the photograph was in front of City Hall. (Courtesy of Bill Henderson.)

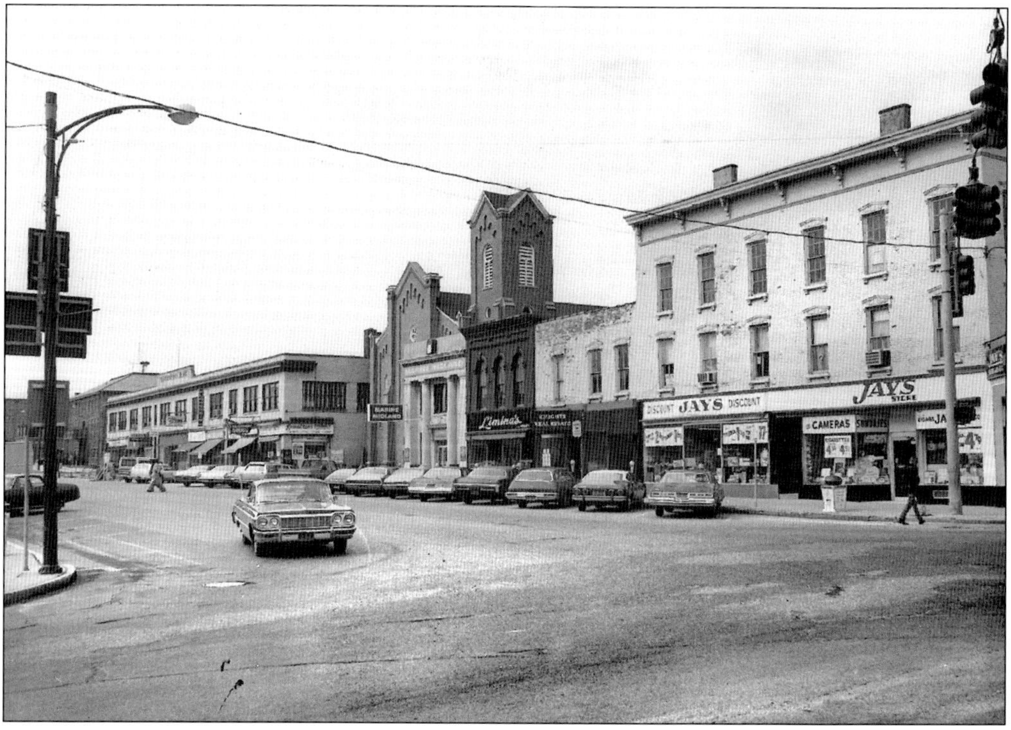

Main Street, 1975. The Cook building is seen at left, with the west side of Main Street being photographed from Park Avenue. The Presbyterian church is in the center of the photograph. (Courtesy of Richard Nellist.)

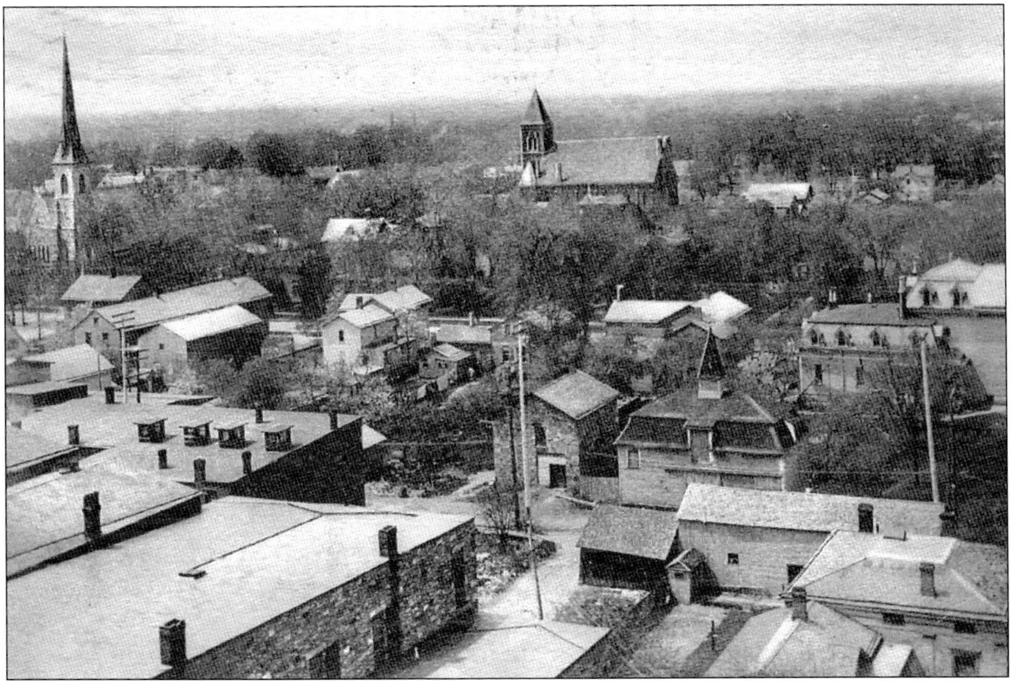

BIRD'S-EYE VIEW. The tops of the buildings are not as pleasing to the eye as the two churches in the background in this 1910 photograph. (Courtesy of Bill Henderson.)

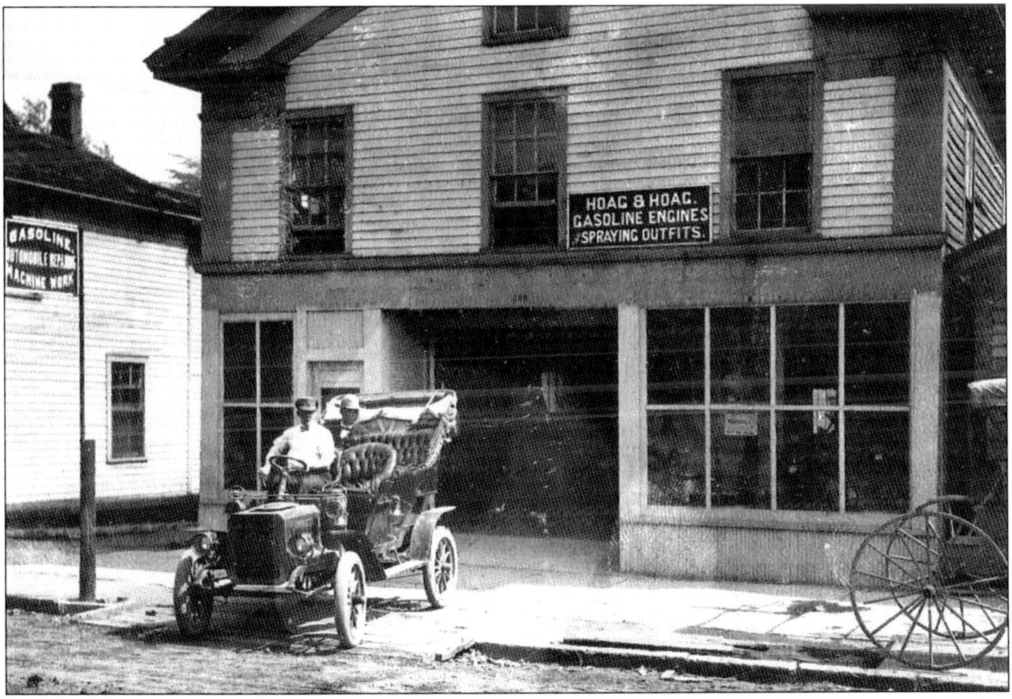

EAST CENTER STREET, 1909. This open touring car pulls out of Hoag and Hoag, while the wheels of a horse-drawn carriage are seen at the right. This was the era of both horses and buggies and horseless carriages. (Courtesy of Richard Nellist.)

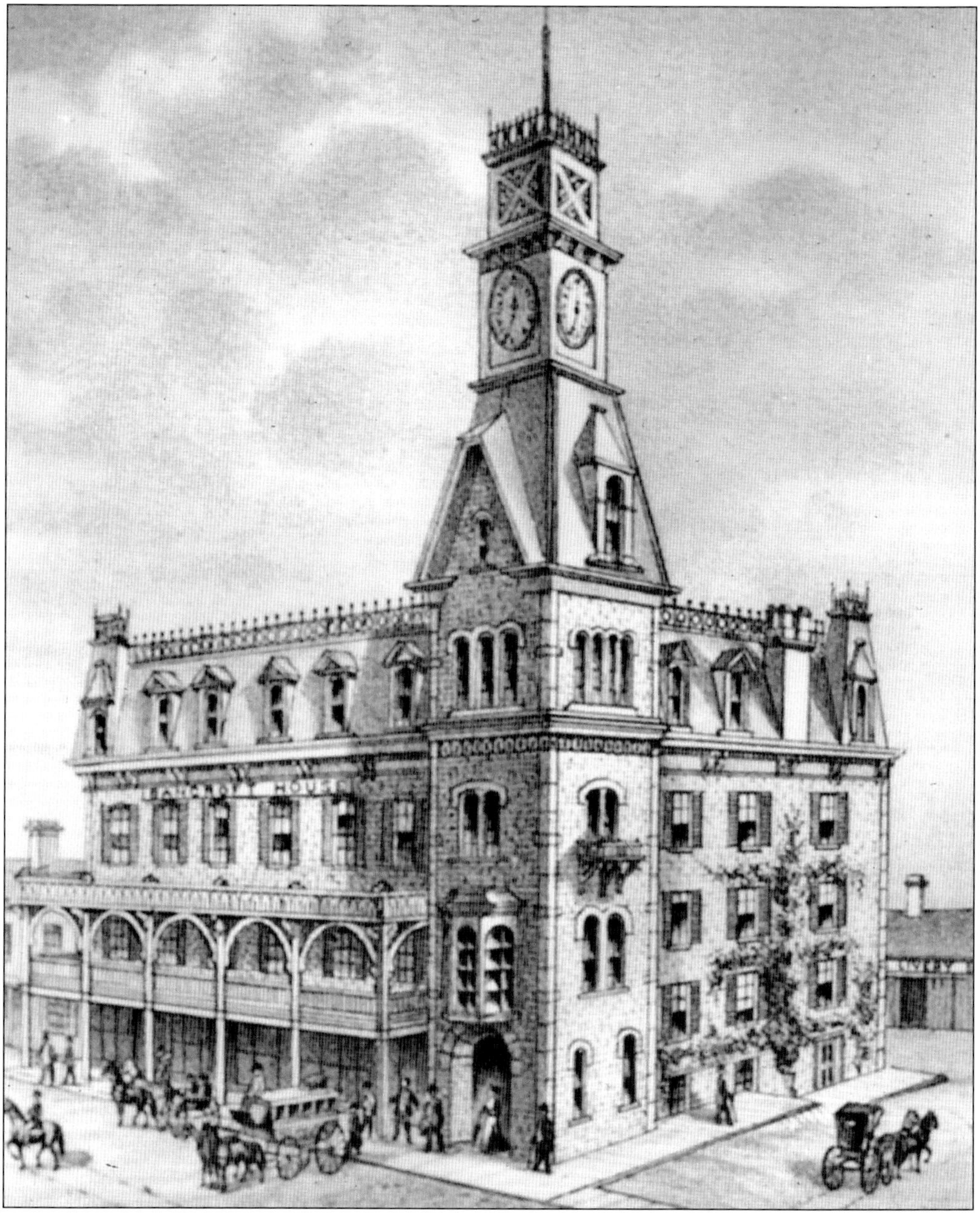

THE BANCROFT HOUSE. Before it became the White Hotel, and before cameras were available, an artist drew a sketch of the Bancroft House, Medina's posh landmark hotel for many years. A livery stable was located directly in back of the hotel, to allow for visitors' horses to be housed while their human counterparts visited. (Courtesy of Mrs. Elmer Chatt.)

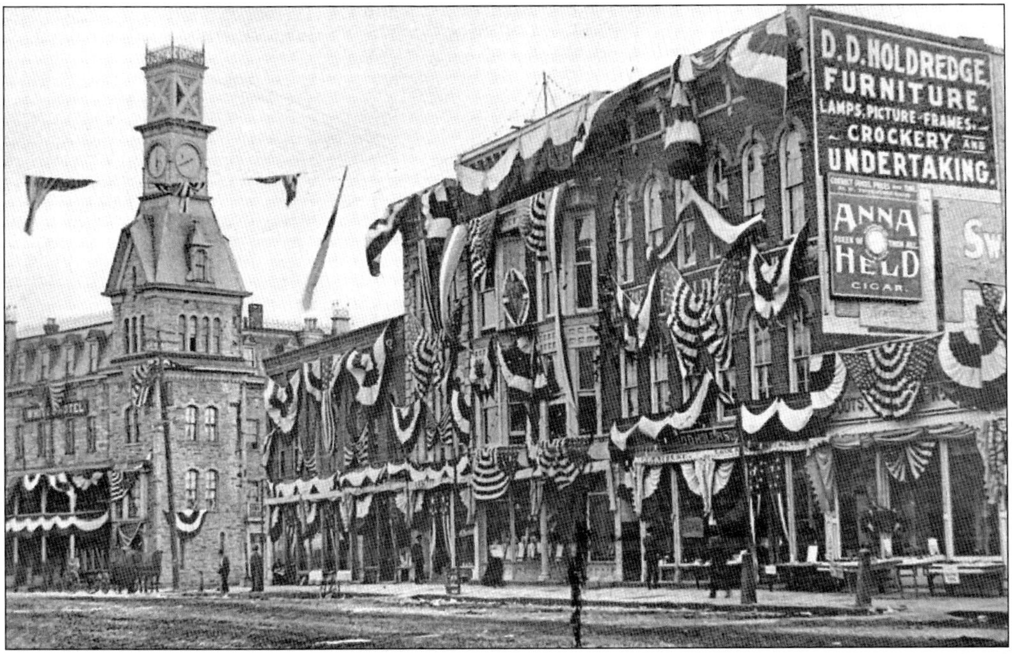

THE WHITE HOTEL. This hotel loomed over Medina for many years, its steeple being a focal point for visitors to travel to as they entered the area. It could be seen for miles, from the canal and points south. When the building burned, it was rebuilt, but the steeple was not. (Courtesy of Richard Nellist.)

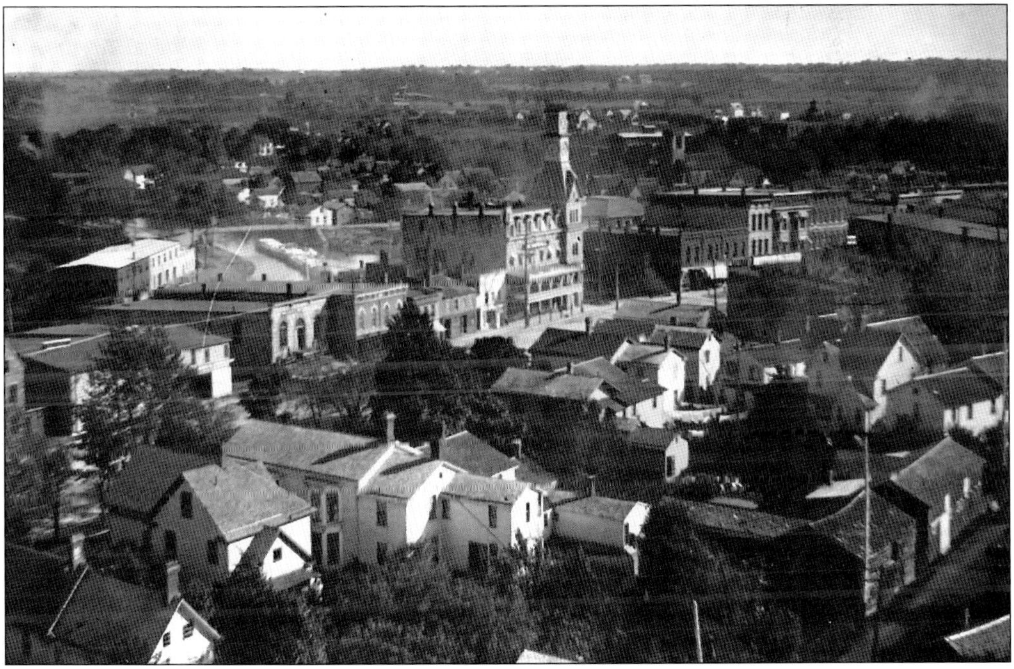

BIRD'S-EYE VIEW. The White Hotel is seen from the steeple of St. Mary's Church. Because of its height, the tower appeared in many of the photographs prior to 1923, the year when it burned. (Courtesy of Mrs. Elmer Chatt.)

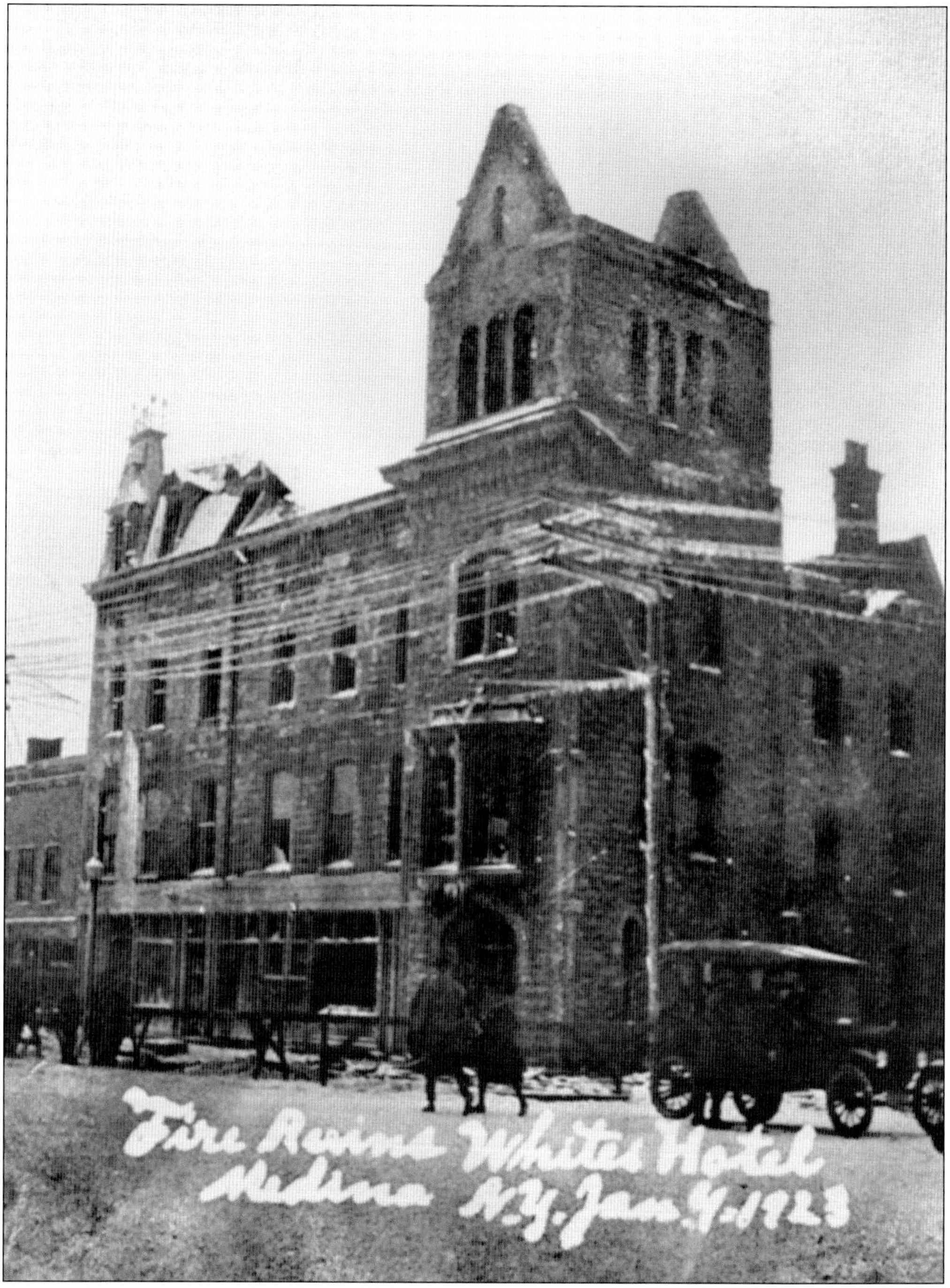

HOTEL RUINS. Fire destroyed the White Hotel in January 1923. In this photograph, taken the day after the fire, the power wires are covered with ice from the water sprayed on the structure. The tower would no longer loom over Medina, nor beckon travelers as they followed their trail toward it. Fortunately the building was solidly built and is still standing, home of the NAPA Auto Parts store today. In staring at it, one can imagine the grandeur of the building, people milling in and out, less than 100 years before. (Courtesy of Richard Nellist.)

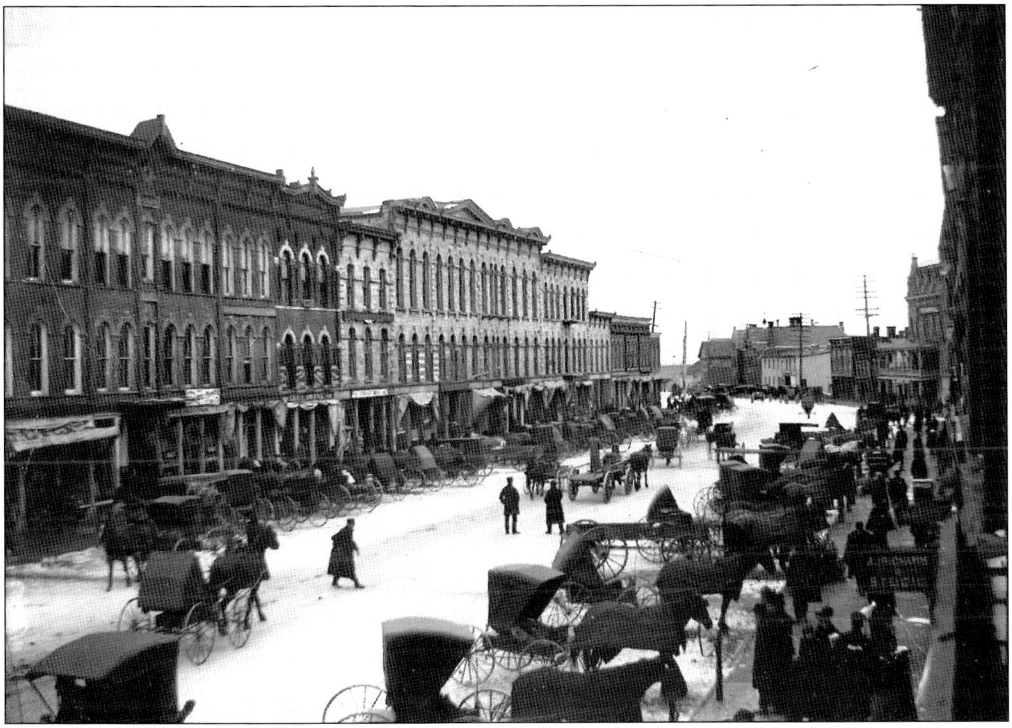

FRIGID MAIN STREET. Even the horses wore coats in this photograph taken around 1900 as buggies lined up on Main Street, the horses tethered to hitching posts, waiting for their owners to return. Notice the snow on the roadway. (Courtesy of Mrs. Elmer Chatt.)

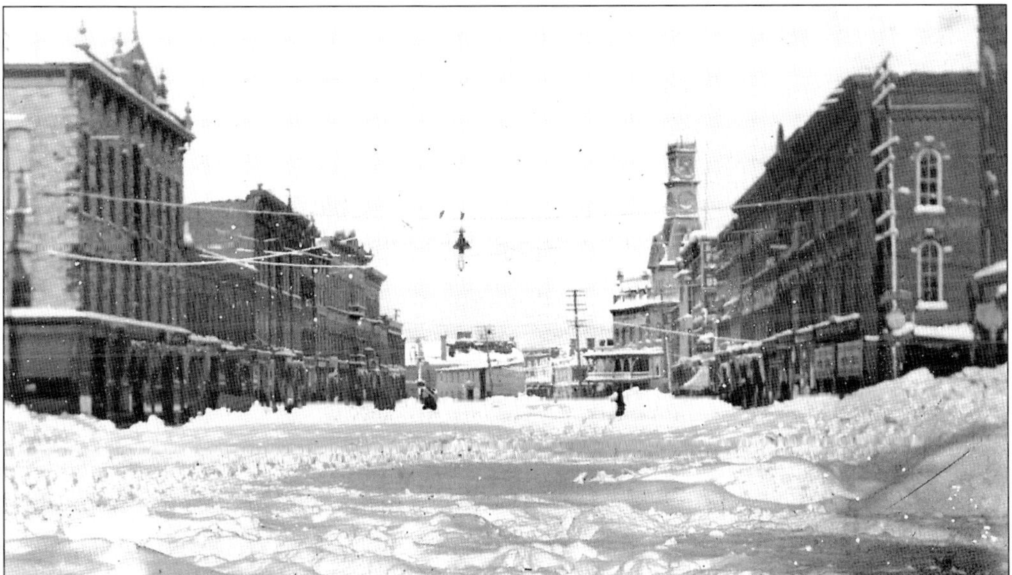

NO SNOW PLOWS. During the horse-and-buggy days, after a snowstorm people would have to walk or drive to town with cutters, sleighs with runners. On this particular day around 1915, not even a sleigh could maneuver through these deep drifts. (Courtesy of Mrs. Elmer Chatt.)

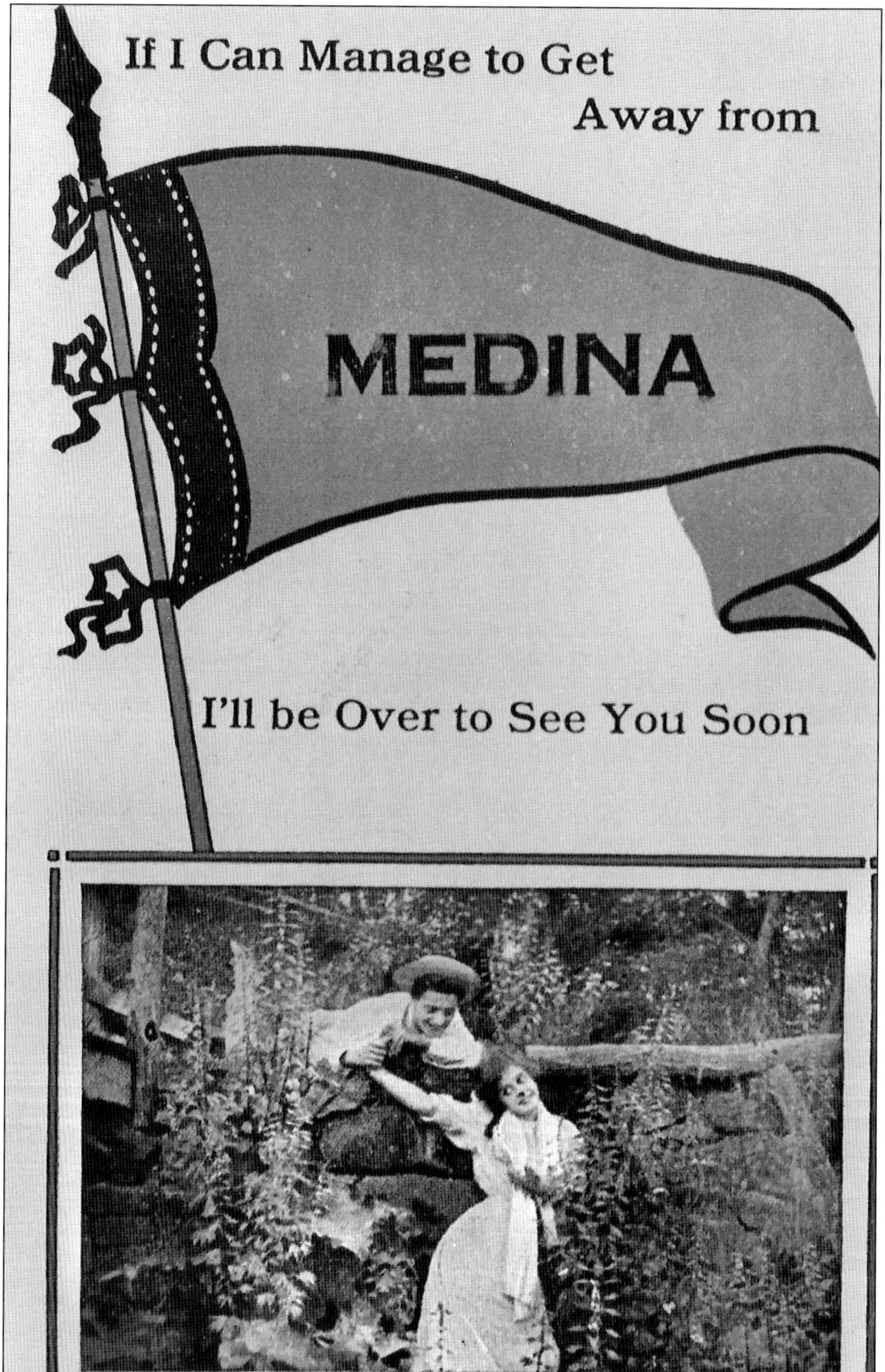

BANNER ADVERTISEMENT. This advertisement from about 1908 states, "If I Can Manage to Get Away from Medina I'll be Over to See You Soon." These advertisements were placed in newspapers and souvenir booklets of the era. (Courtesy of Richard Nellist.)

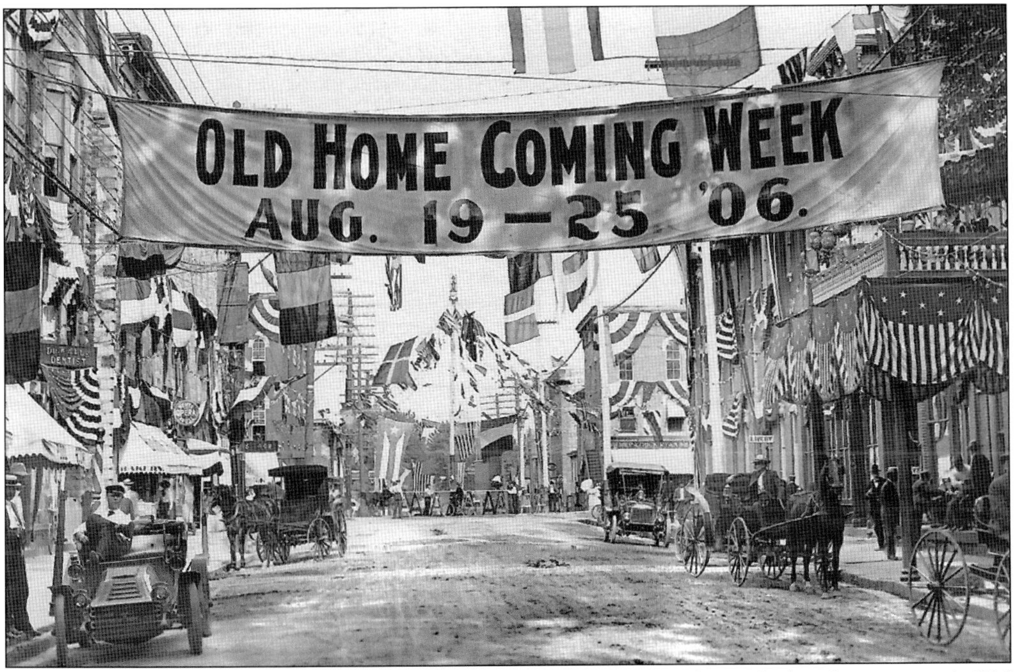

OLD HOMECOMING WEEK. Some signs said Old Home Week, and this banner said Old Homecoming Week. Whatever it was called, buildings were highly decorated and people were happy in August 1906. Old Home Week was celebrated on a smaller scale after the first one. (Courtesy of Bill Henderson.)

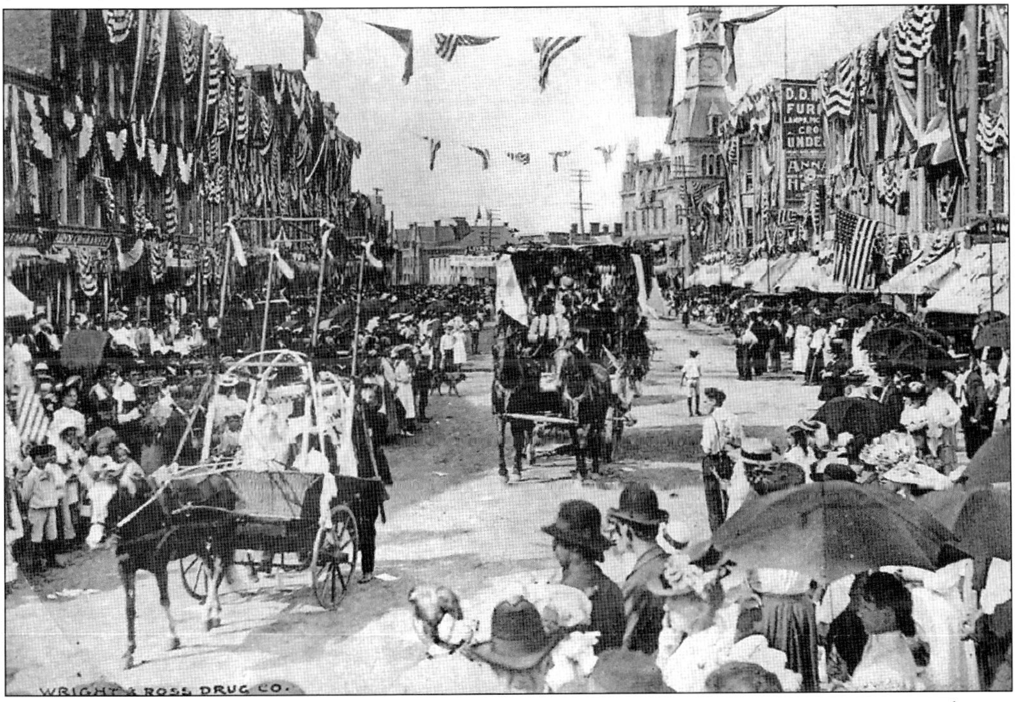

WATCHING THE PARADE. People line up in droves to see the parade down Main Street during Old Homecoming Week. (Courtesy of Bill Henderson.)

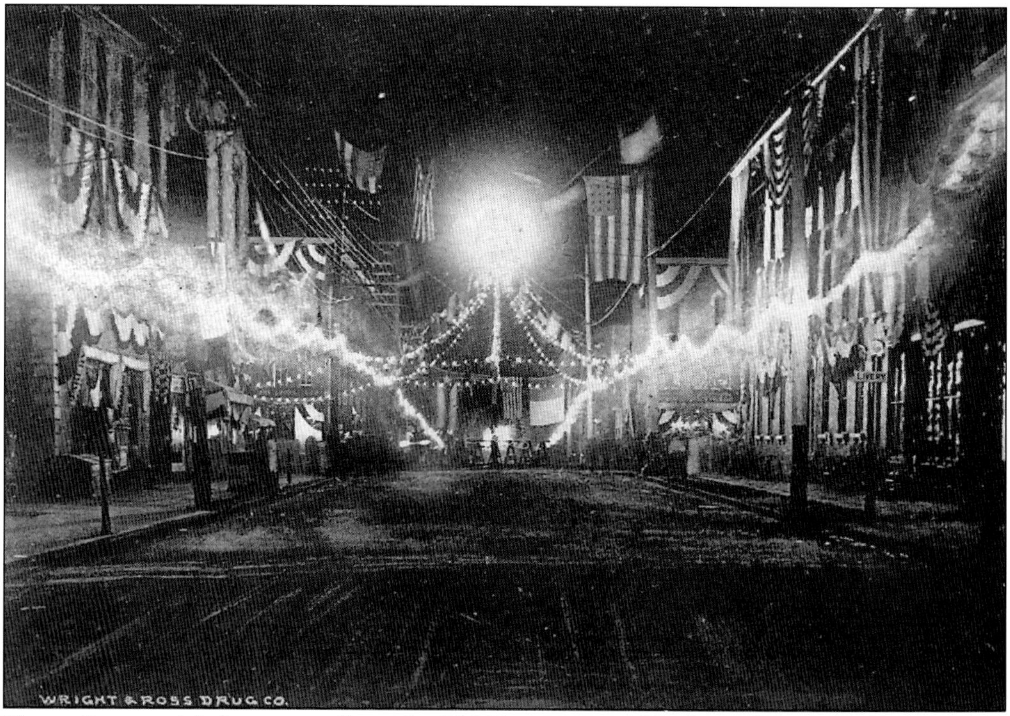

NIGHT LIGHTS. Medina went all out for Old Homecoming Week, to the point of lighting the streets brightly at night. (Courtesy of Bill Henderson.)

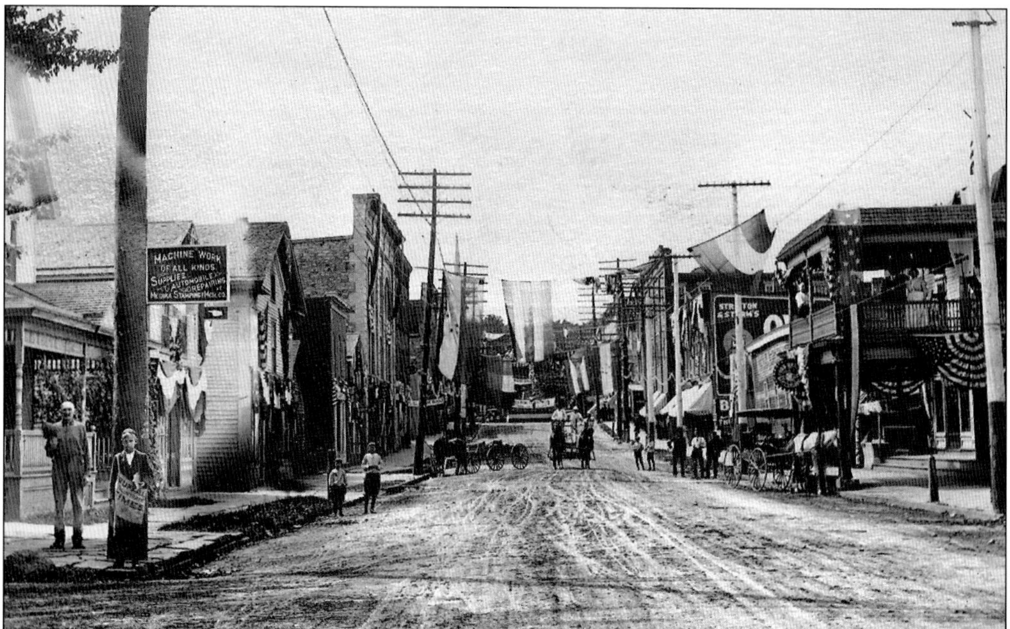

PEOPLE AND FLAGS. The church steeple can be seen behind the banners crossing a side street for Old Home Week. (Courtesy of Bill Henderson.)

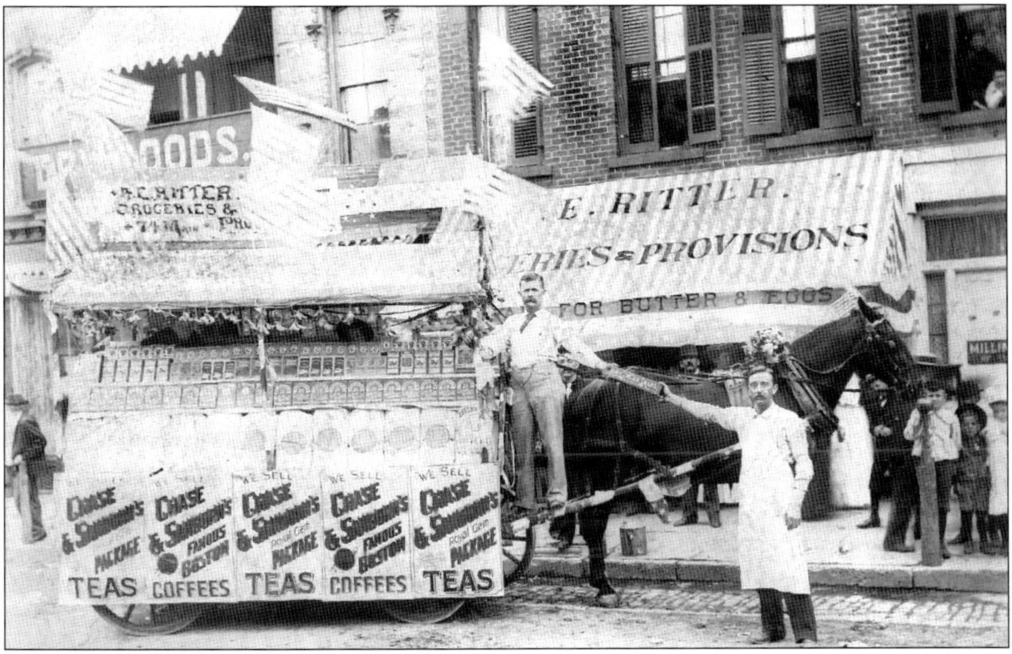

COFFEE, TEA, AND FLOUR. John Stork, left, joins hands with this brother-in-law, L. E. Ritter, in front of Ritter's Store at 435 Main Street. The flag-decorated horse-drawn wagon in front displays Chase and Sanborn teas and coffees, and there are sacks of Gold Medal flour on the wagon. John Stork was chief of police, and there is a street named after him off of South Main Street. (Courtesy of Frank Berger.)

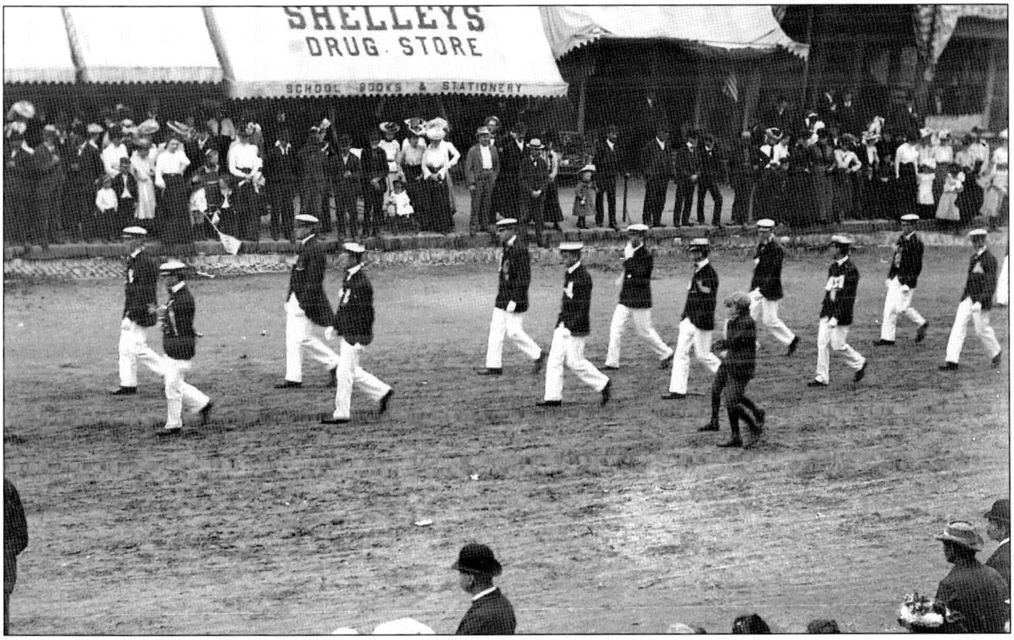

COLORFUL SPECTATORS. The people watching this parade around 1910 were more colorful than the marchers. Note the two boys running along the side of the marchers. Were they trying to cross or did they get caught up with the moment? (Courtesy of Mrs. Elmer Chatt.)

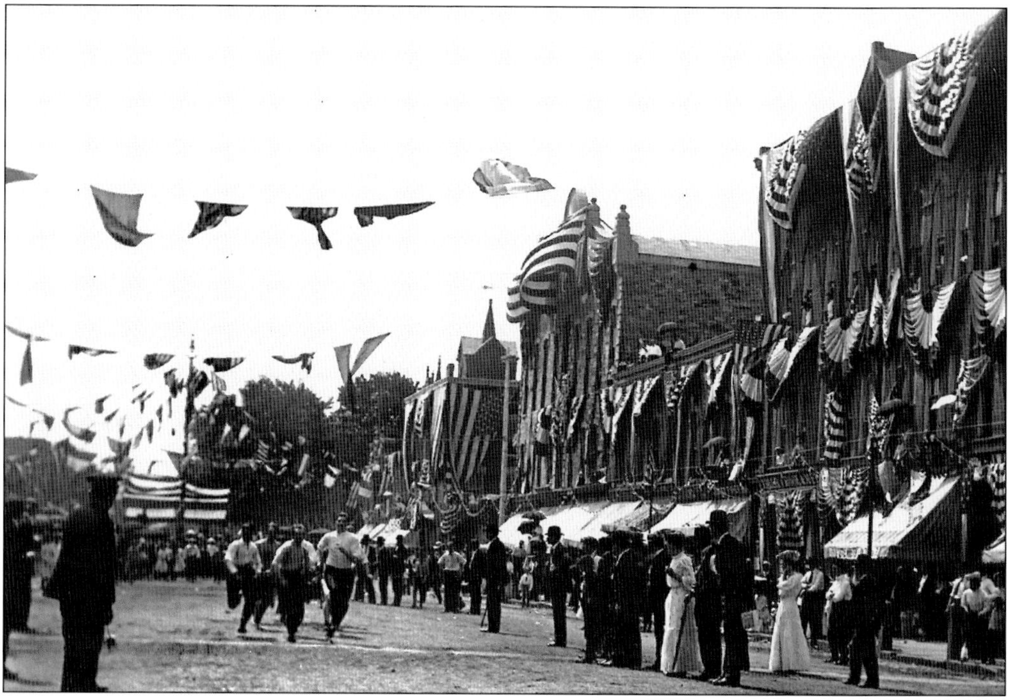

Watching a Race. A group of men run down Main Street as onlookers stand in the street and on the sidewalks to watch their progress. Note the white dresses on the ladies. (Courtesy of Mrs. Elmer Chatt.)

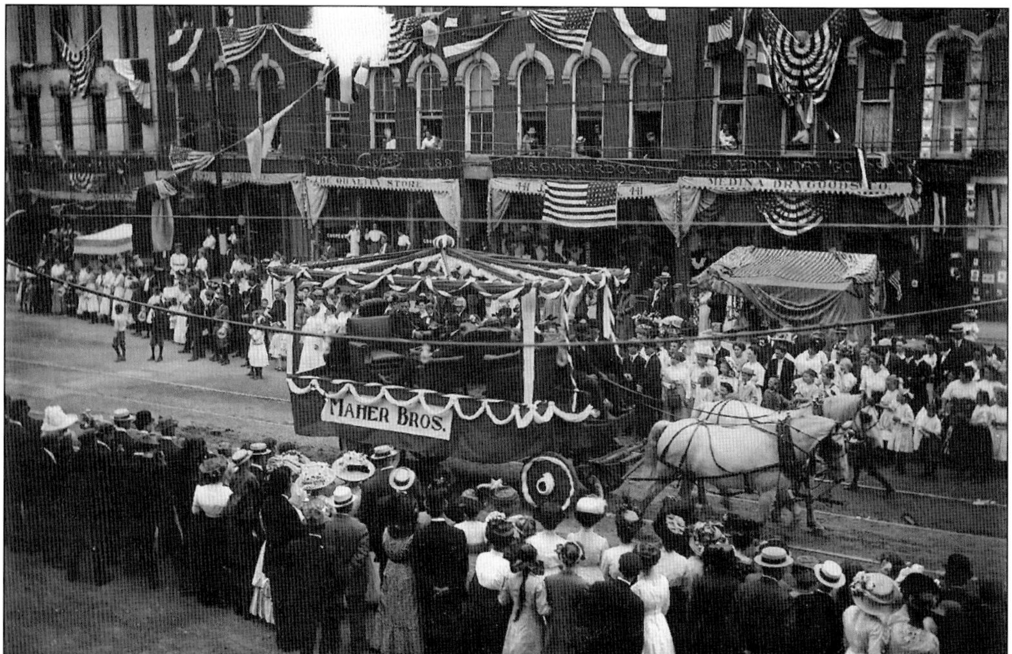

Maher Brothers Float. This was one of many floats that traveled down Main Street in August 1906 during Old Homecoming Week. (Courtesy of Richard Nellist.)

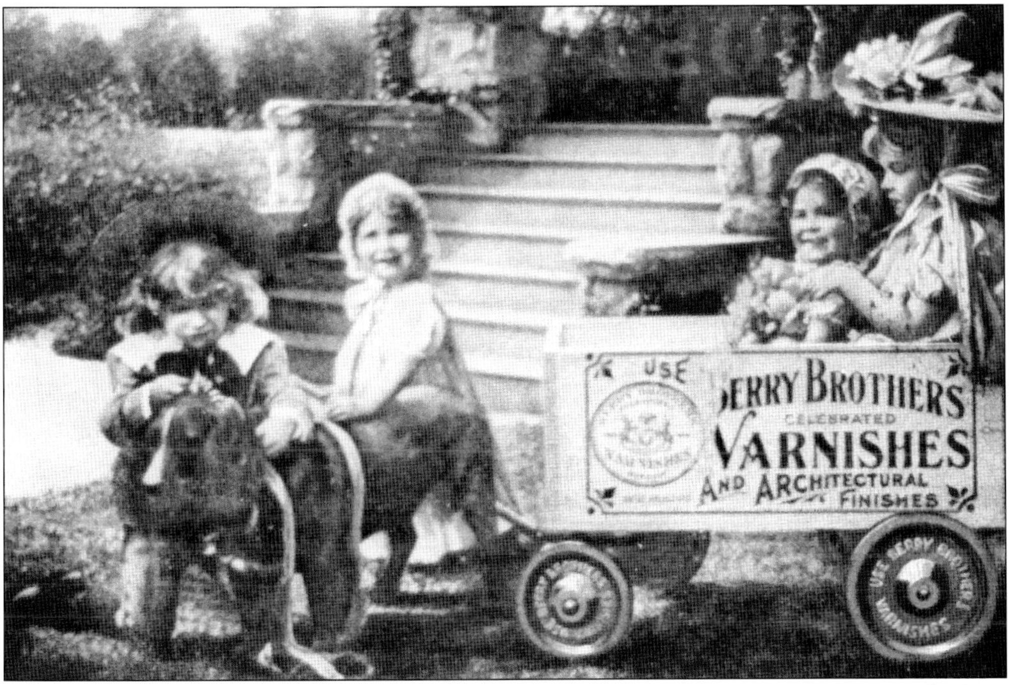

ACER AND WHEDON FLOAT. Situated on the canal, where the Acme Company now stands, Acer and Whedon made furniture and woodworking supplies. This advertisement was for varnish, one of the items Acer and Whedon sold. (Courtesy of Richard Nellist.)

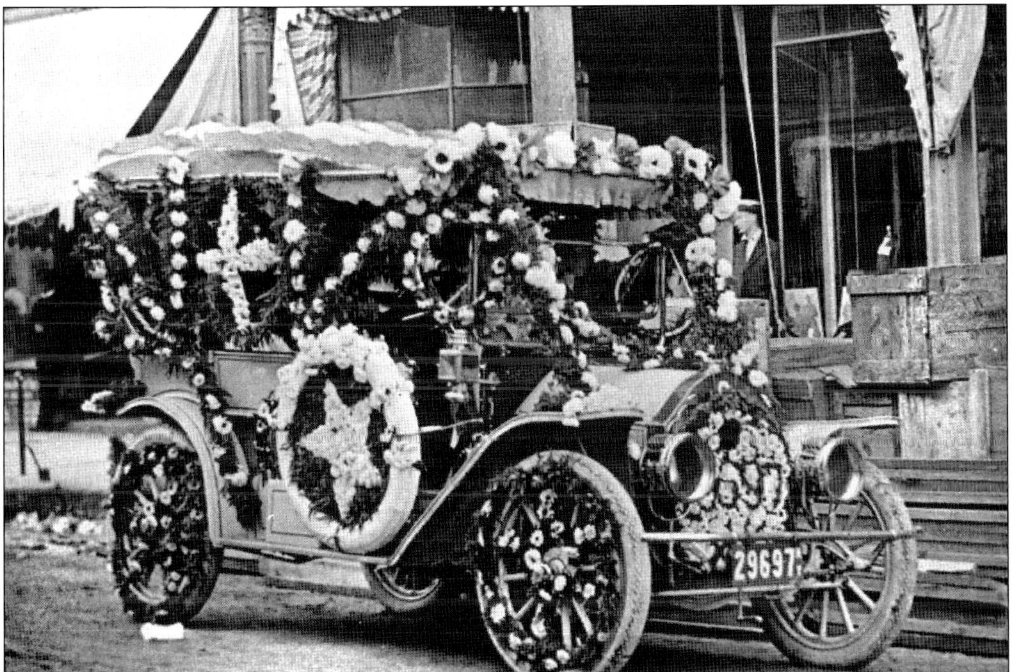

STARS AND FLOWERS. This car waits to join in the Main Street parade around 1910. (Courtesy of Richard Nellist.)

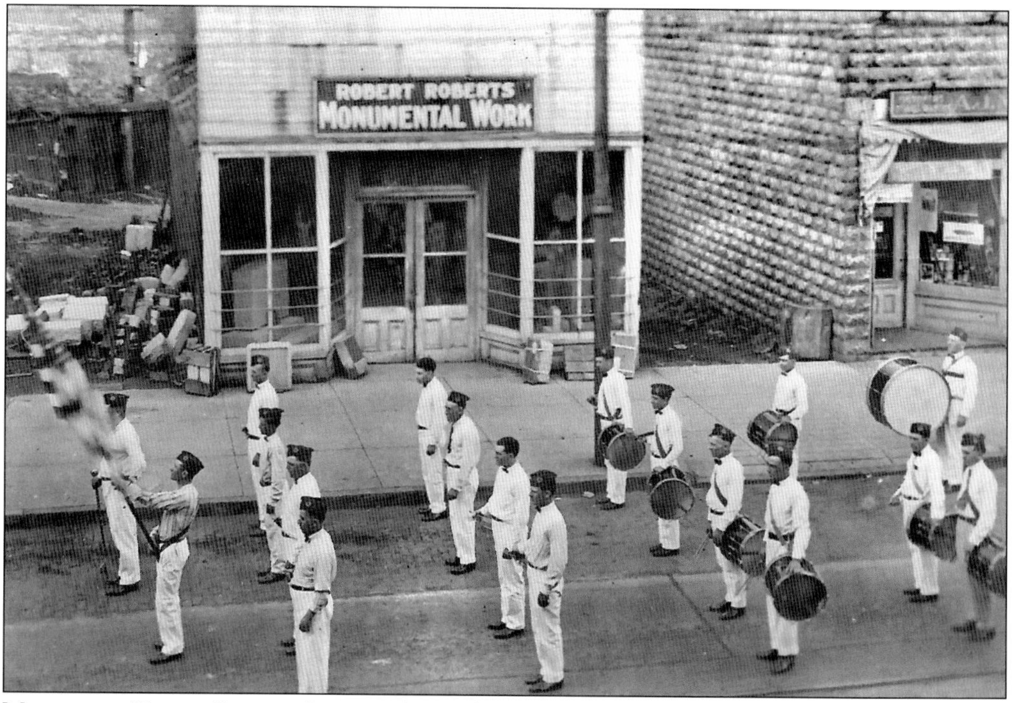

Marching Down Center Street. Around 1930, veterans parade on Center Street in front of Robert Roberts Monumental Work. (Courtesy of Frank Berger.)

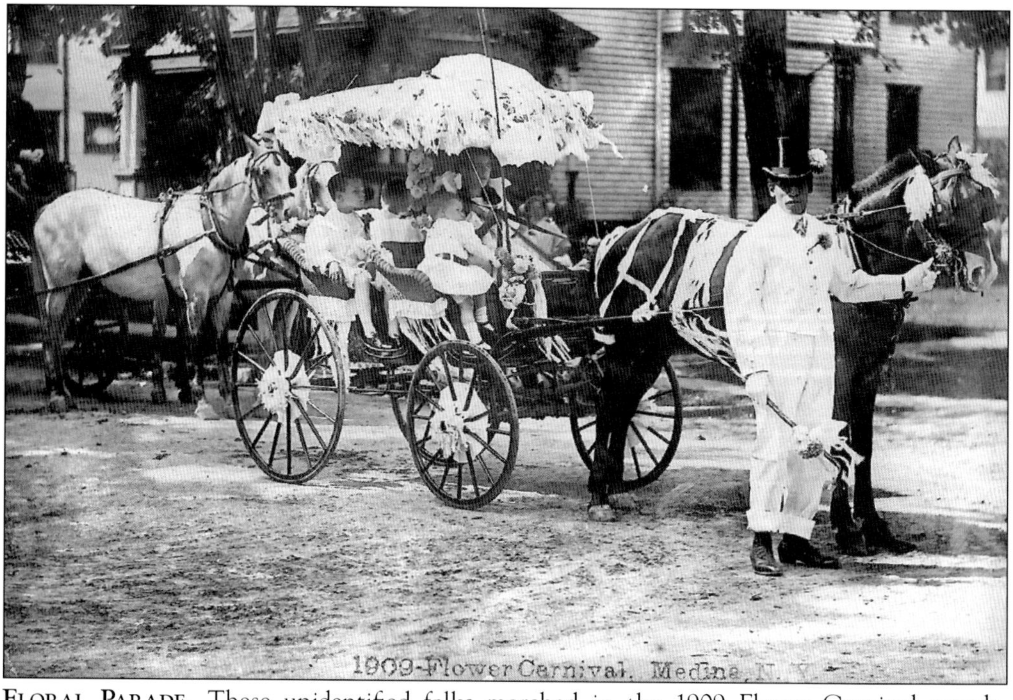

Floral Parade. These unidentified folks marched in the 1909 Flower Carnival parade. (Courtesy of Bill Henderson.)

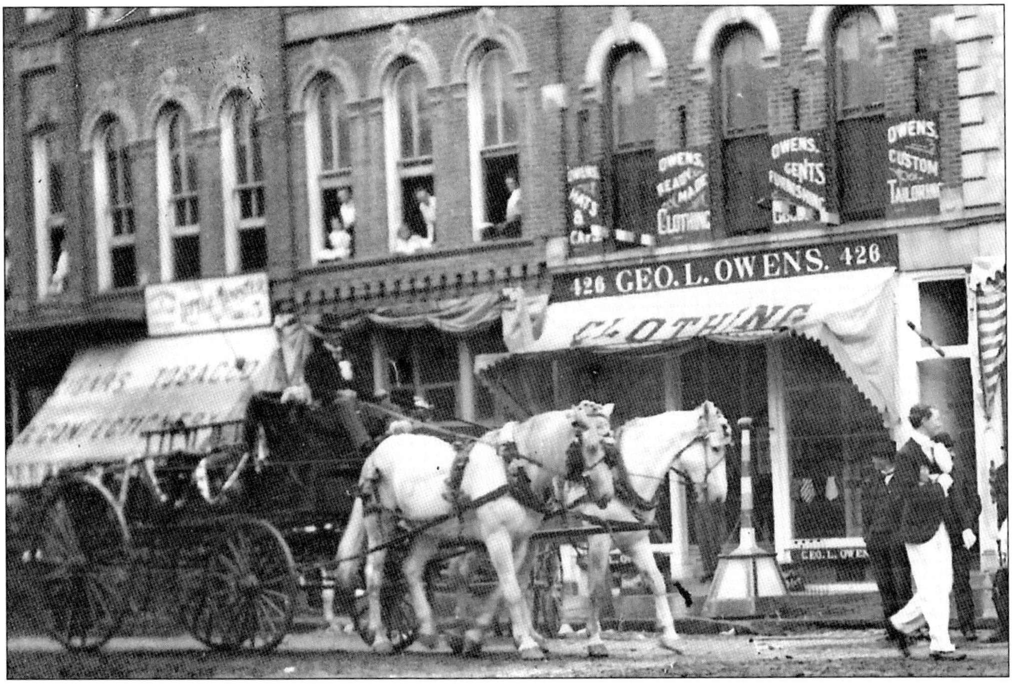

IN THE WINDOWS. Residents peer out of their upstairs apartment windows as the final marcher of a parade makes his way down Main Street, followed by a team of horses pulling a wagon. (Courtesy of Mrs. Elmer Chatt.)

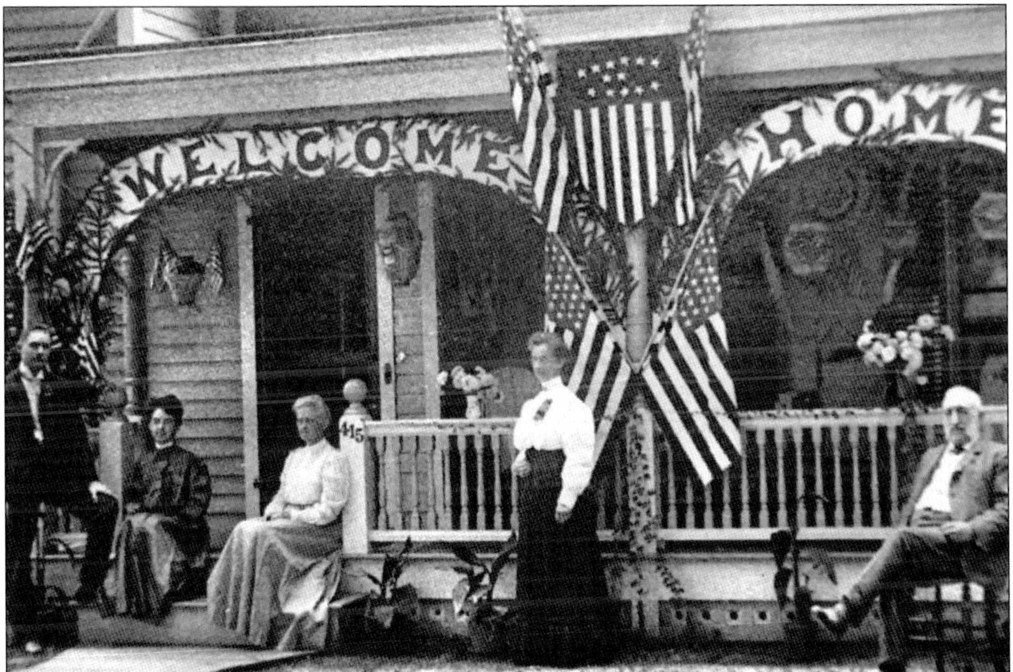

WELCOME HOME. The Murdocks of 445 Commercial Street display the Welcome Home sign proudly in August 1906 for Old Homecoming Week. (Courtesy of Richard Nellist.)

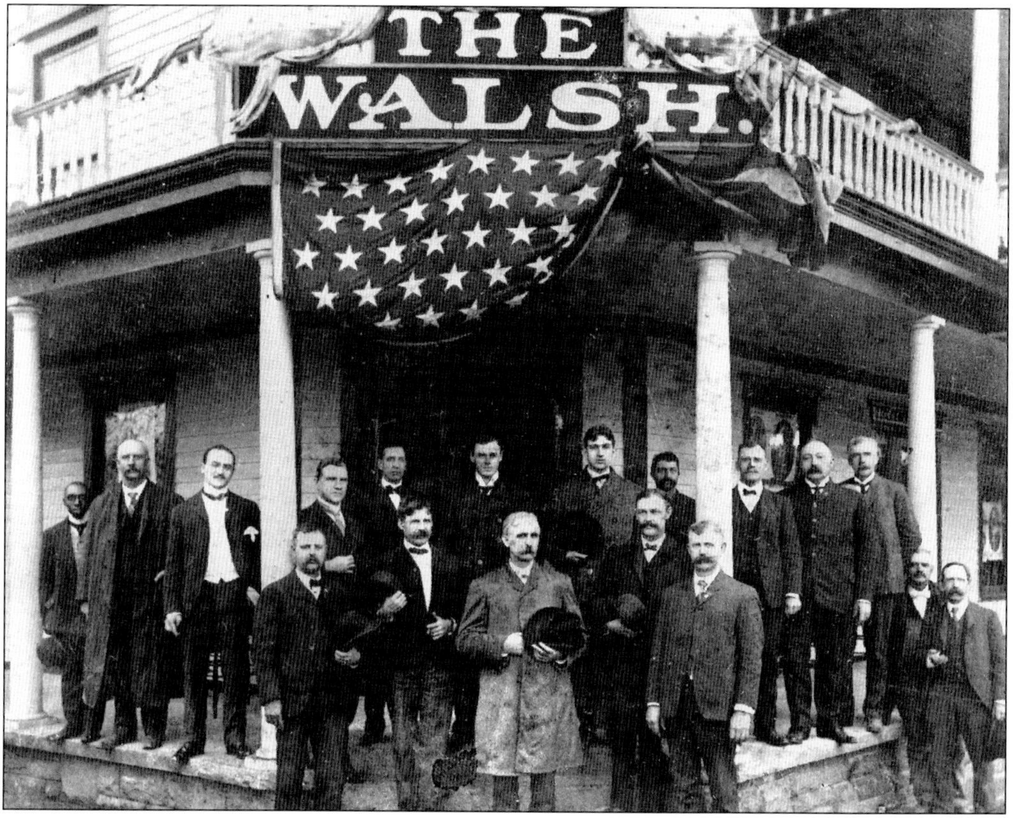

MEN AT THE WALSH. This group of dignitaries poses for the camera at the southeast corner of the Walsh House, which was also decorated with bunting. (Courtesy of Mrs. Elmer Chatt.)

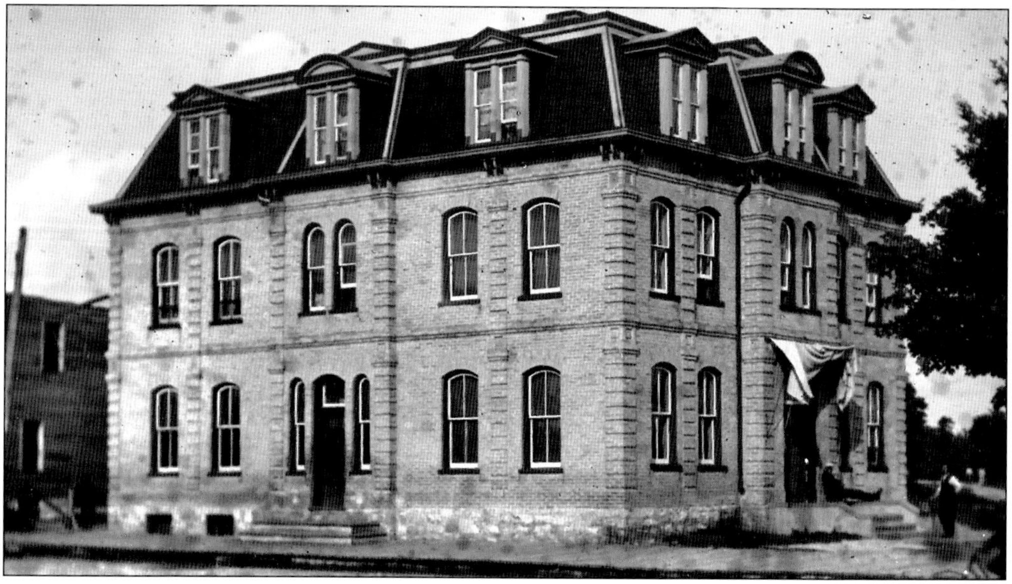

THE WALSH HOUSE. The Walsh has been a longtime establishment, opening in the late 19th century and continuing to operate today in the same location on West Avenue, next to the old train depot. (Courtesy of Mrs. Elmer Chatt.)

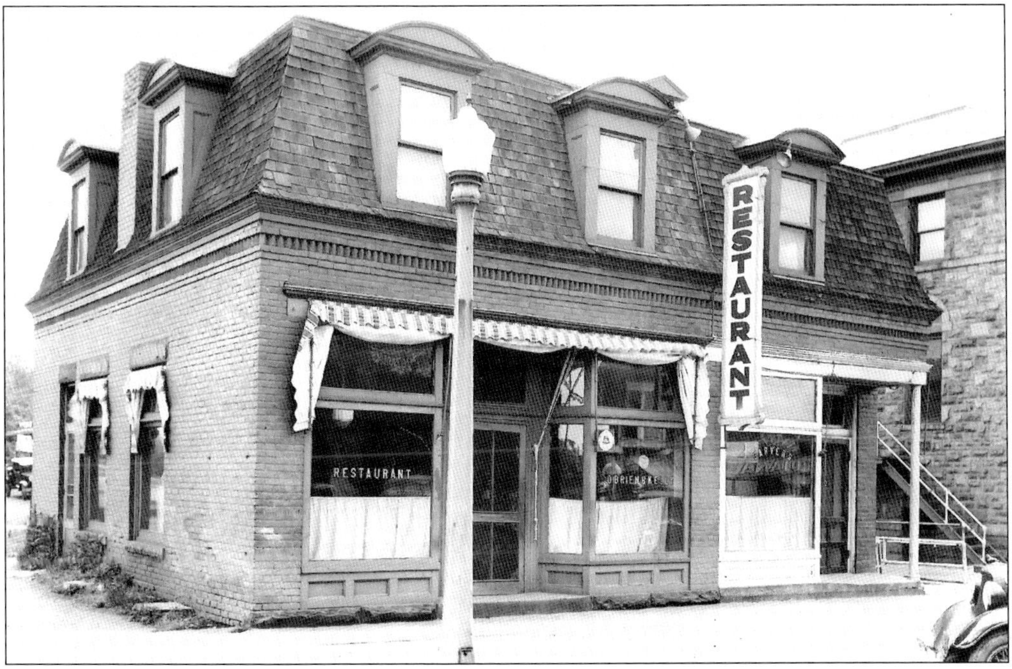

O'BRIEN AND KELLY, 1940. This was the forerunner of O'Brien's Inn, situated directly south of City Hall. Note the streetlamp in front, the awning, and the two front entrances, with the right entrance entering Garver's Restaurant. It was directly across the street from the Diana Theater, which is closed now. (Courtesy of Martin Hobbs.)

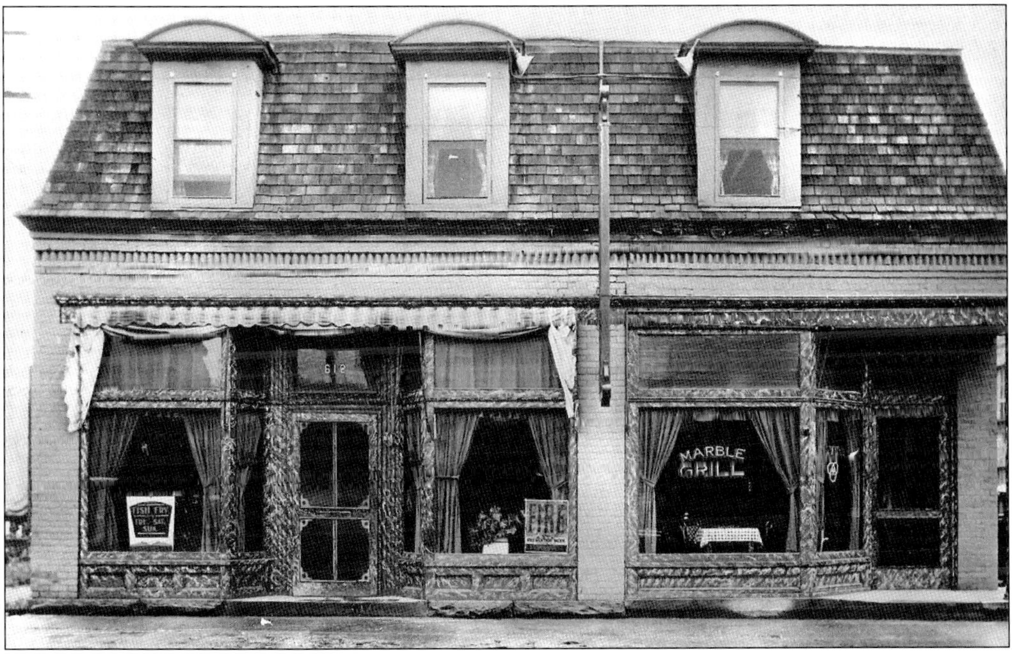

THE MARBLE GRILL, 1935. Before it was O'Brien's or Garver's, this was the Marble Grill, and it advertised fish fries on Friday nights. This was before the streetlamps were installed. (Courtesy of Martin Hobbs.)

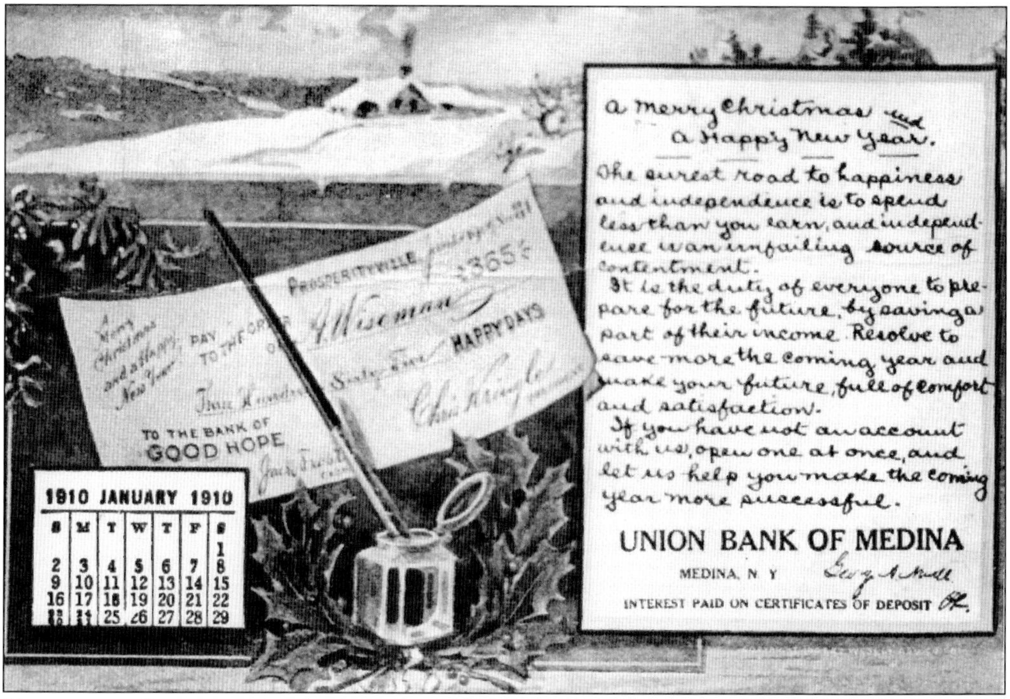

Christmas Card, 1910. This unique card was sent to the customers of the Union Bank of Medina. The check is made to the order of A. Wiseman for the amount of 365 Happy Days. It is paid by the Bank of Good Hope, Jack Frost proprietor. It is signed by Chris Kringle. The letter advises people to save for the coming year. The Union Bank went bankrupt in 1931. (Courtesy of Richard Nellist.)

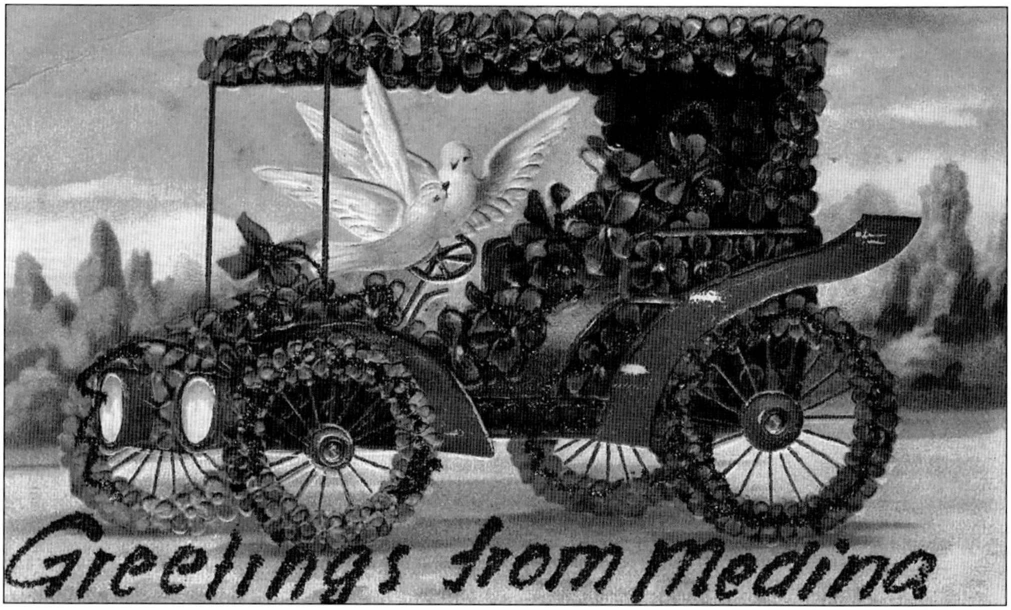

Beautiful Greetings. This postcard from around 1930 greets people to Medina in a beautiful way. The wagon and wheels are trimmed in purple violets, a common wildflower in western New York. (Courtesy of Bill Henderson.)

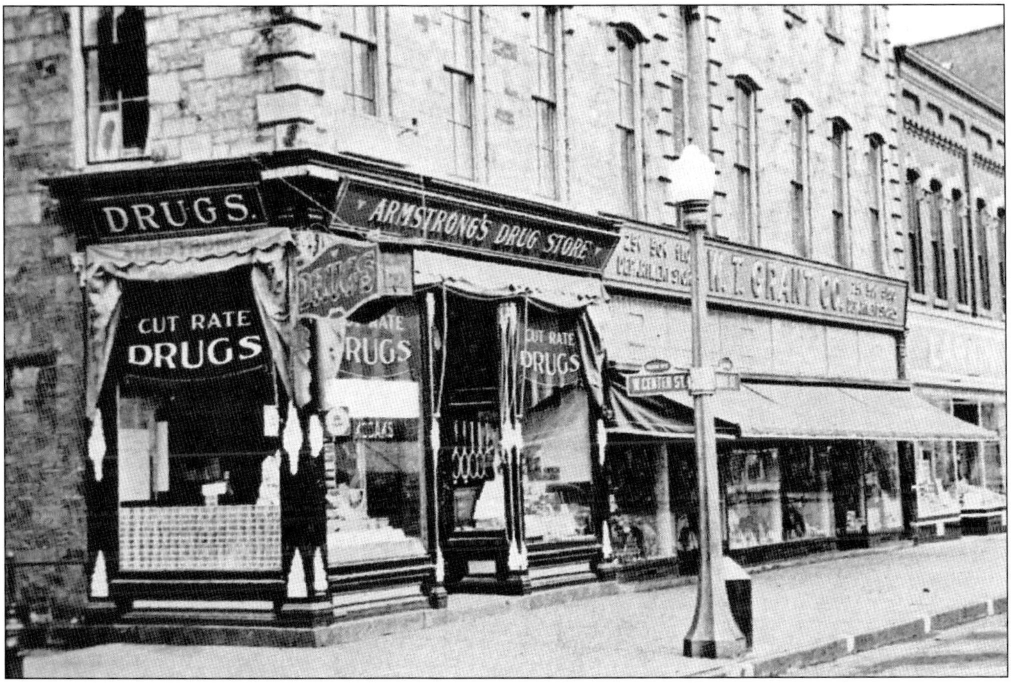

ARMSTRONG'S DRUG STORE. This was one of three drugstores in Medina during the 1930s and 1940s. On the corner of Main and West Center Streets, it was also a bus station stop. W. T. Grant Company, a popular 5¢ and 10¢ store, was next to it. (Courtesy of Richard Nellist.)

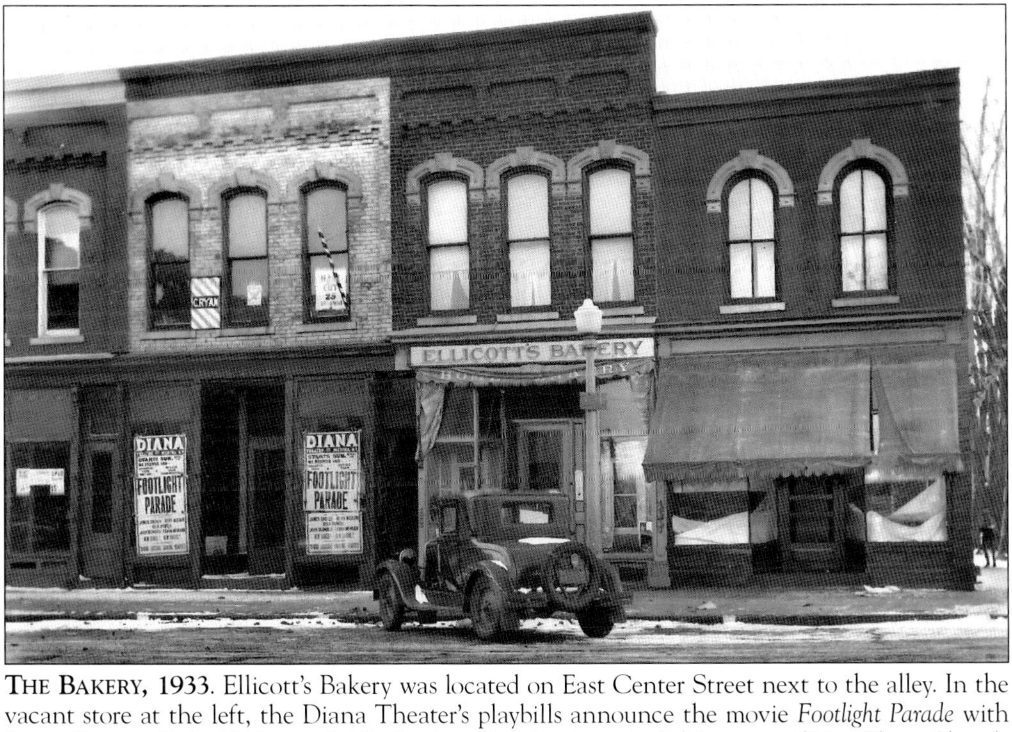

THE BAKERY, 1933. Ellicott's Bakery was located on East Center Street next to the alley. In the vacant store at the left, the Diana Theater's playbills announce the movie *Footlight Parade* with James Cagney, Ruby Keeler, and "300 luscious dancing beauties." (Courtesy of Mrs. Elmer Chatt.)

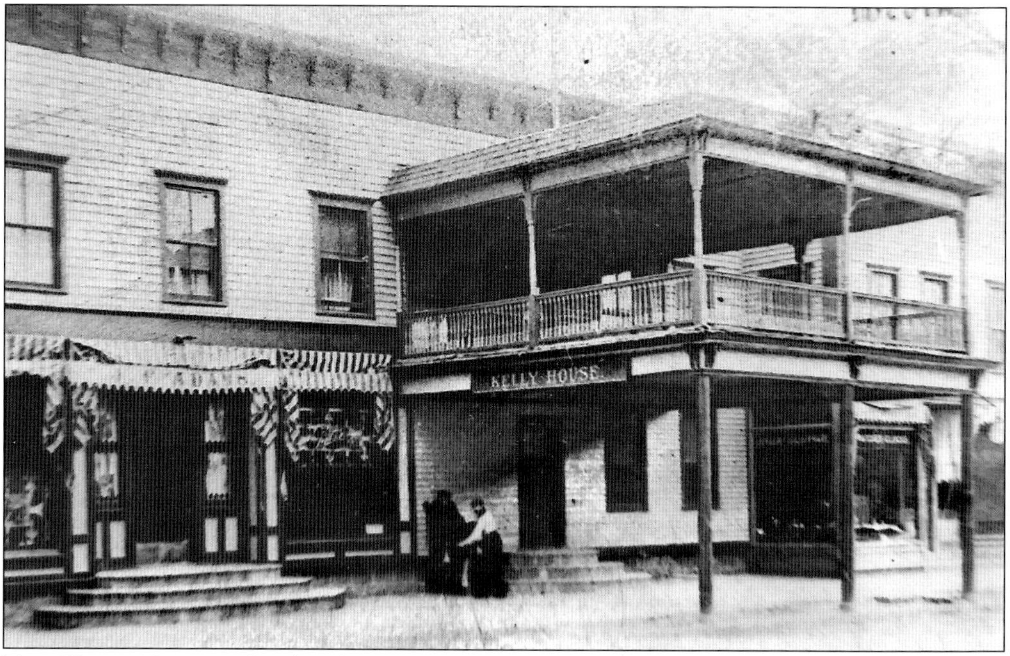

THE KELLY HOUSE. This hotel was on the north side of East Center Street around 1915. (Courtesy of Richard Nellist.)

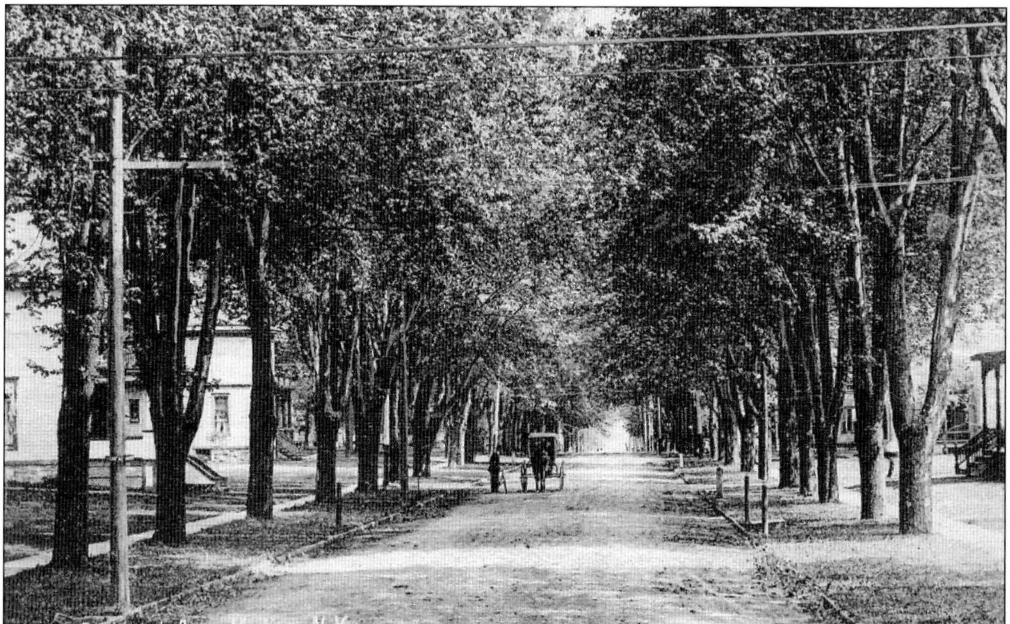

PROSPECT AVENUE, 1909. A quiet, tree-lined street is the ideal place to take a buggy ride or walk a dog in the days before automobiles. (Courtesy of Bill Henderson.)

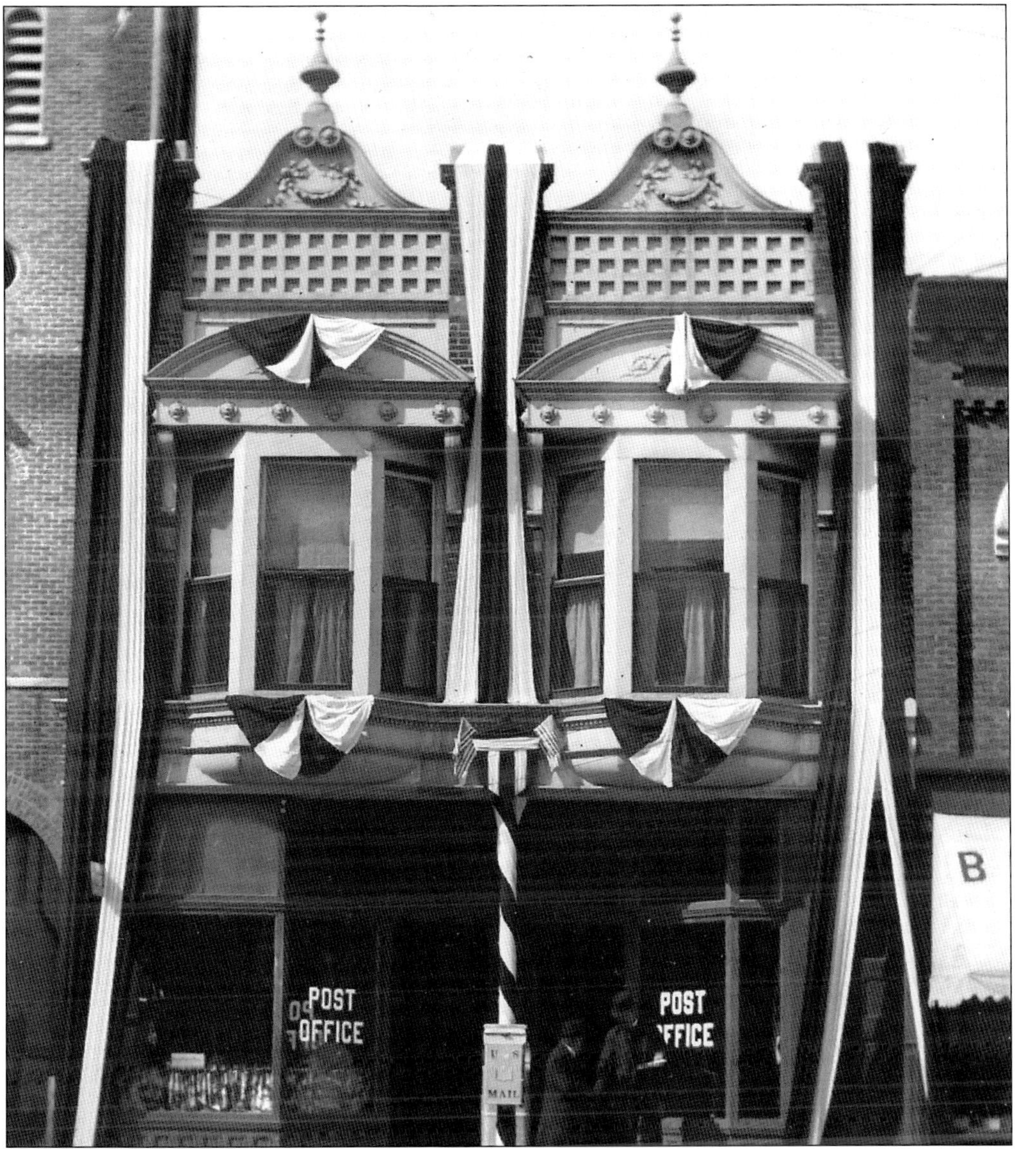

ORIGINAL POST OFFICE. The first post office was on the west side of Main Street between the Presbyterian church and Johnson's boot shop. The building is now HSBC Bank. (Courtesy of Mrs. Elmer Chatt.)

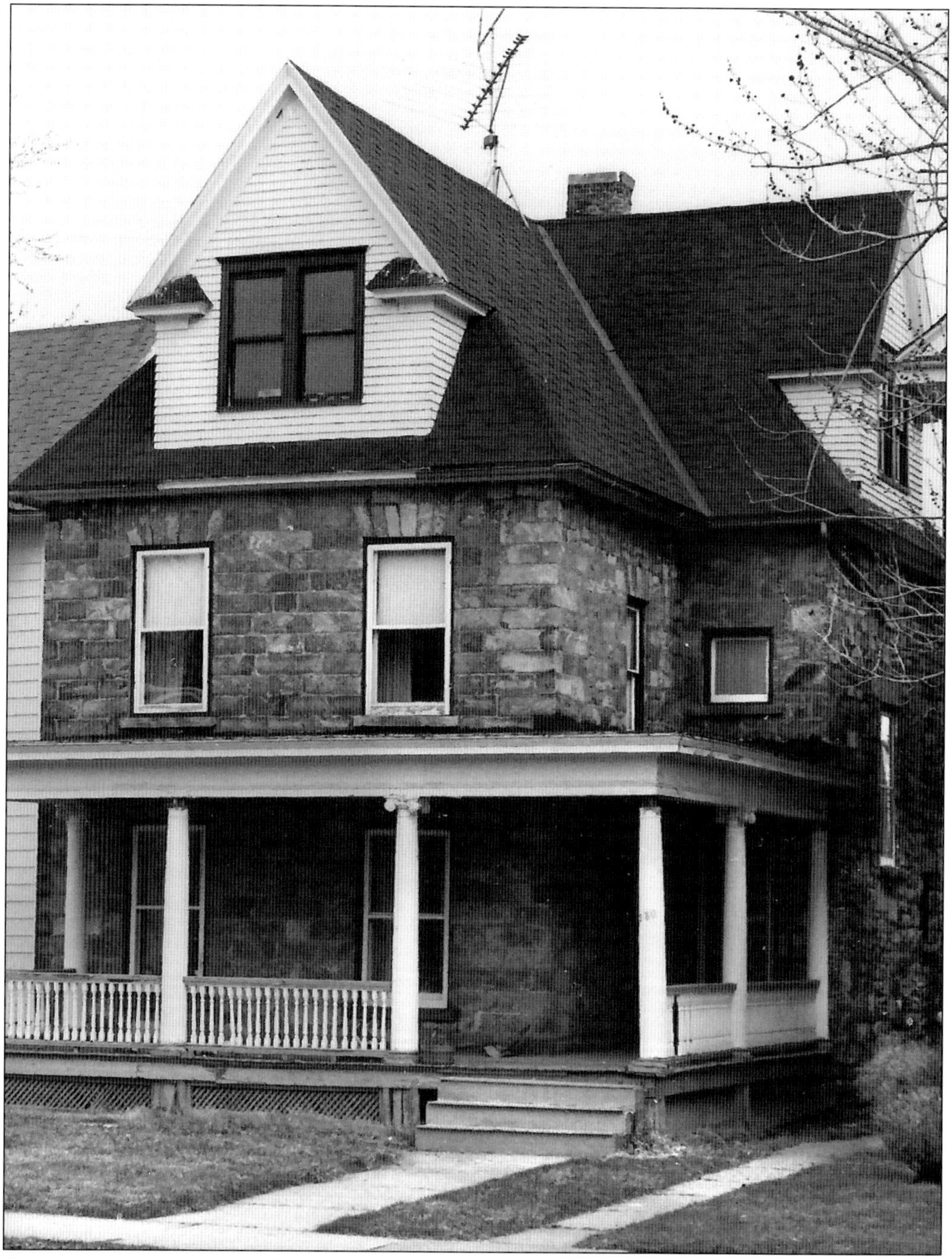

SANDSTONE AND WOOD. This house was built of sandstone, but subsequent owners added dormers and a porch made of wood. (Courtesy of Richard Nellist.)

Five

Majestic Buildings

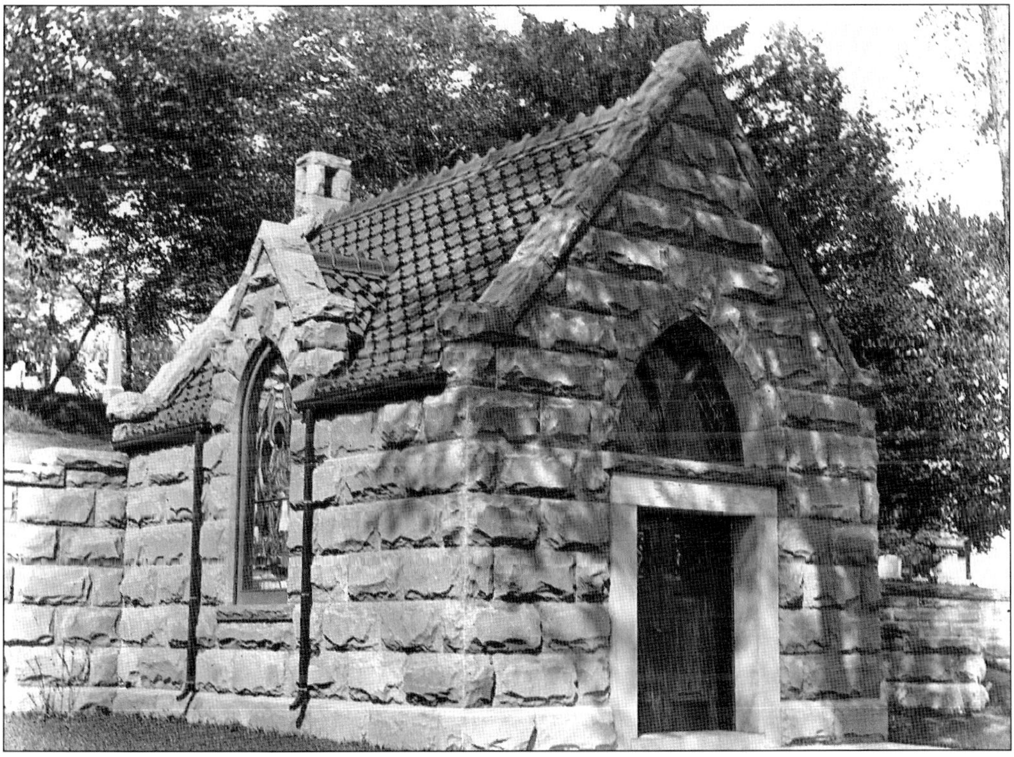

Boxwood Sandstone. This lovely red structure, made of Medina sandstone, is at Boxwood Cemetery, located on North Gravel Road. The property is adjacent to Glenwood Lake. (Courtesy of Mrs. Elmer Chatt.)

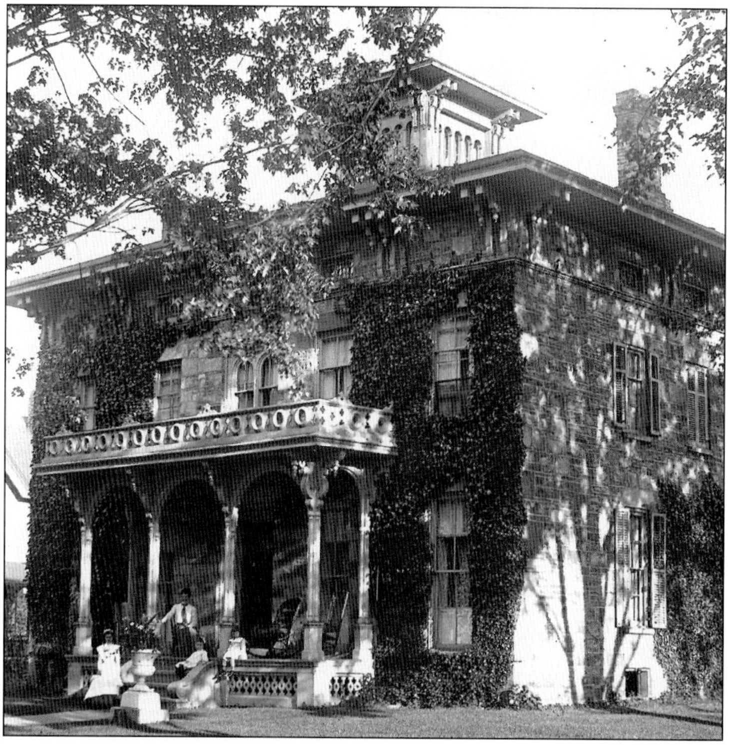

Stone Mansion. This home is located at 321 West Center Street and is now an apartment house. (Courtesy of Mrs. Elmer Chatt.)

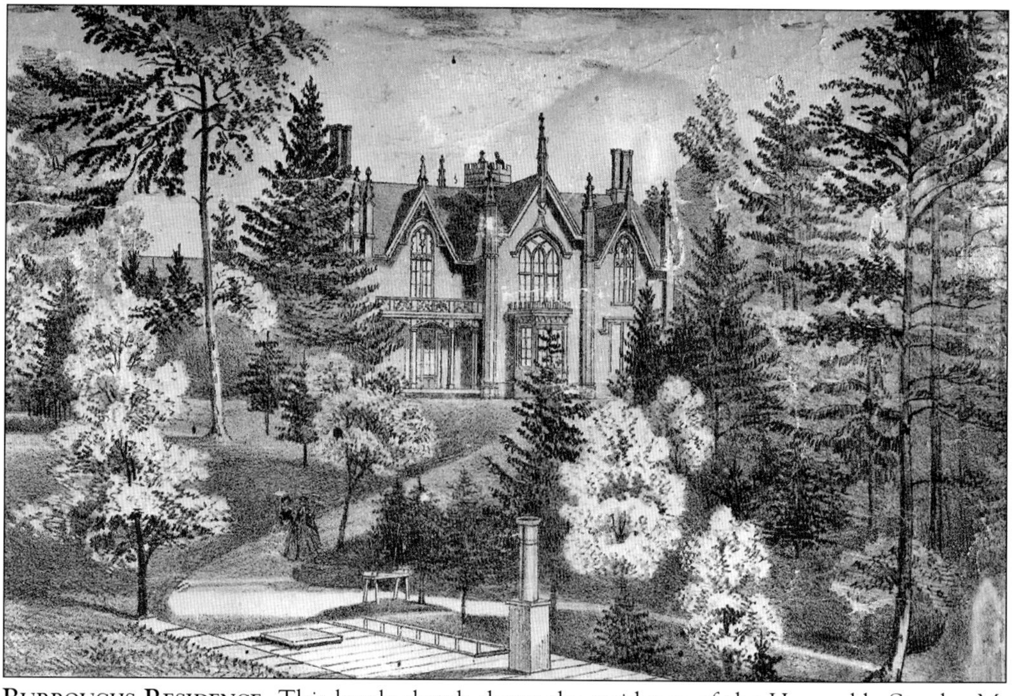

Burroughs Residence. This lovely sketch shows the residence of the Honorable Stanley M. Burroughs. It was located where State Street Park is now, near the spot where the Erie Canal flows over the Oak Orchard Creek, and had a marvelous view of the waterfall. The Burroughses had a lovely view from all their windows. (Courtesy of Mrs. Elmer Chatt.)

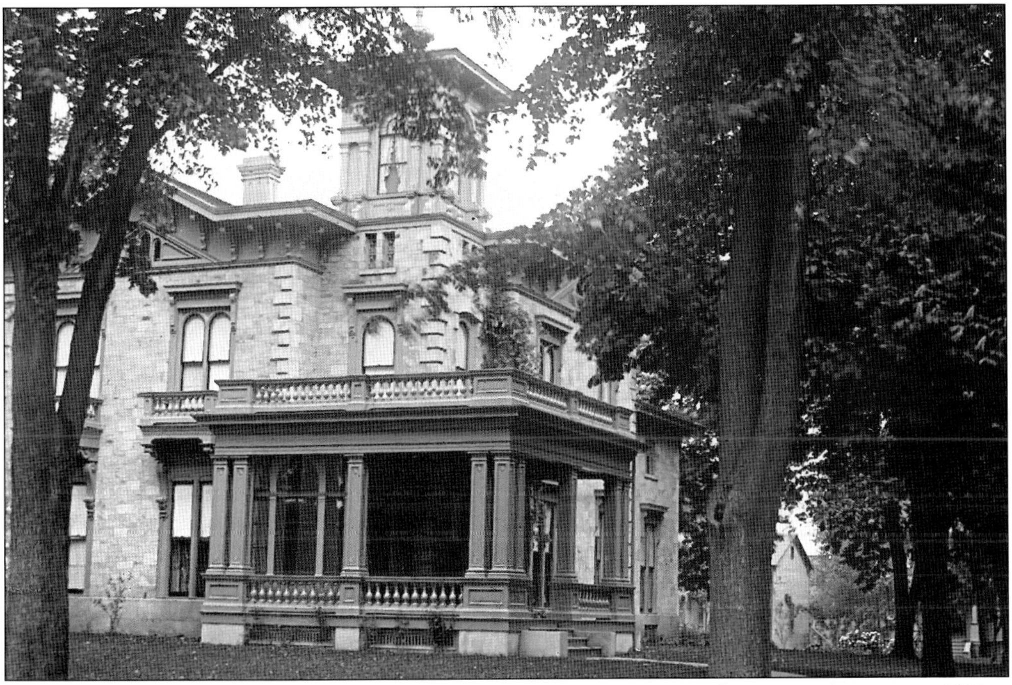

West Center Street. This was the Luther Home on the corner of Prospect Avenue and West Center Street. The tower looks out over Medina and the canal and was once called Stonehurst. This photograph was taken in the 1960s when the home became an apartment complex. (Courtesy of Mrs. Elmer Chatt.)

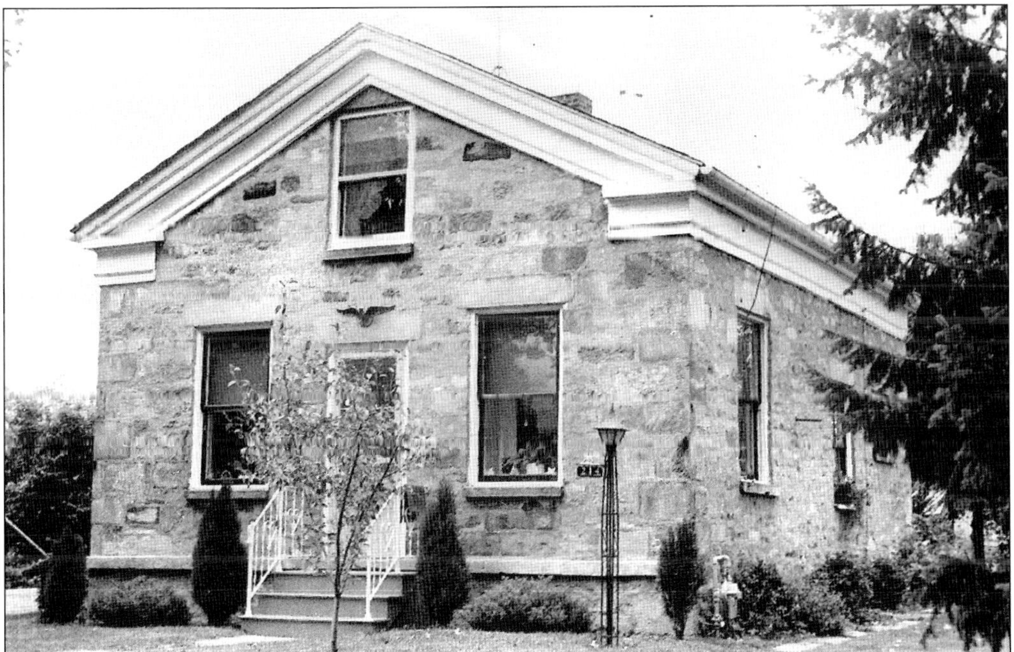

Sandstone Schoolhouse. This former schoolhouse on Pleasant Street was converted into a home. (Courtesy of Richard Nellist.)

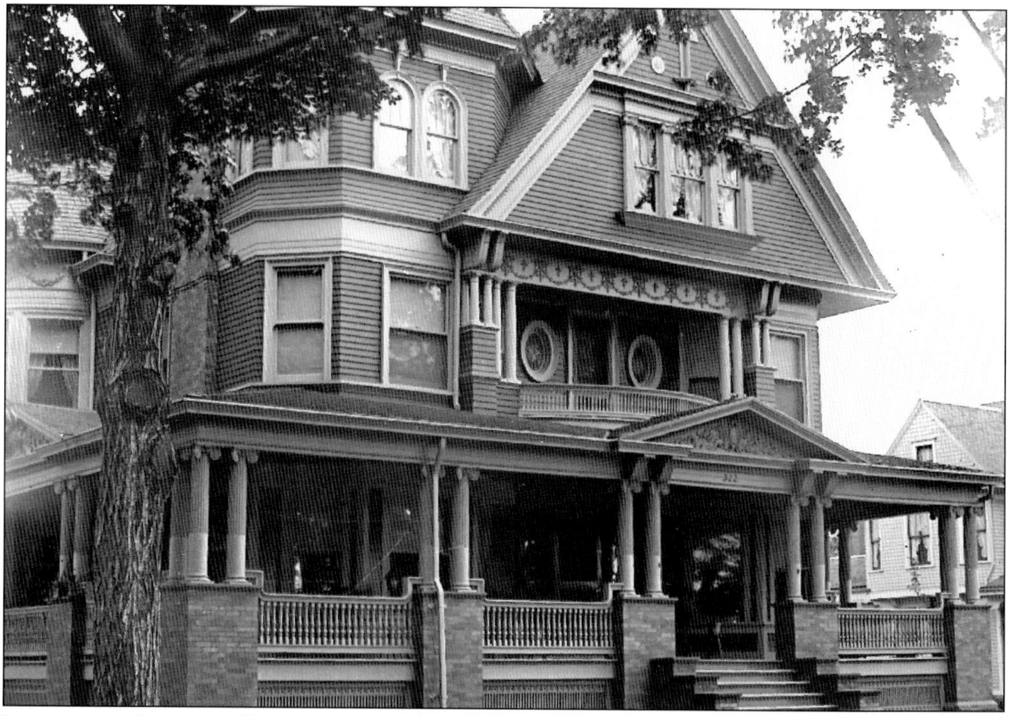

Large and Lovely. This magnificent home at 322 West Center Street is an apartment house today. (Courtesy of Mrs. Elmer Chatt.)

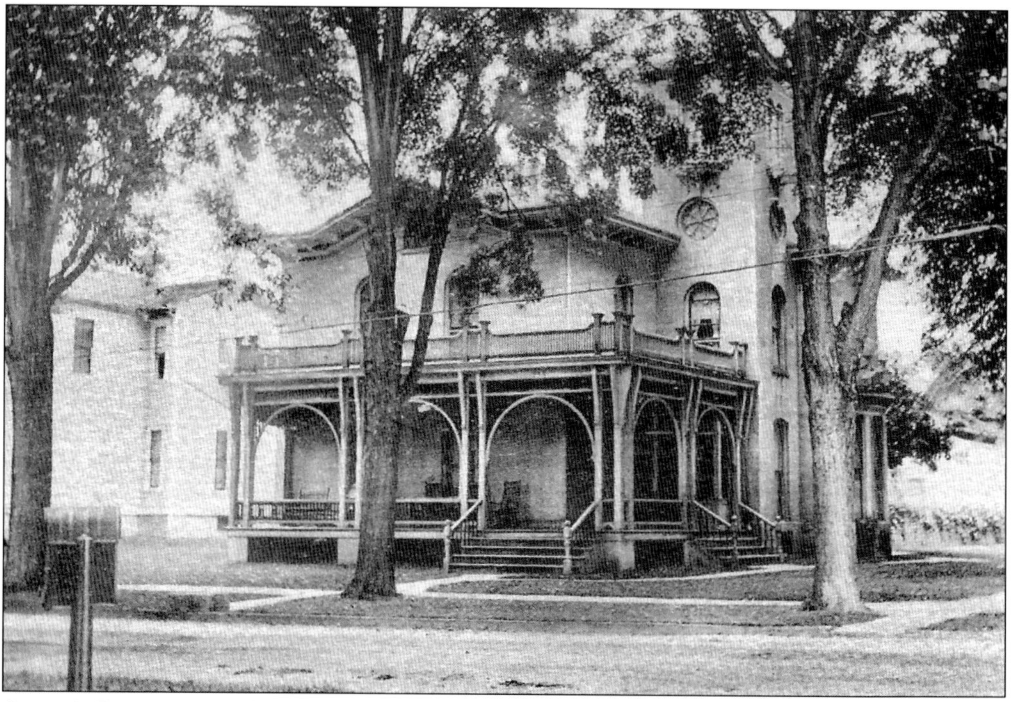

Child's Residence. This home, photographed about 1915, was located on 503 West Center Street. (Courtesy of Grant-Pollard Insurance Office.)

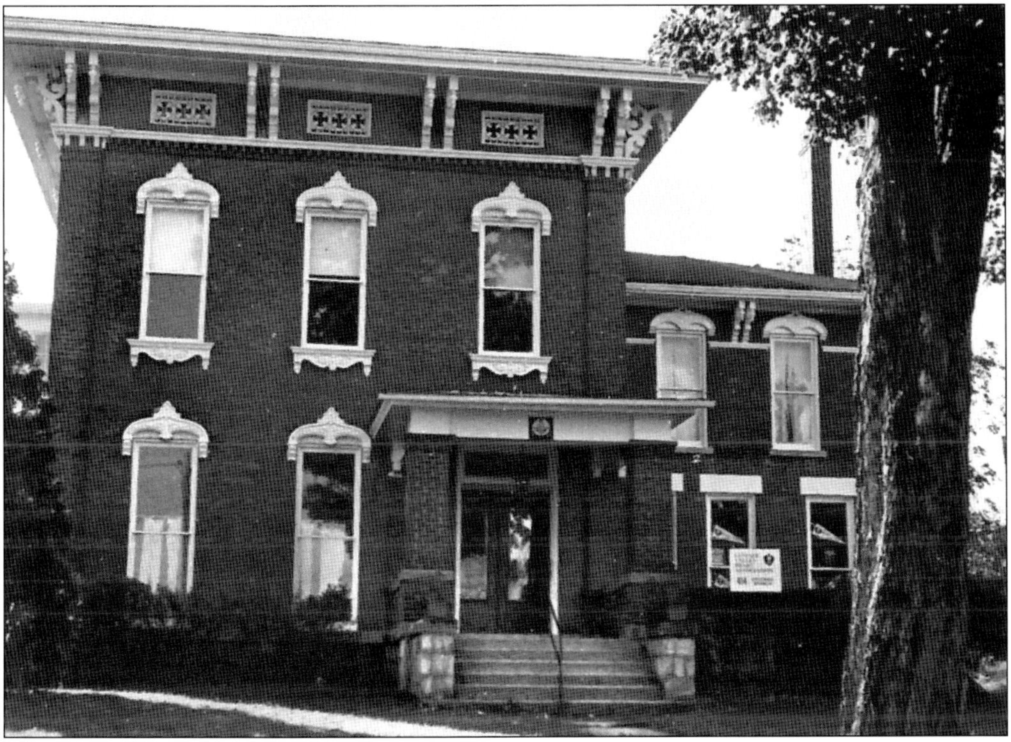

MASONIC TEMPLE. This is the Masonic temple on West Avenue. (Courtesy of Richard Nellist.)

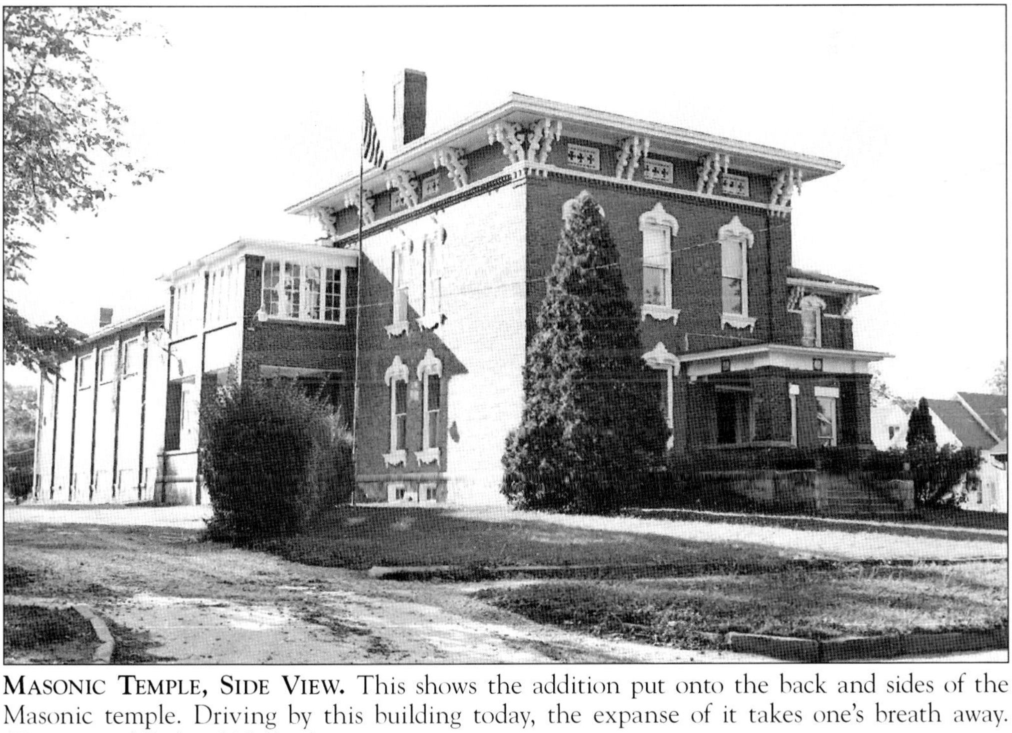

MASONIC TEMPLE, SIDE VIEW. This shows the addition put onto the back and sides of the Masonic temple. Driving by this building today, the expanse of it takes one's breath away. (Courtesy of Richard Nellist.)

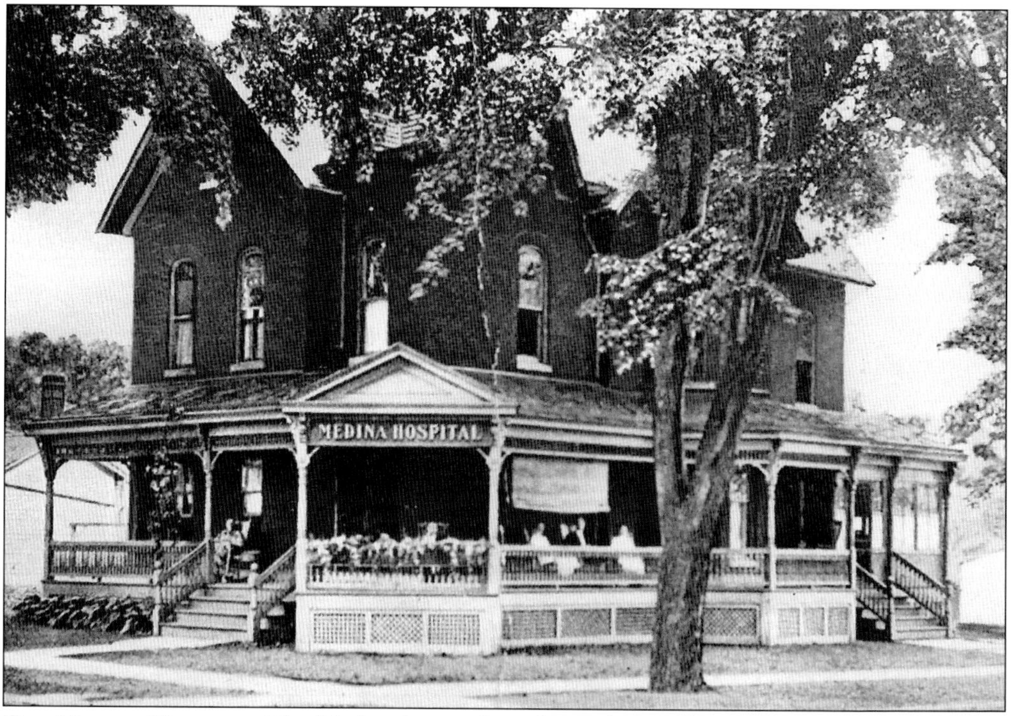

OLD MEDINA HOSPITAL. The Medina hospital was located on Eagle Street and Prospect Avenue until a new one was built on Ohio Street near the banks of the Erie Canal. This building became the YMCA. (Courtesy of Richard Nellist.)

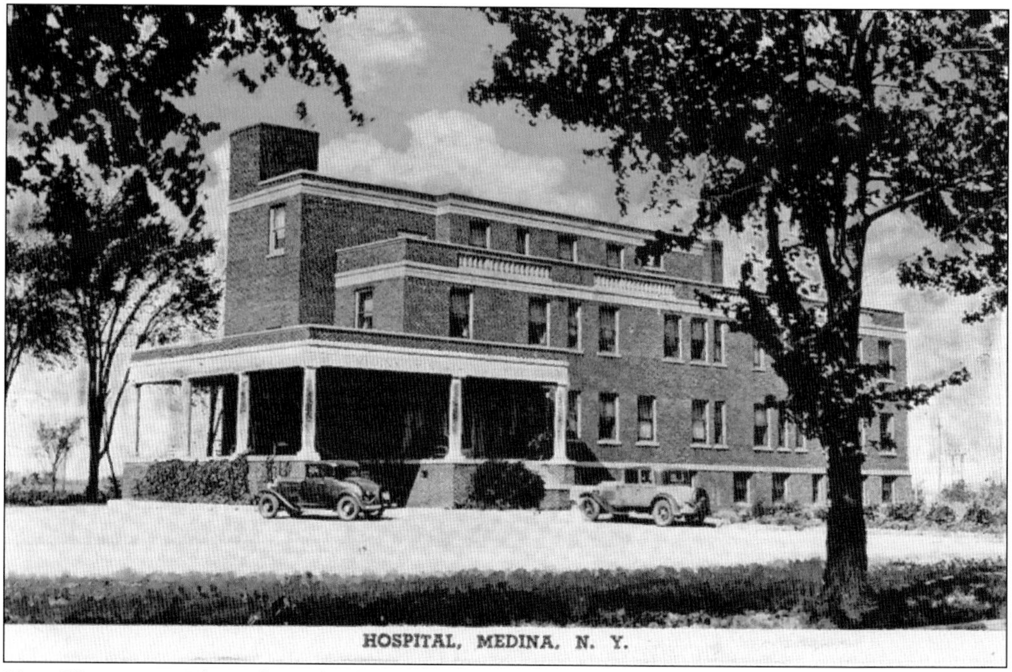

NEW HOSPITAL. This is how the hospital looked in the 1920s. It was a modern building for the times. (Courtesy of Mrs. Elmer Chatt.)

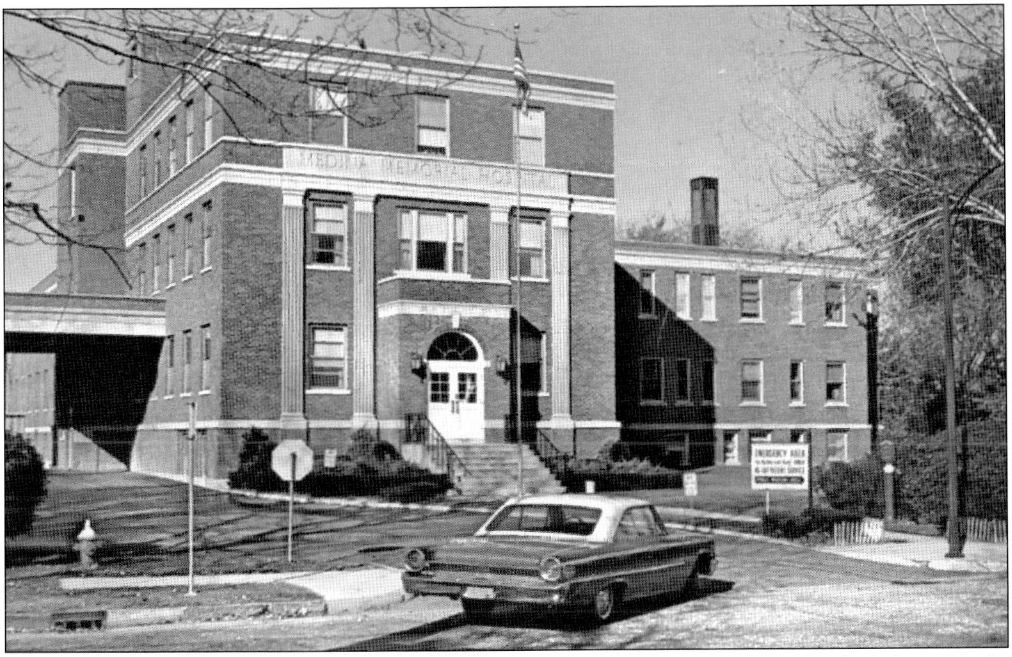

NEW HOSPITAL ADDITION. You can see where the hospital has expanded in this photograph, compared to the previous one. Where the overhang once overshot the front of the hospital, it is now recessed with a new story added to the north side and additional footage to the front. (Courtesy of Mrs. Elmer Chatt.)

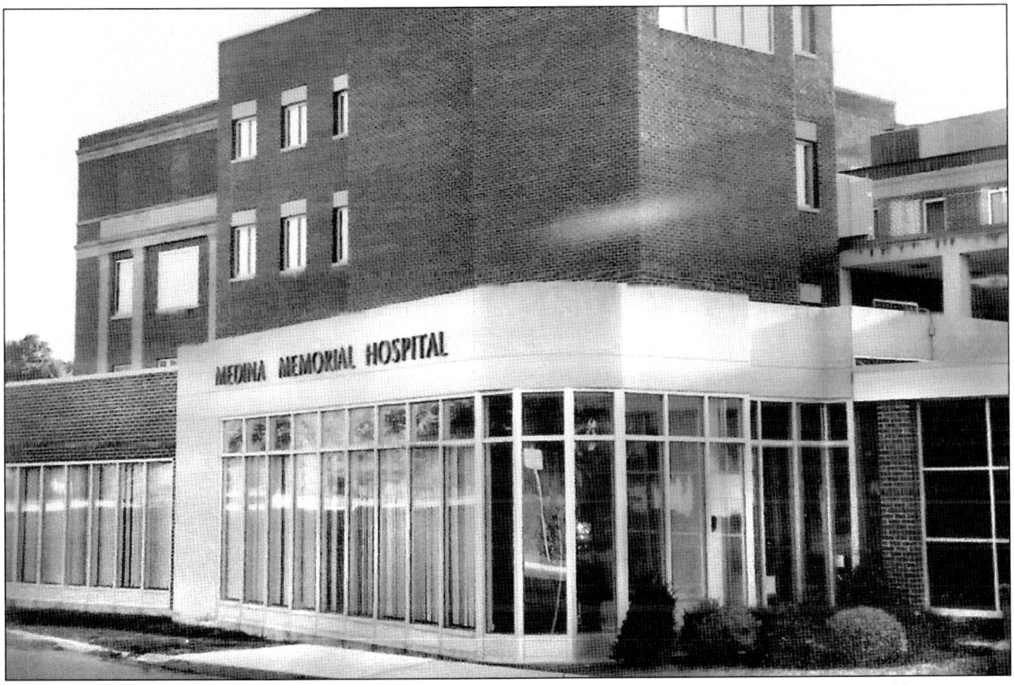

HOSPITAL TODAY. The overhang is now enclosed with glass panels, and another addition runs parallel to the south, also lined with glass. The building is in a quiet section at the west end of Medina, with additional parking facilities and medical buildings located on adjacent streets.

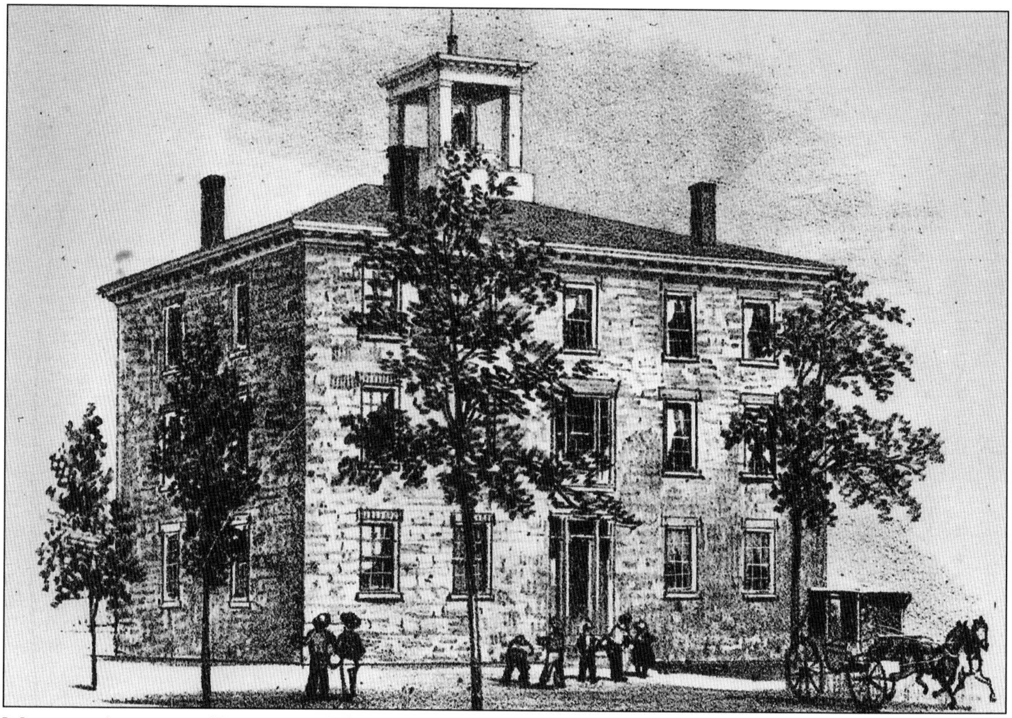

Medina Academy Drawing. This c. 1890 lithograph shows the Medina Academy in its prime. The academy was located at the end of Pearl Street, near the Medina Armory. (Courtesy of Mrs. Elmer Chatt.)

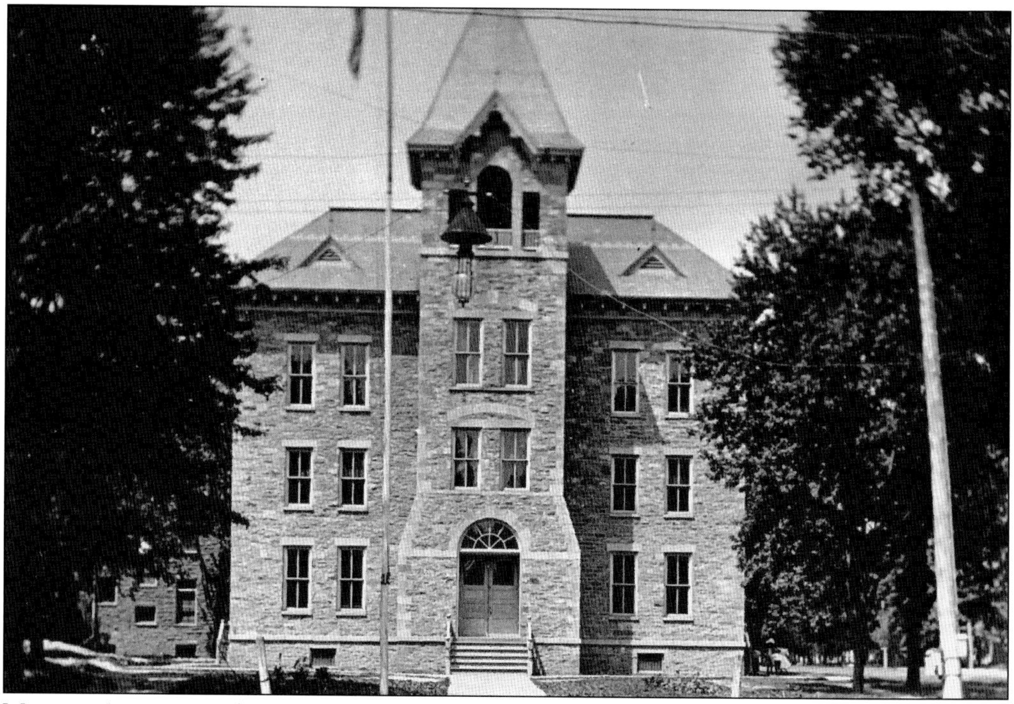

Medina Academy. The old high school is in the background. (Courtesy of Bill Henderson.)

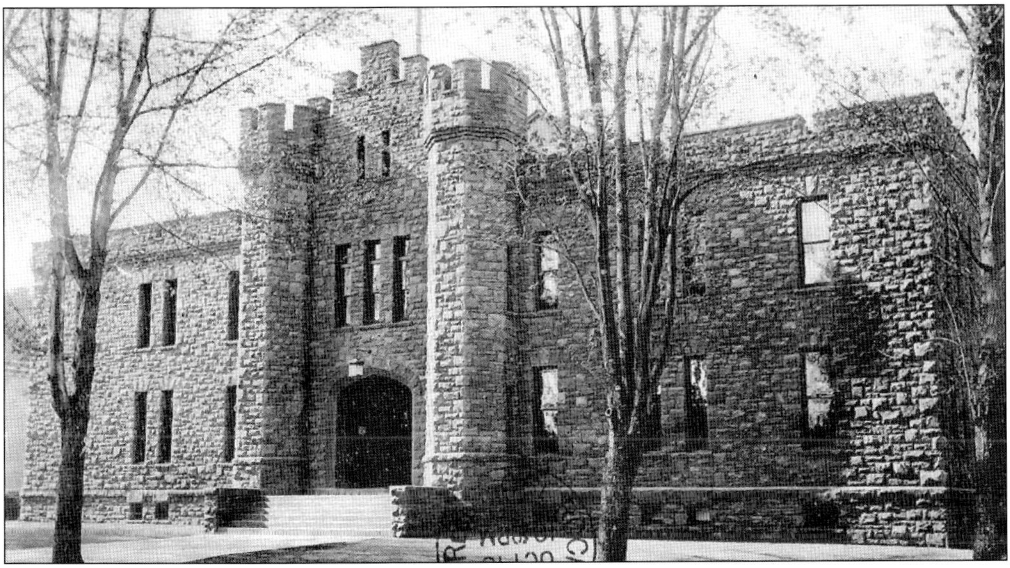

THE ARMORY. This is a front view of the armory, which was another huge structure that took up almost an entire block. (Courtesy of Grant-Pollard Insurance Office.)

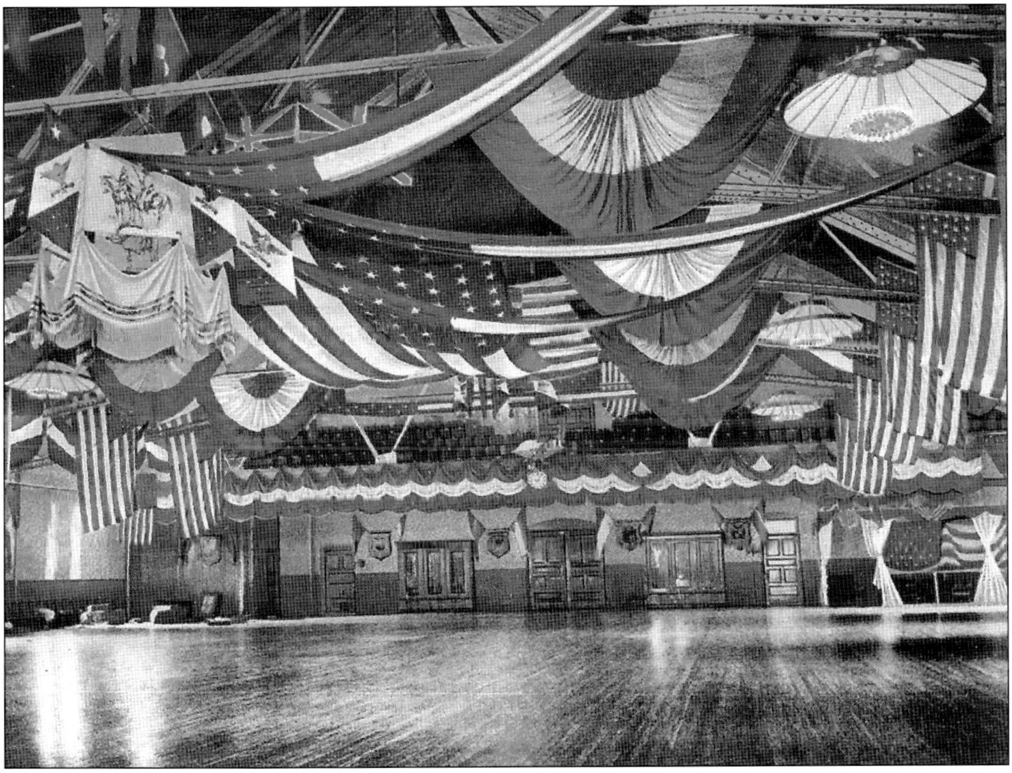

INSIDE THE ARMORY. This was the drill hall in the 29th Separate Company's armory. (Courtesy of Bill Henderson.)

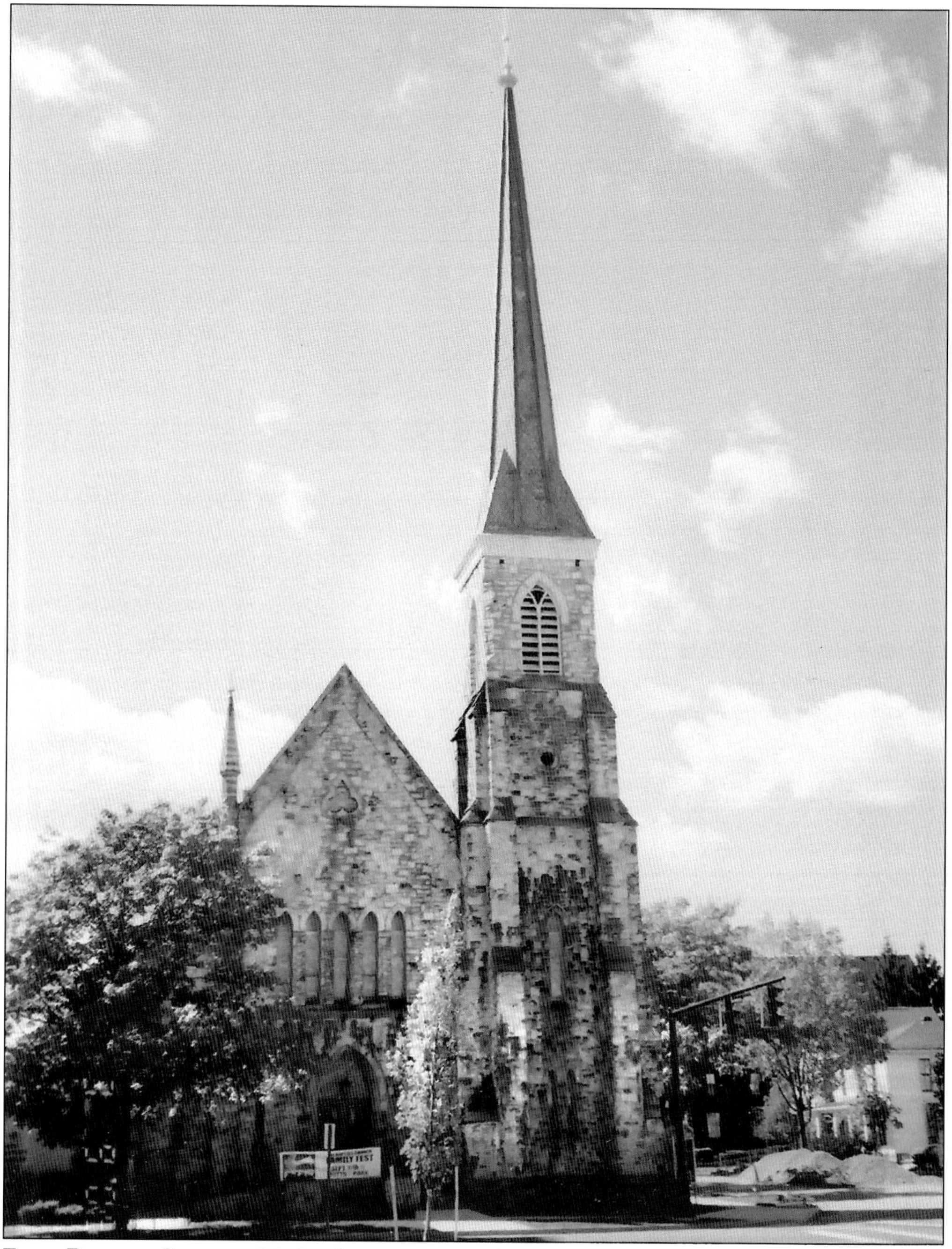

First Baptist Church. Made of rustic gray sandstone, this original church was built between 1870 and 1873 and stands majestically on the corner of West Avenue and West Center Street.

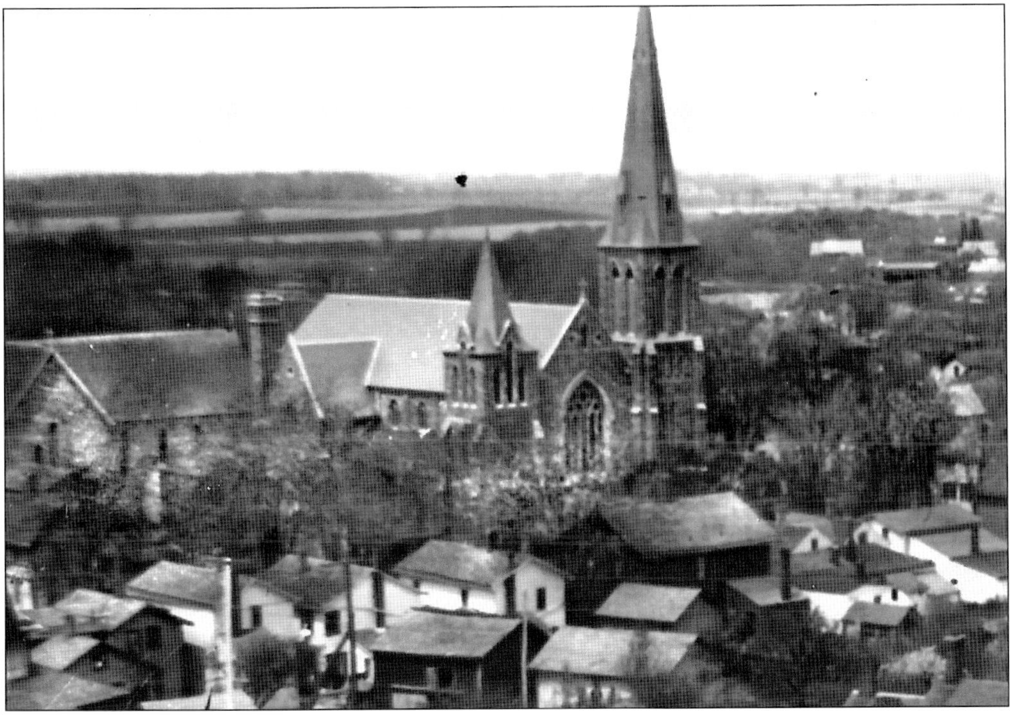

ST. MARY'S CHURCH. This bird's-eye view of St. Mary's Roman Catholic Church on Main Street is thought to have been taken from the tower of the White Hotel around 1910. The church was rebuilt after the original burned in 1870. (Courtesy of Mrs. Elmer Chatt.)

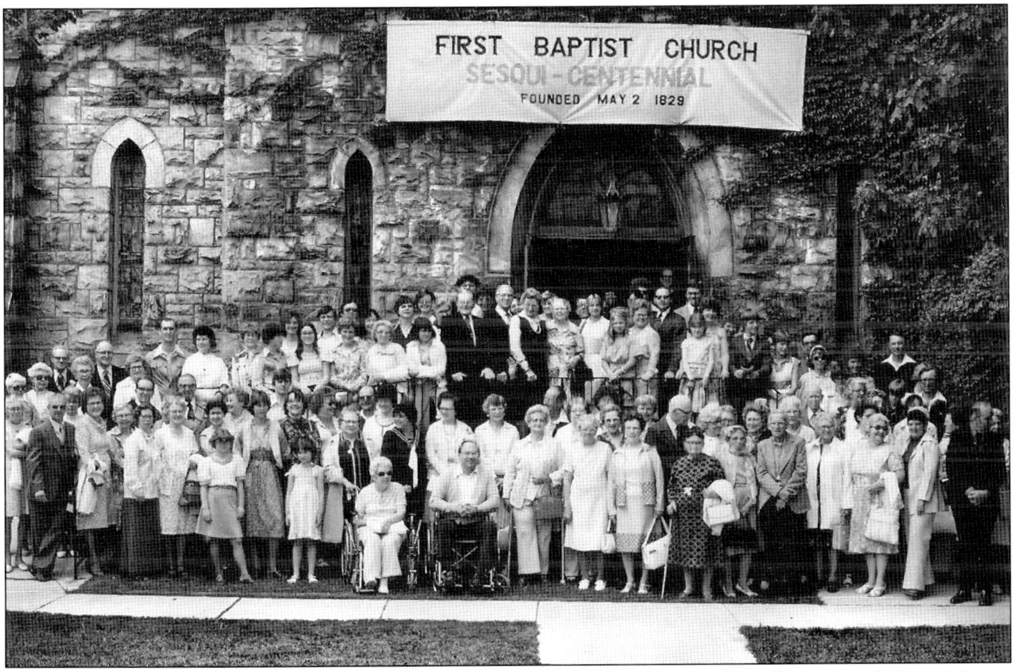

FIRST BAPTIST'S SESQUICENTENNIAL. Members of the First Baptist Church, seen at left, celebrate the 150th anniversary of the church in Medina on May 2, 1979. (Courtesy of Richard Nellist.)

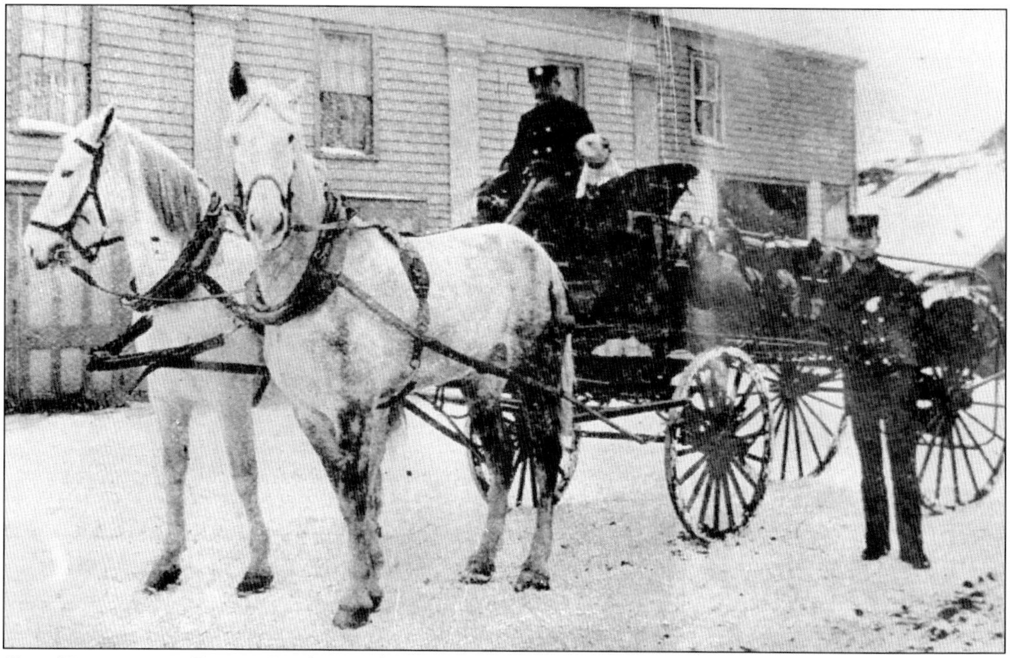

OLD FIREHOUSE. Driver Fred Beard Sr. tries out a new team of gray horses owned by William Smith as Dunk O'Brien looks on around 1890. The firehouse burned down in 1906, and the site now holds City Hall. The fire dog is unidentified. (Courtesy of Frank Berger.)

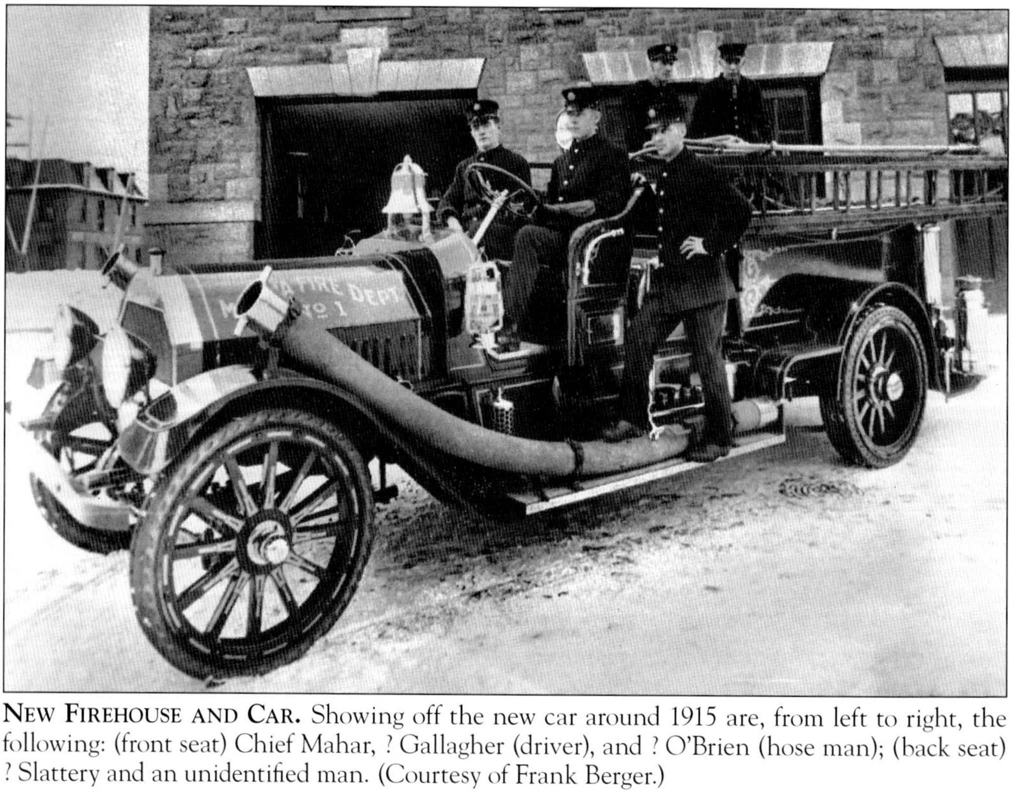

NEW FIREHOUSE AND CAR. Showing off the new car around 1915 are, from left to right, the following: (front seat) Chief Mahar, ? Gallagher (driver), and ? O'Brien (hose man); (back seat) ? Slattery and an unidentified man. (Courtesy of Frank Berger.)

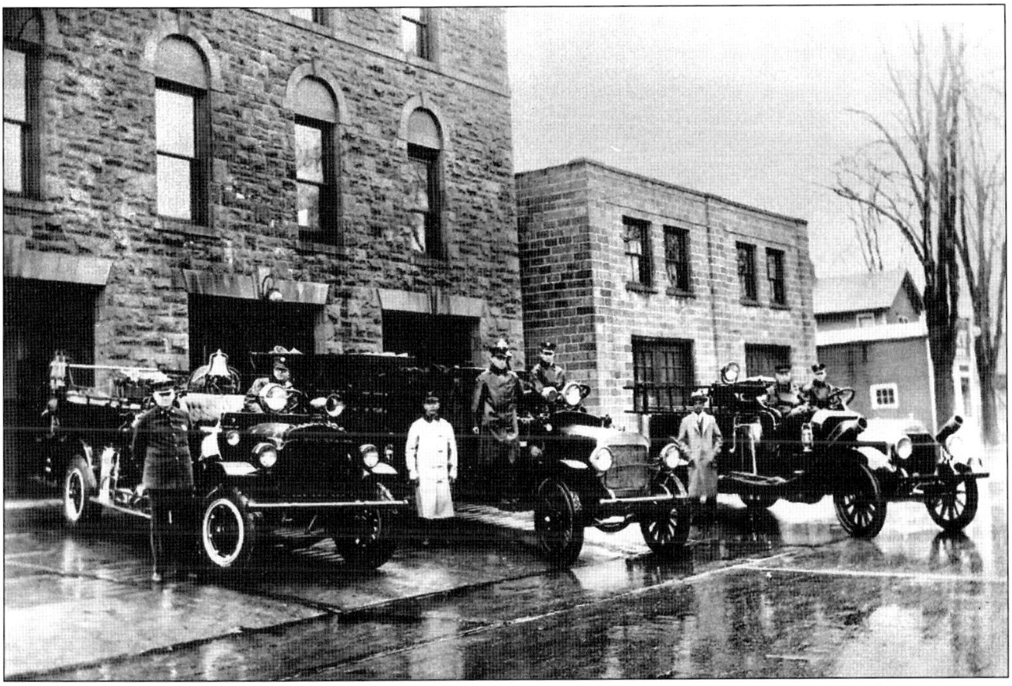

MEDINA FIRE COMPANY, 1933. Members of the Medina Fire Company pose in the rain on a cold, rainy day. From left to right are Chief James Schooley, Leo Ronallo, Art Whalen, William Maxon, Frank Eppolito, Carl Carrello, Michael McGraw, and Joseph Stillwell. (Courtesy of Frank Berger.)

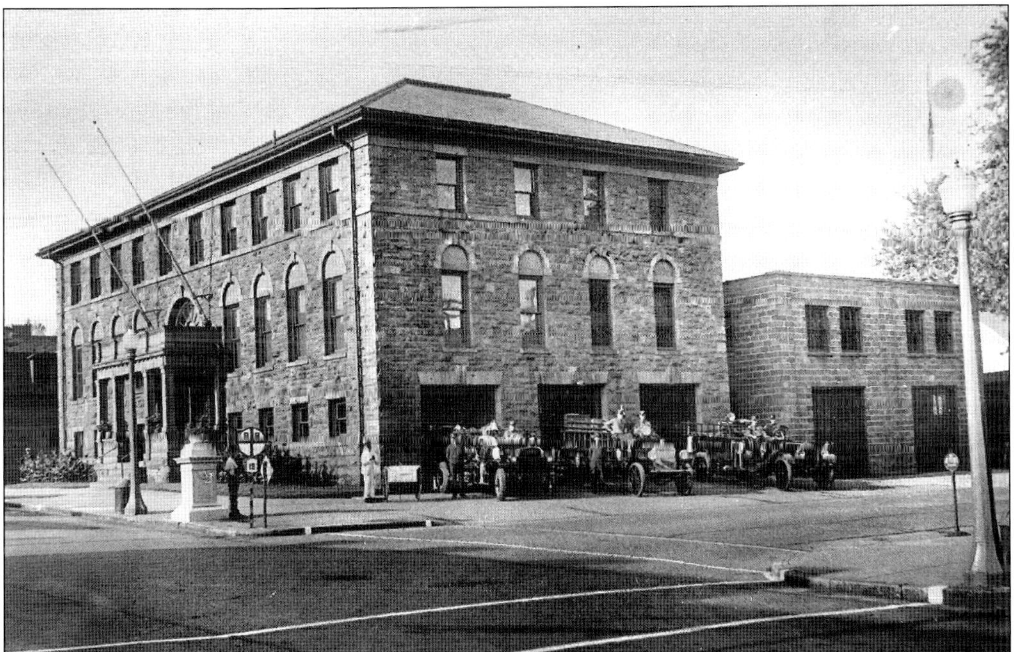

NEW FIREHOUSE. The same group of men as in the above photograph pose for a shot around 1933 of their impressive firehouse, which is also City Hall. (Courtesy of Frank Berger.)

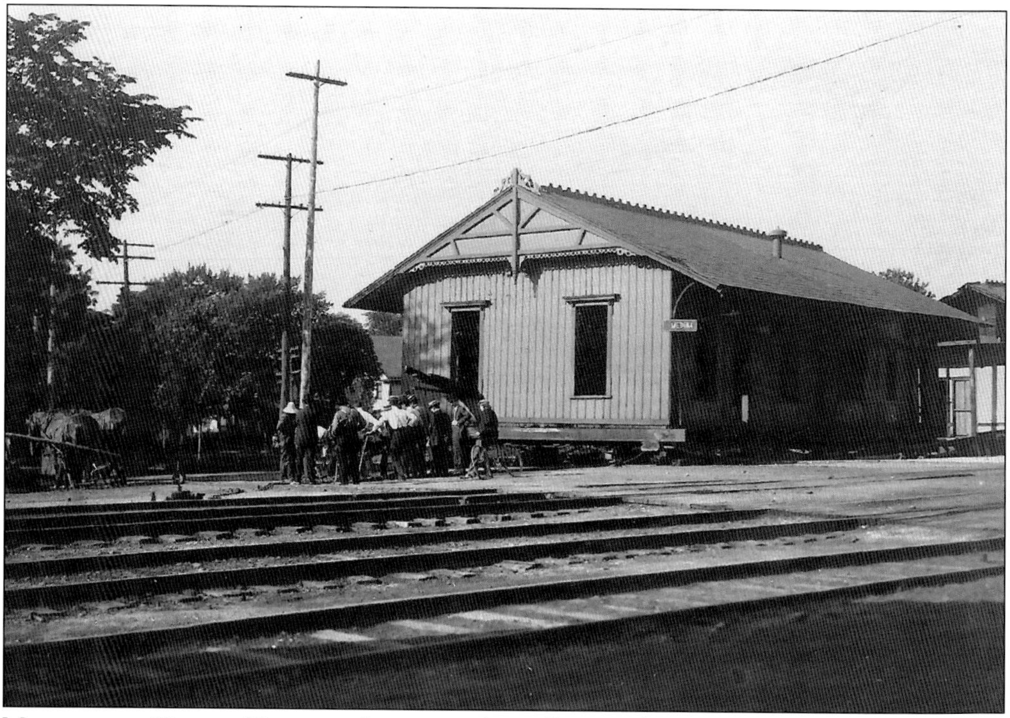

Moving the Depot. The train depot is on log rollers, ready to move to a different location, on West Avenue next to the Walsh Hotel around 1903. It now houses the Railroad Museum. (Courtesy of Bill Henderson.)

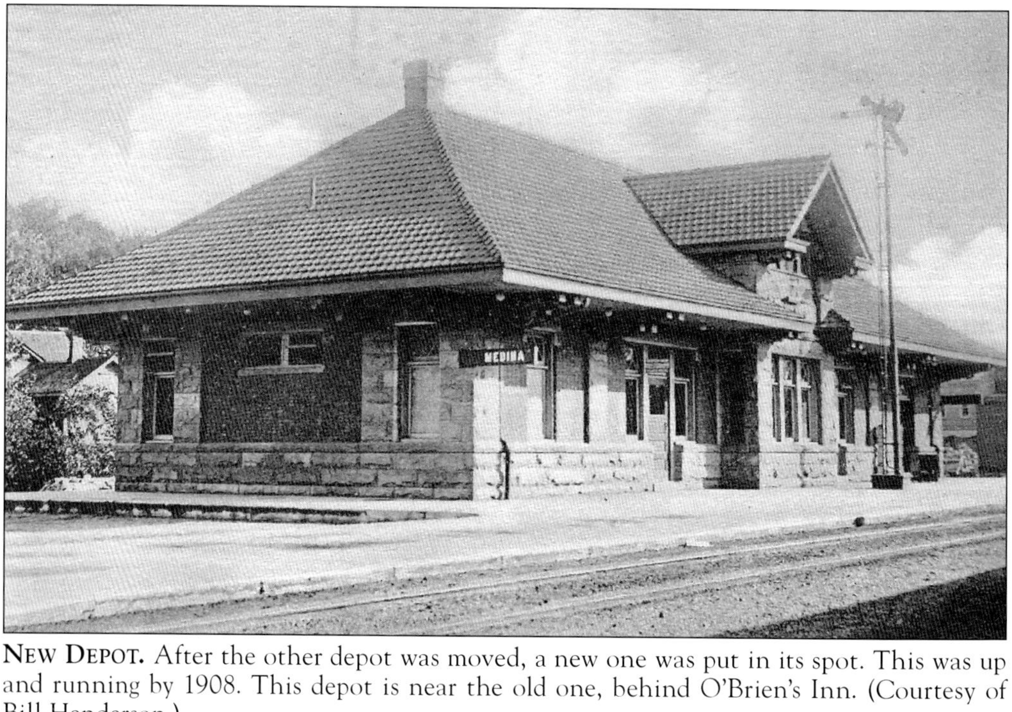

New Depot. After the other depot was moved, a new one was put in its spot. This was up and running by 1908. This depot is near the old one, behind O'Brien's Inn. (Courtesy of Bill Henderson.)

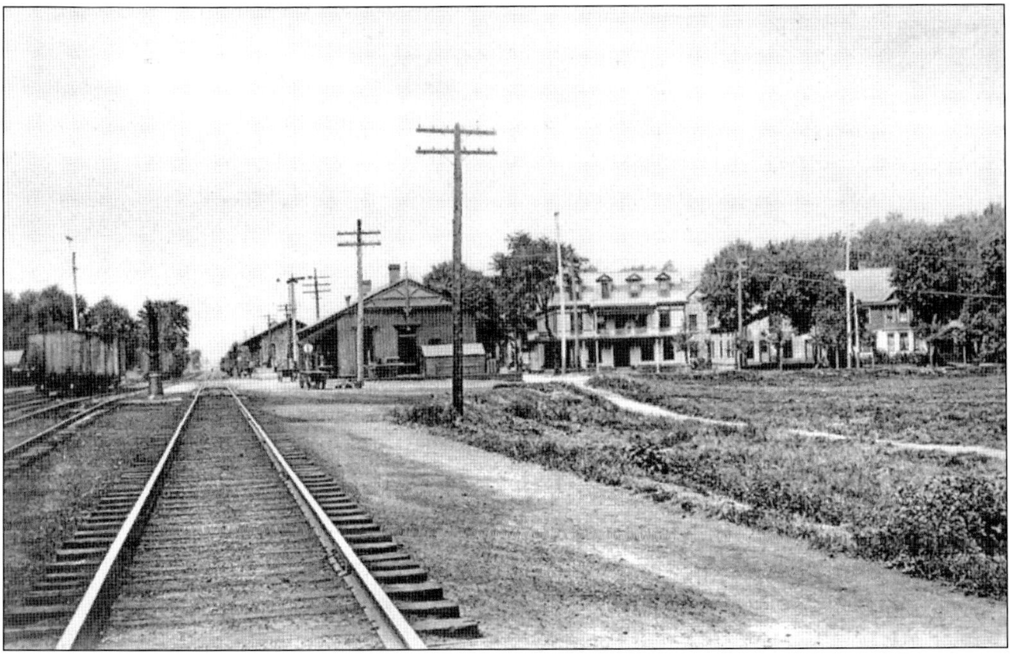

Old Depot in Place. The old depot is in its place next to the Walsh Hotel, where it remains today. (Courtesy of Bill Henderson.)

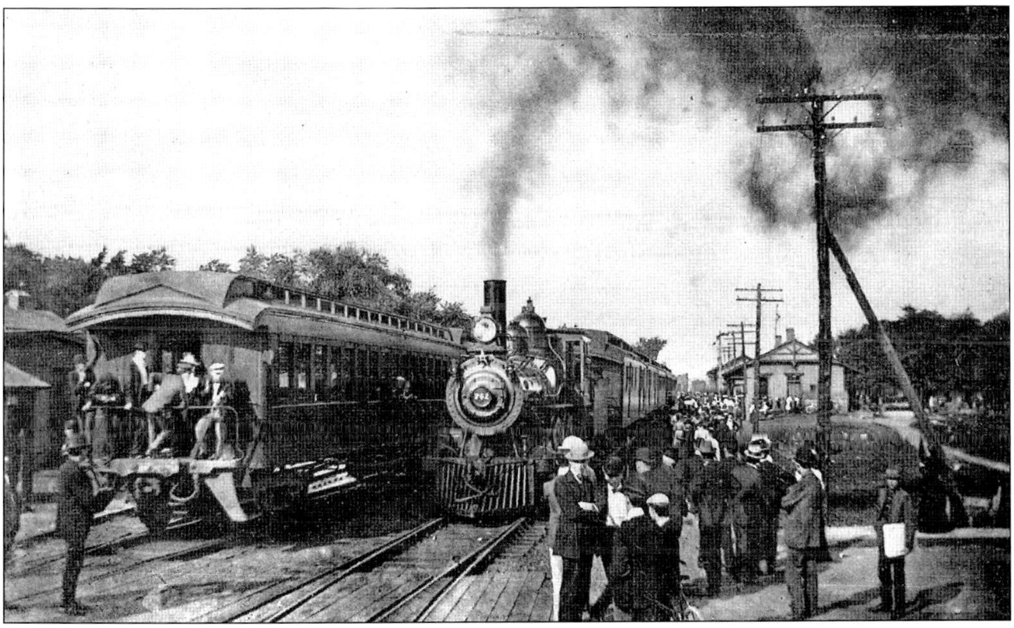

All Aboard! These folks do not seem to be too concerned about the close proximity of a train and a trolley as they wait by the tracks around 1900. At that time, there were many trains stopping each day, going in both directions. (Courtesy of Bill Henderson.)

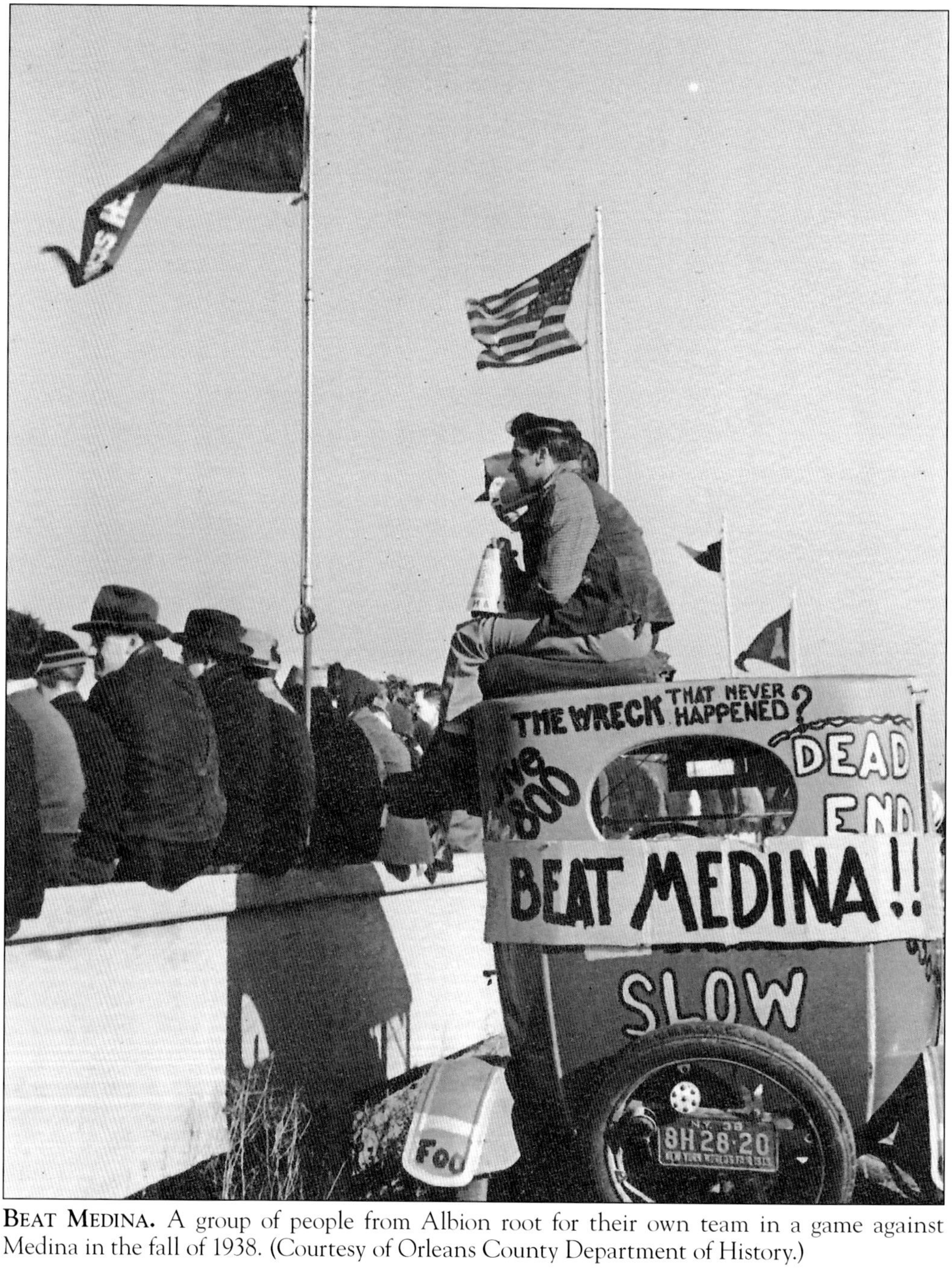

BEAT MEDINA. A group of people from Albion root for their own team in a game against Medina in the fall of 1938. (Courtesy of Orleans County Department of History.)

Six

Outskirts and Later Years

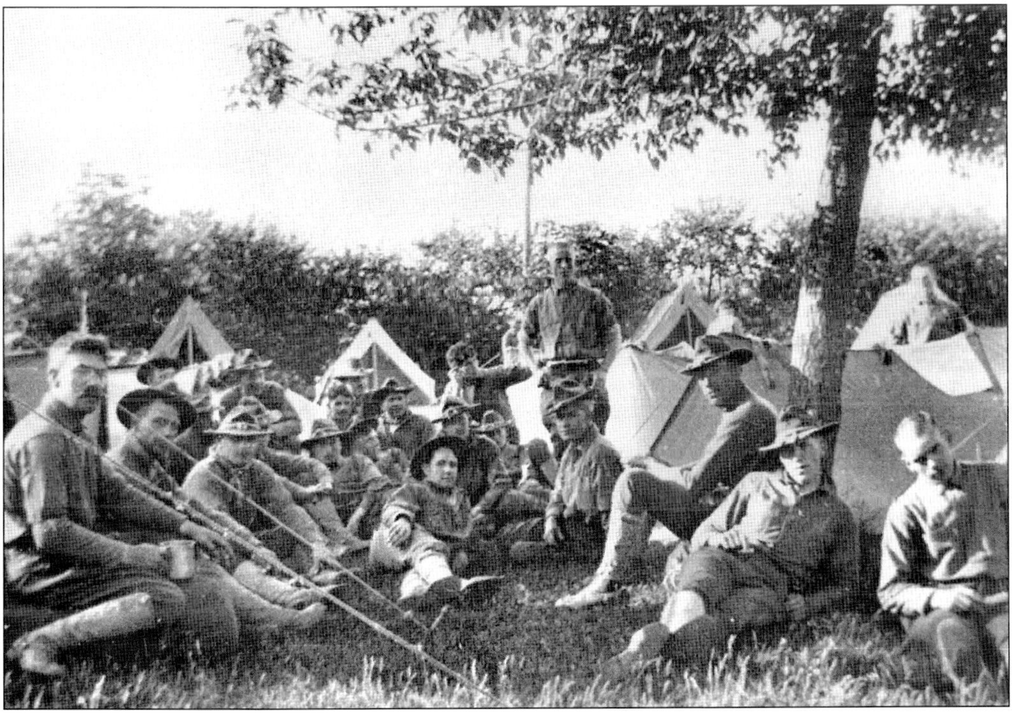

Taking a Break. A group of soldiers takes a break, making camp along Ridge Road around 1915. Soldiers used to march down Ridge Road for practice maneuvers. (Courtesy of Richard Nellist.)

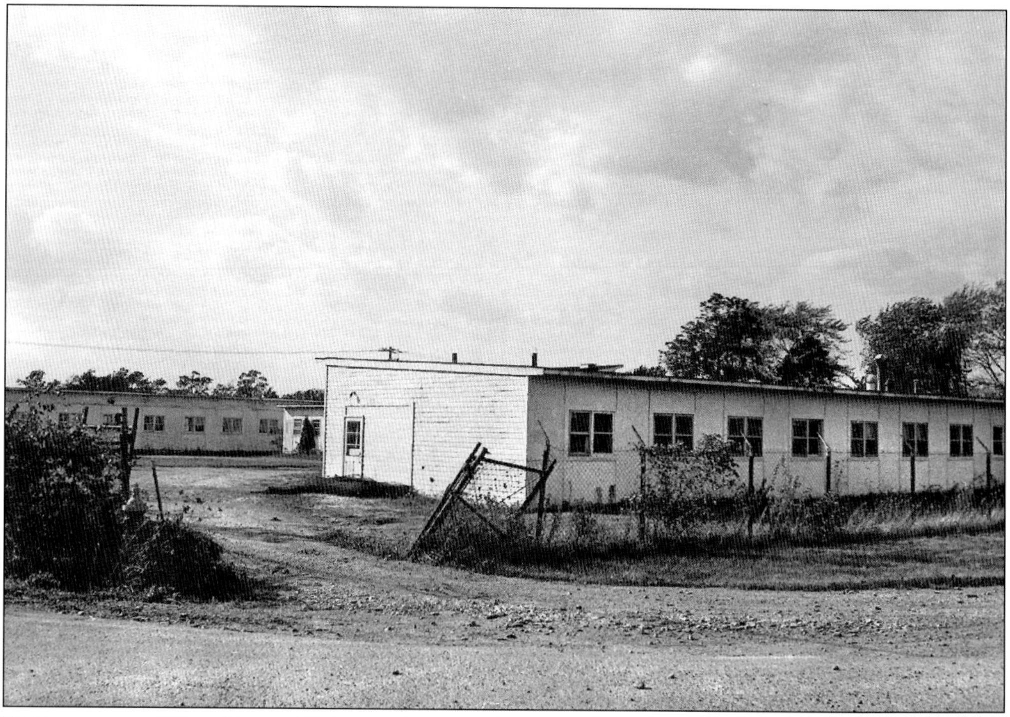

PRISONERS OF WAR CAMP. This was the outside view of the prisoners' barracks housing World War II POWs from Italy and Germany. Located on Park Avenue next to the H. J. Heinz Company, Heinz used the prisoners as workers in his factory. After they left, local residents began to tear the fence down, many looking for memorabilia. The camp became a school for several years, then was torn down. (Courtesy of Richard Nellist.)

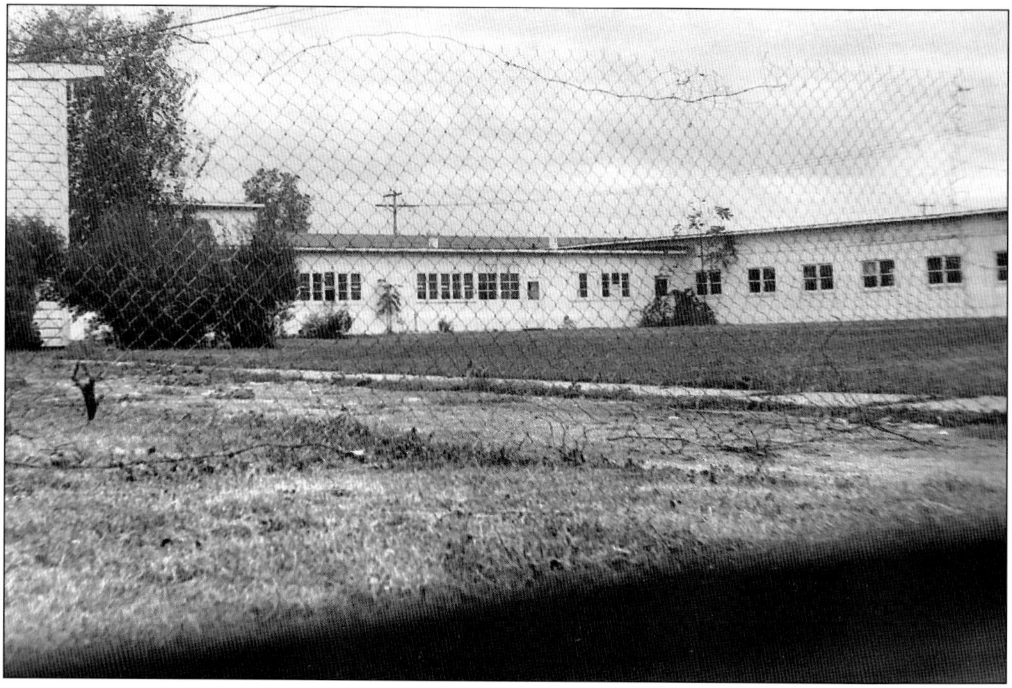

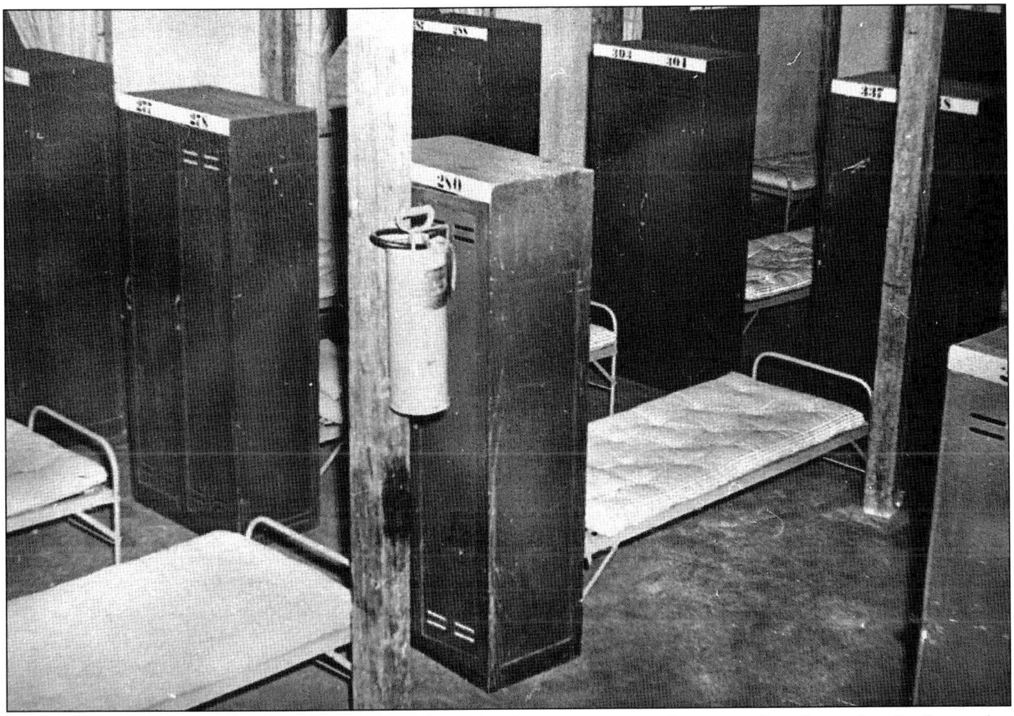

INSIDE THE BARRACKS. Prisoners lived in stark quarters, with just a bunk and a bed, at the POW camp on Park Avenue in World War II. The photograph above shows that each bunk is attached to a locker. The photograph below looks more "lived in." Although the door looks easy to escape through, the camp was fenced in, with armed guards around the perimeter. (Courtesy of Richard Nellist.)

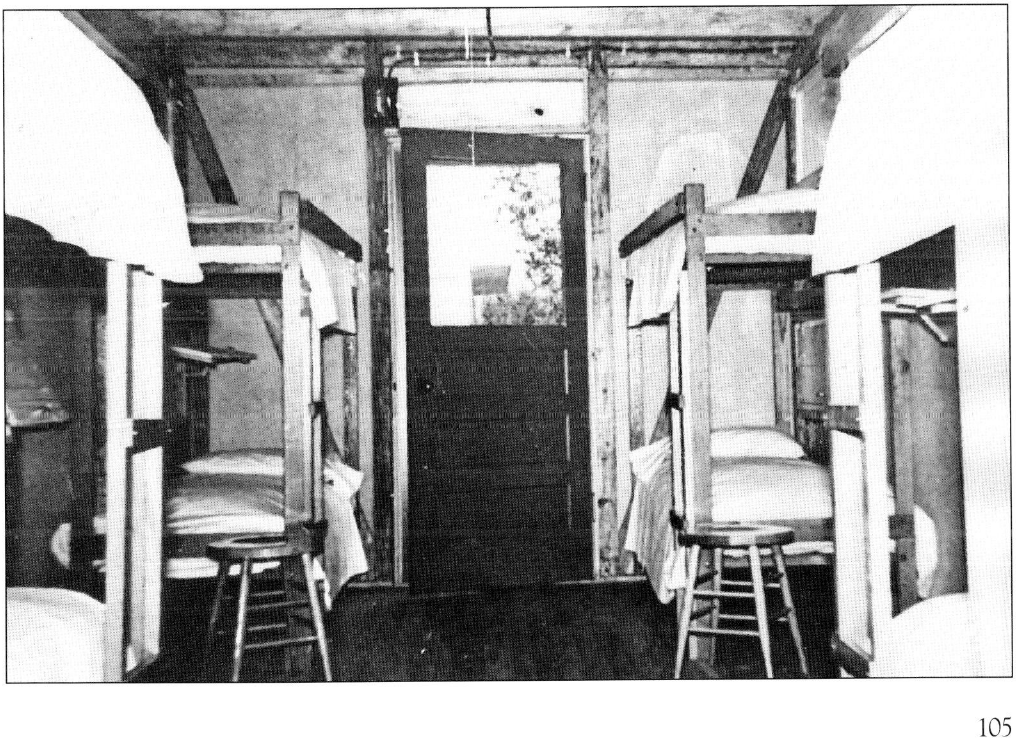

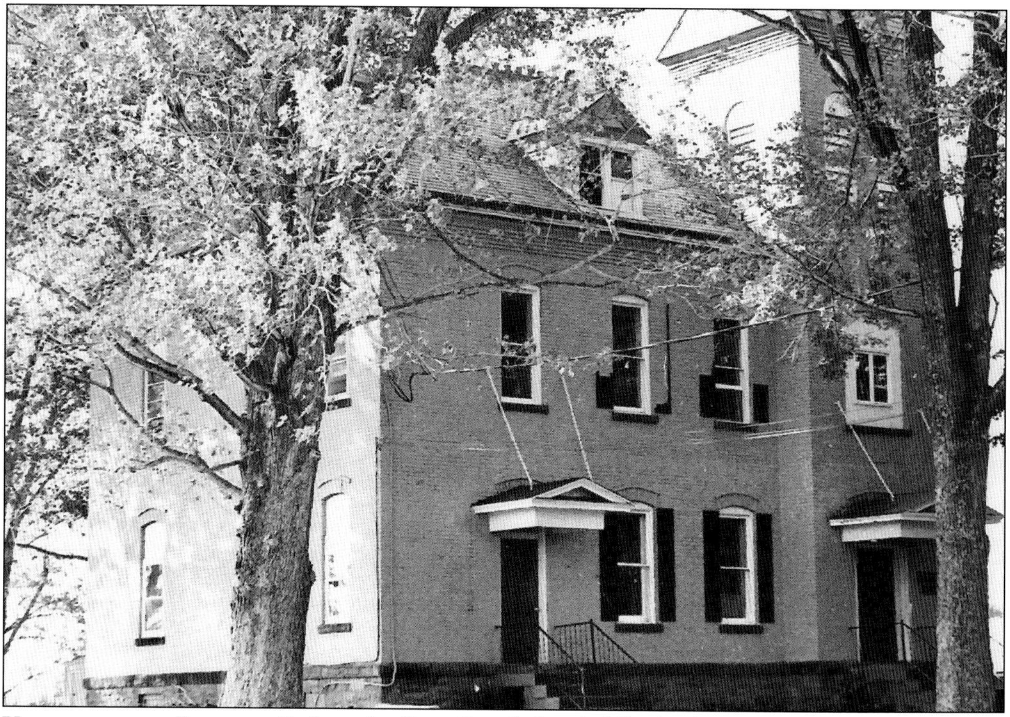

KNOWLESVILLE SCHOOL. Before the Erie Canal, local folks looked to Knowlesville for their future, but it was not meant to be. This building was a school for many years until the Knowlesville District dissolved and blended into the Medina School District. The building is an apartment house now. (Courtesy of Richard Nellist.)

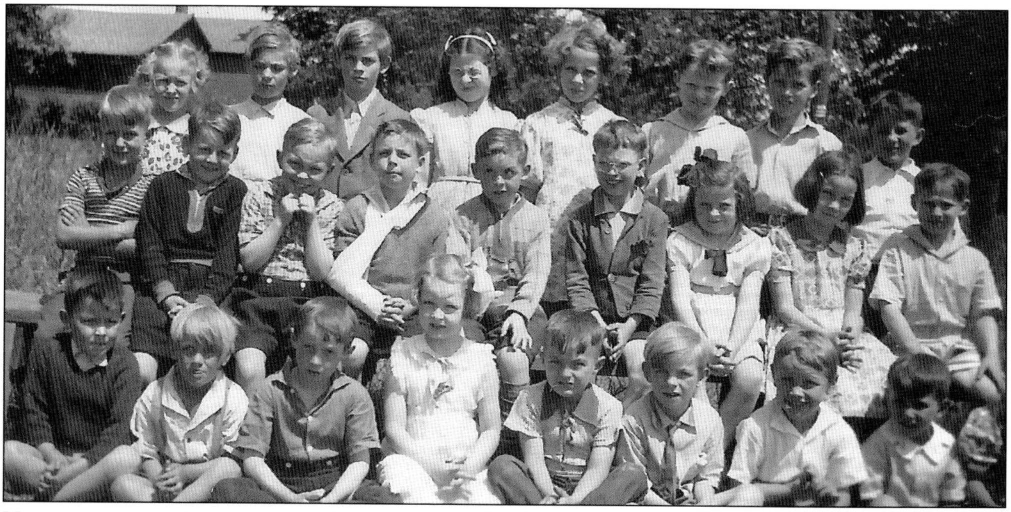

KNOWLESVILLE ELEMENTARY. Students pose for the camera on the playground at Knowlesville Elementary School around 1938. From left to right are the following: (first row) Milfred Woodroe, two unidentified boys, Alice Knights, Bob Ames, ? Bennett, Tom Kimball, and Don Martin; (second row) Bill Ames, Wesley Bennett, Roger Kenyon, Charles Bennett, unidentified, Harold Allen, Madelyn Higgins, Verona Reed, and Joe Curtin; (third row) Mildred Bandemere, two unidentified boys, Shirley Baker, Virginia Forsythe, Tom Curtin, Chet Kimball, and Norm Martin. (Courtesy of Susan Fuller.)

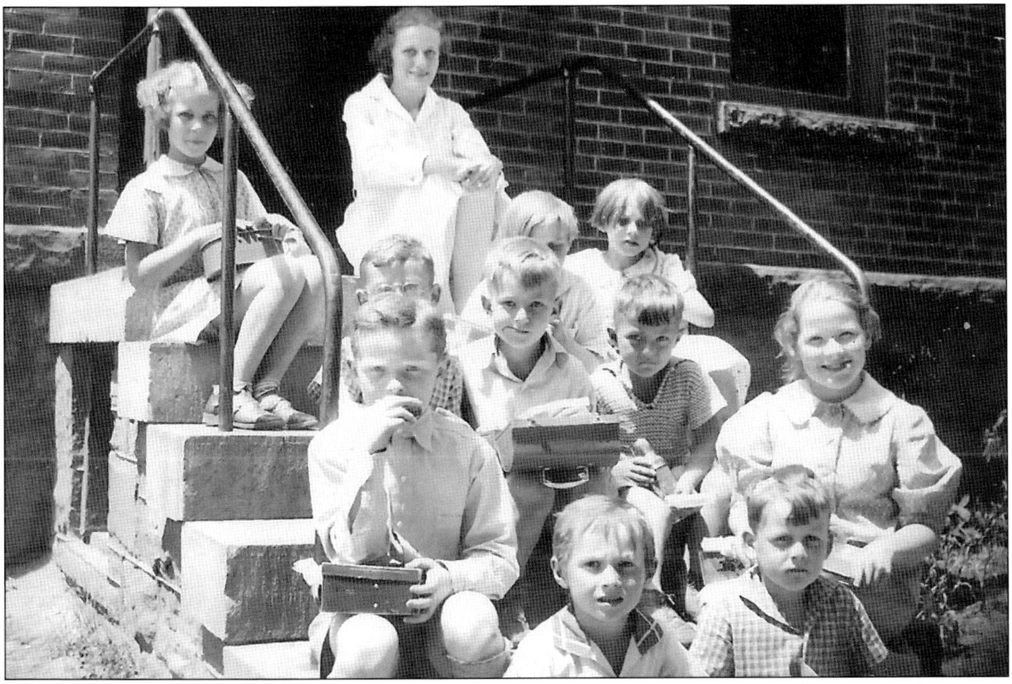

ON THE STEPS. In this *c.* 1939 photograph, students pose with their dental hygienist, who is not identified. From left to right are as follows: (first row) unidentified and Charles Bennett; (second row) Tom Curtin and Mary Curtin Kingsley; (third row) Harold Allen, William Ames, and Robert Ames; (fourth row) three unidentified children and the unidentified dental hygienist. (Courtesy of Susan Fuller.)

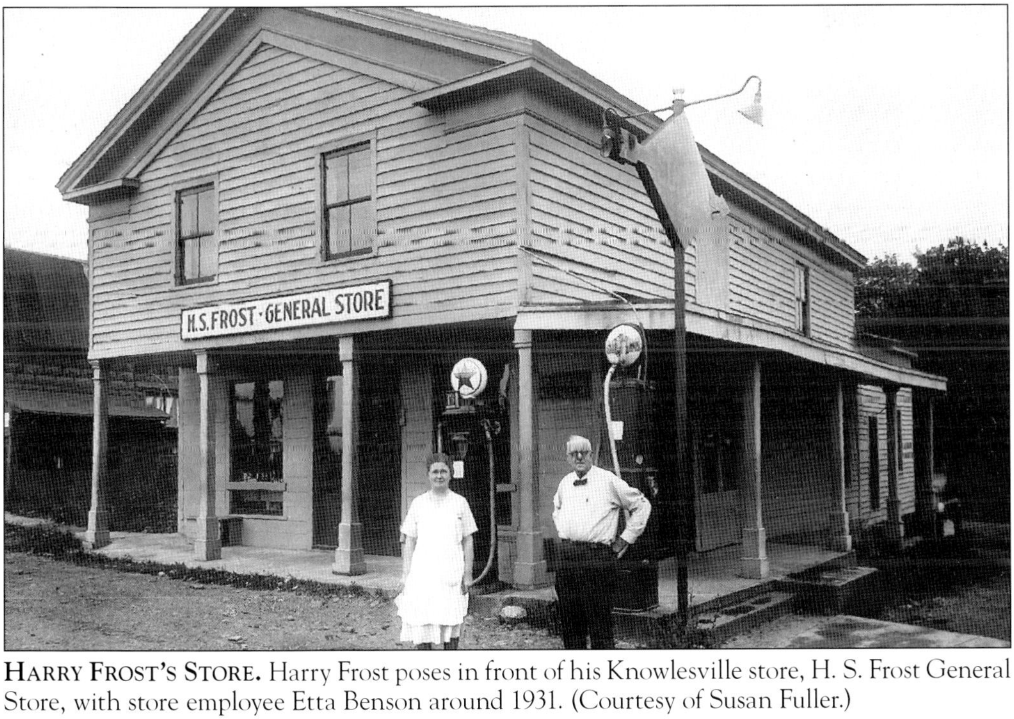

HARRY FROST'S STORE. Harry Frost poses in front of his Knowlesville store, H. S. Frost General Store, with store employee Etta Benson around 1931. (Courtesy of Susan Fuller.)

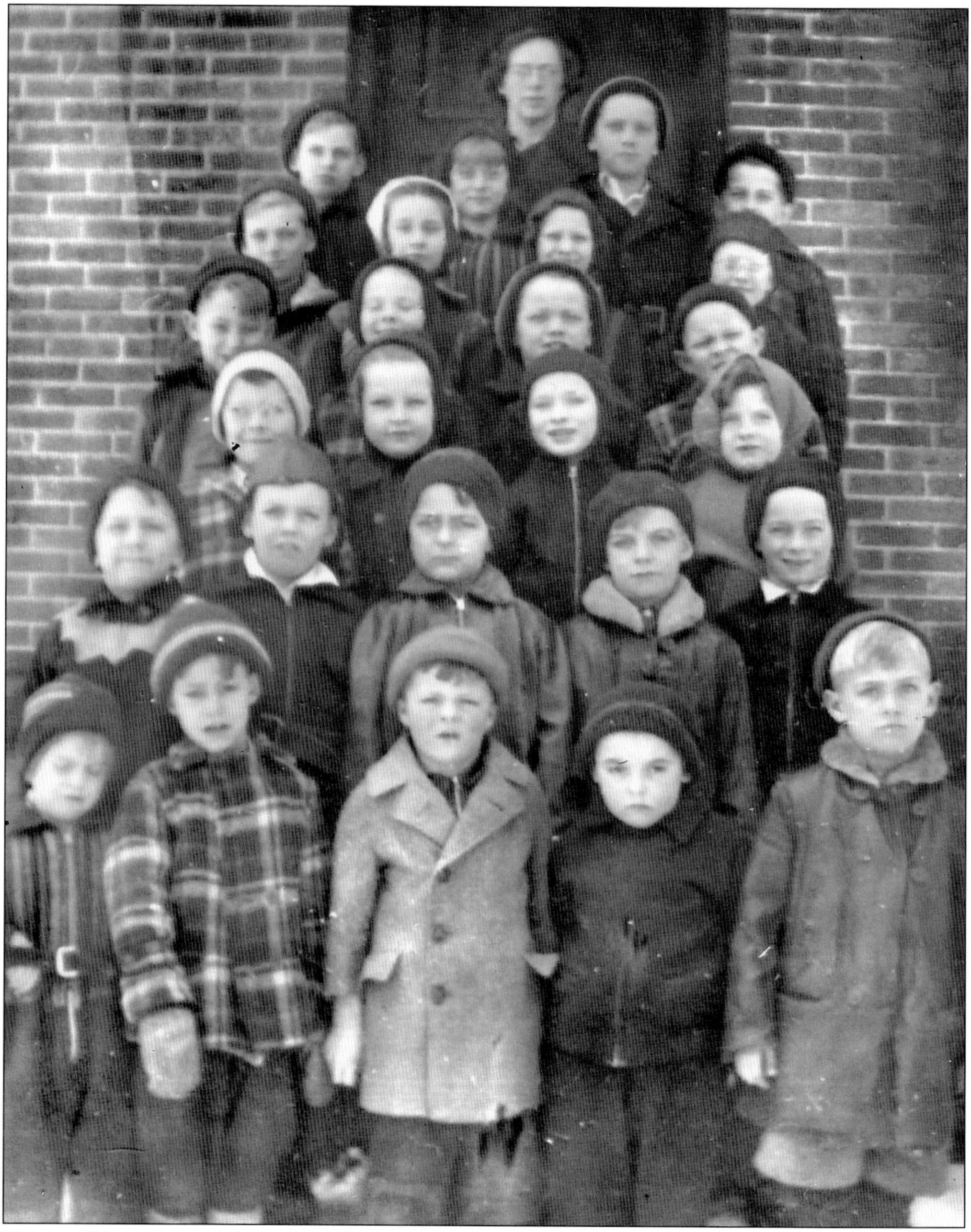

COATS, HATS, AND MITTENS: These students are all bundled up and standing in the snow with their teacher around 1940. From left to right are the following: (first row) unidentified, Lloyd Baker, Joseph Curtin, Stella Dewing, and Richard Scott; (second row) Donald Martin, Charles Brunett, Robert Ames, Foster Bennett, and Robert Tucker; (third row) Larry Bowen, Alice Knights Martin, Shirley Baker, and Madilyn Higgins Enderby; (fourth row) William Ames, Barbara Achillies, Tom Kimball, and Roger Kenyon; (fifth row) unidentified, Verona Reed Pritchard, unidentified, and Harold Allen; (sixth row) two unidentified students, Chet Kimball, and Norm Martin. At the top of the class is teacher Anna May Higgins Wheatly. (Courtesy of Susan Fuller.)

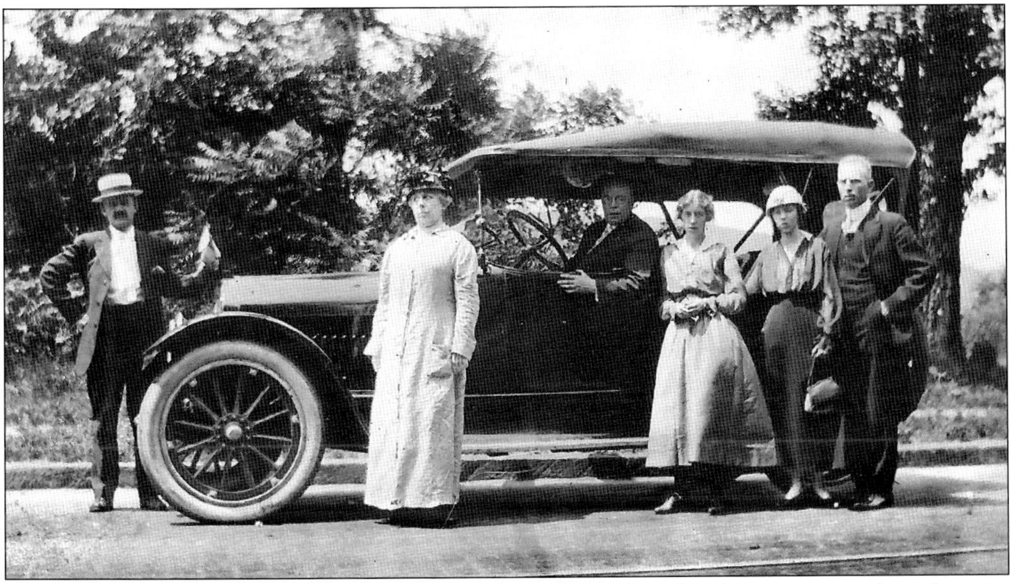

TAKING A TRIP. Posing outside their car, members of the Hartt family prepare to take a day trip. From left to right are Mr. and Mrs. Hartt, their chauffeur, Addis Hartt, Elaine Hartt, and their brother. (Courtesy of the A. Hartt estate.)

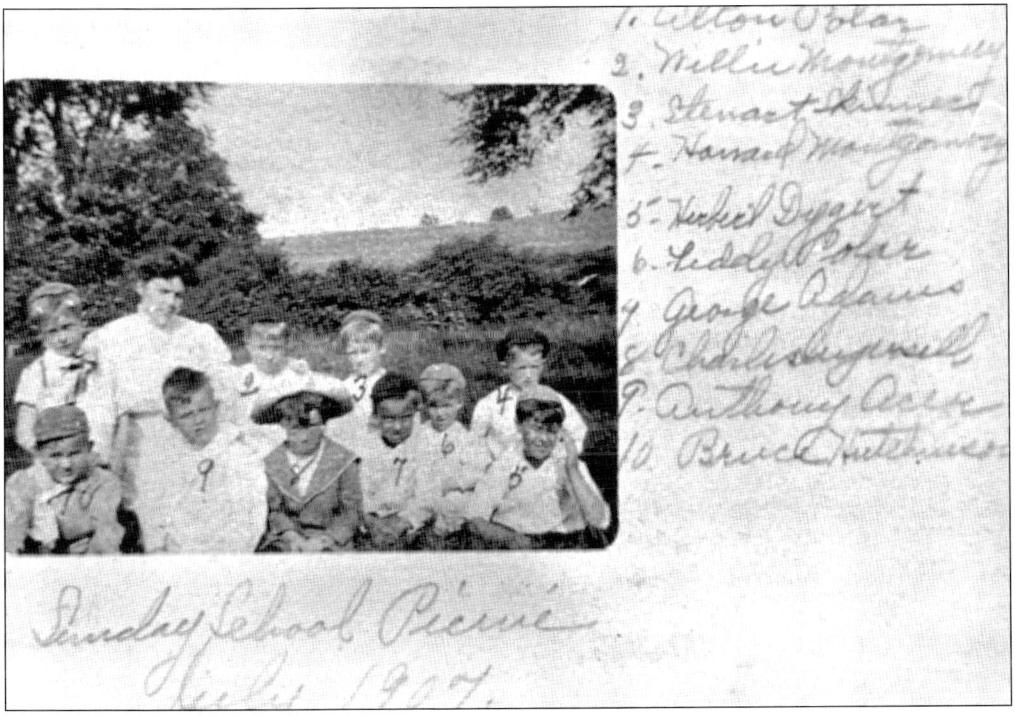

SUNDAY SCHOOL BOYS. Although the teacher is unidentified, the boys at the Sunday school picnic in July 1907 are, from left to right, the following: (front row) Bruce Hutchison, Anthony Acer, Charles Ingersoll, George Adams, Freddy Polar, and Herbert Daggert; (back row) Alton Polar, Willie Montgomery, Stewart Skinner, and Howard Montgomery. (Courtesy of Richard Nellist.)

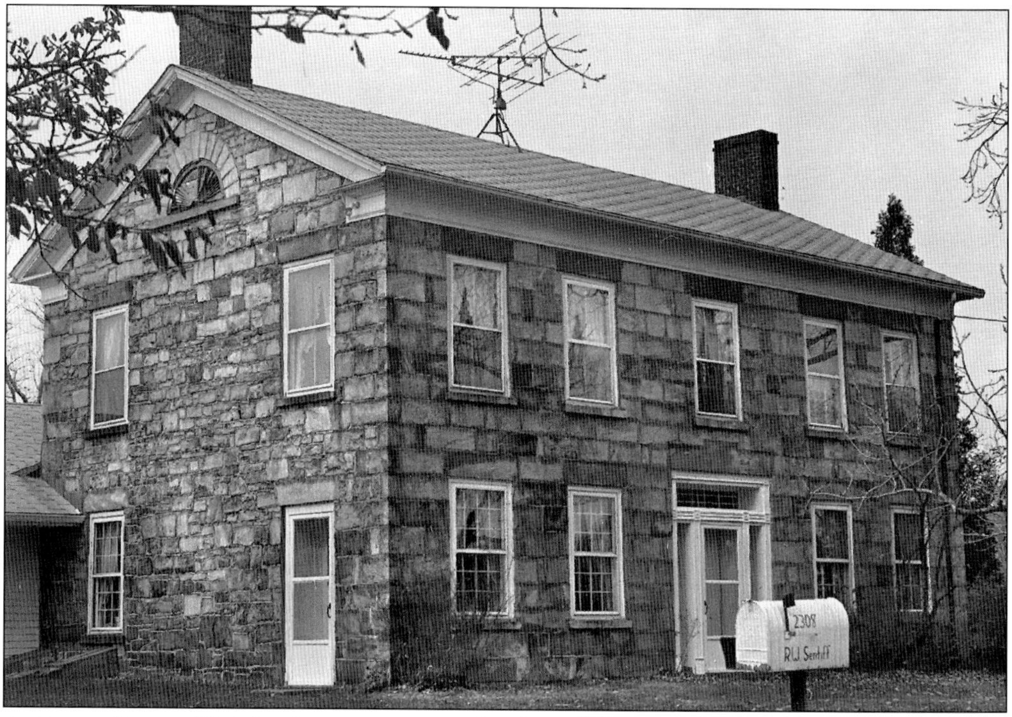

ANGLING ROAD. This lovely structure was the Sentiff House. The flag is up on the mailbox, telling the postman to stop because there is mail. (Courtesy of Richard Nellist.)

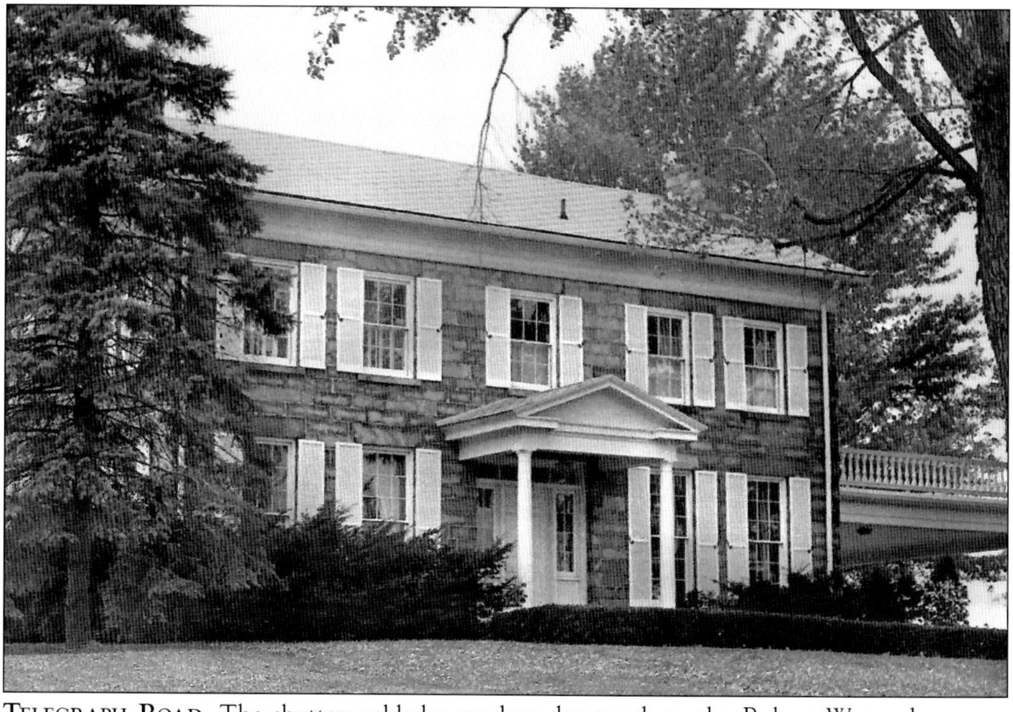

TELEGRAPH ROAD. The shutters added a modern-day touch to the Robert Waters home on Telegraph Road. (Courtesy of Richard Nellist.)

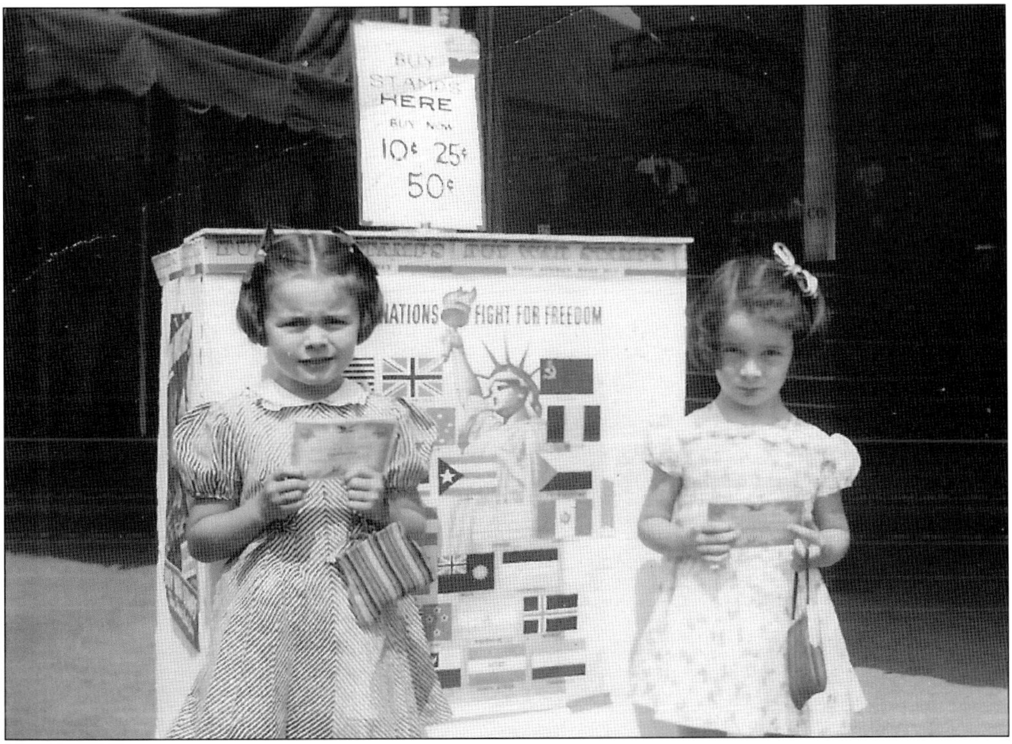

KELLEY GIRLS. Sisters Marilyn (left) and Elaine Kelley pose in front of the J. C. Penney store on Main Street, Medina, around 1942 during a World War II bond drive. The small sign above the bond machine says "Buy Stamps Here, Buy Now 10¢, 25¢, and 50¢." The girls were dressed in their "good" dresses, complete with hair ribbons, to go to town. (Courtesy of Elaine Jamele.)

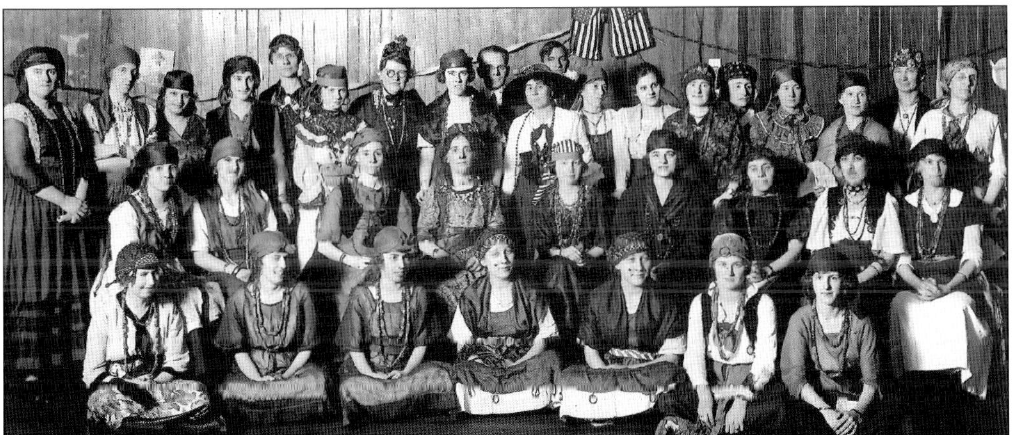

HALLOWEEN GYPSIES, 1920. A bunch of female friends got together and enjoyed dressing like gypsies for a party on October 31, 1920. From left to right are (first row) Ms. Dillon, N. Smith, M. Smith, Ms. Corbin, Ms. Corbin, Ms. Smith, and Ms. Robinson; (second row) Ms. Williamson, Ms. Lum, Ms. Brown, Ms. Turner, Ms. Lyke, Ms. Scheid, Ms. Rutherford, Ms. Warne, and Ms. Ricketts; (third row) Ms. Ford, A. Hartt, Ms. Wodke, Ms. Gray, Ms. Lenihan, N. Davis, Ms. Douglas, Ms. Delaney, Mr. Fancher, Ms. Rugg, Mr. Mattoon, Ms. Hall, Ms. Fancher, Ms. Hall, Ms. Ferguson, Ms. Bartholomew, Ms. Smith, Ms. Tuohey, and Ms. Newnham. (Courtesy of the A. Hartt Estate.)

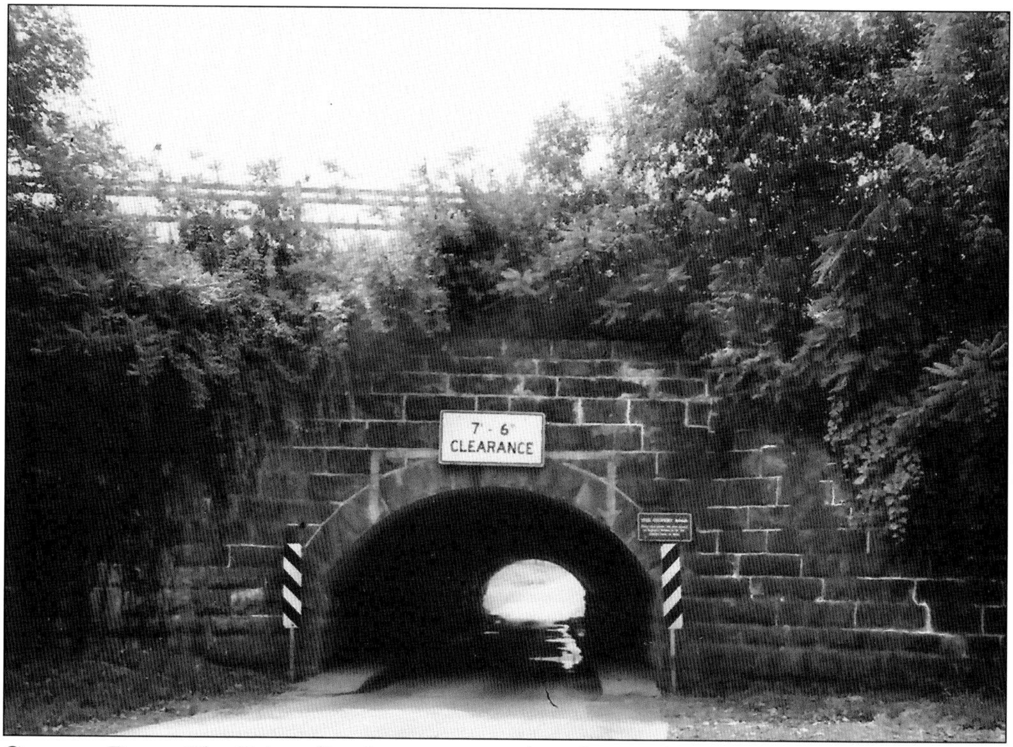

CULVERT ROAD. The Culvert Road got its name after a huge culvert was installed on it, allowing the Erie Canal to flow over the top of the road and allowing automobiles to drive under the canal. Although the culvert leaks and is scary, very low and only allowing shorter cars to drive through it, it is a big attraction for folks visiting the Medina area.

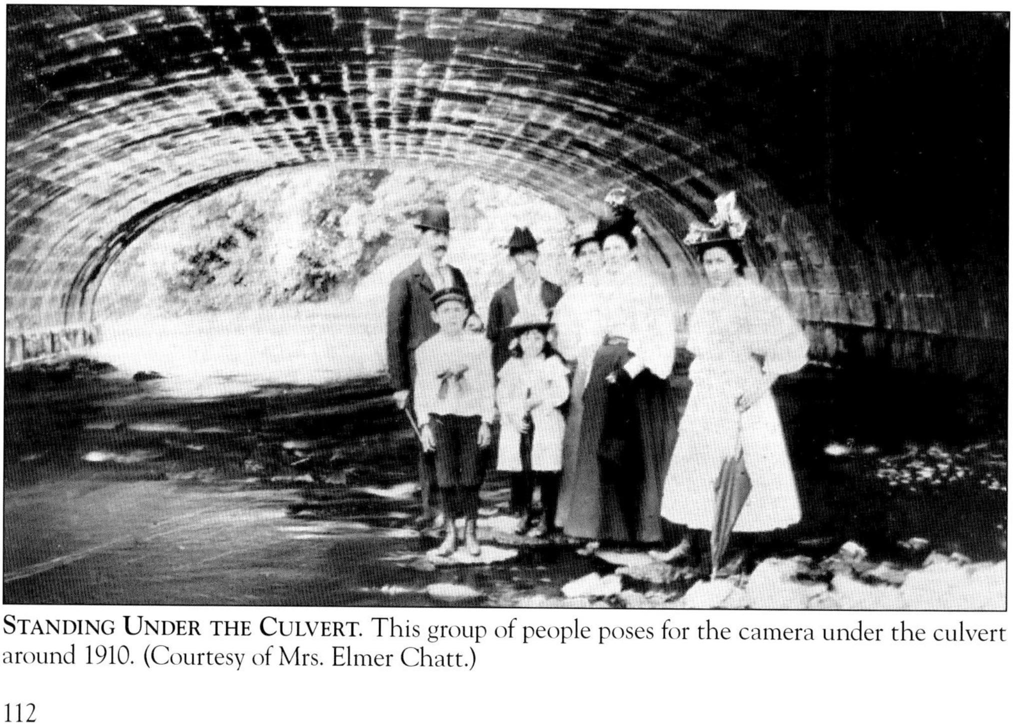

STANDING UNDER THE CULVERT. This group of people poses for the camera under the culvert around 1910. (Courtesy of Mrs. Elmer Chatt.)

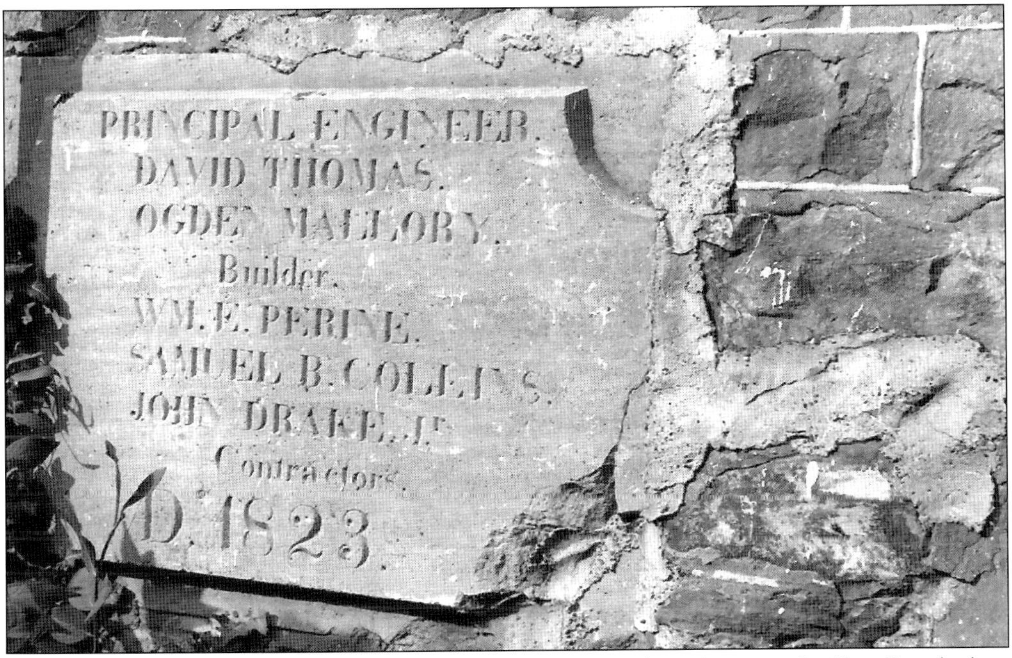

UNIQUE CORNERSTONE. This cornerstone was taken from the culvert on the Erie Canal when it was widened, and it was put in the wall of the Toussaint house on Culvert Road. It states, "Principal Engineer David Thomas, Ogden Mallory, Builder, Wm. E. Perine, Samuel B. Collins, John Drake, Contractors, 1823."

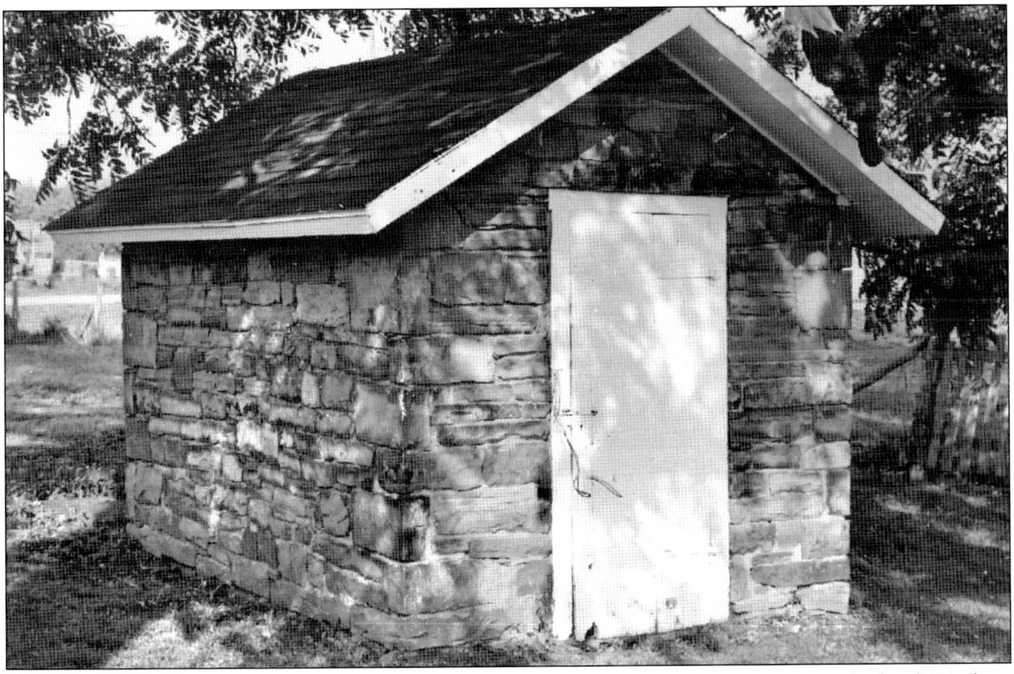

SANDSTONE SMOKEHOUSE. Even a smokehouse looks impressive when crafted of Medina sandstone. This one is on Culvert Road and owned by the Toussaint family. (Courtesy of Richard Nellist.)

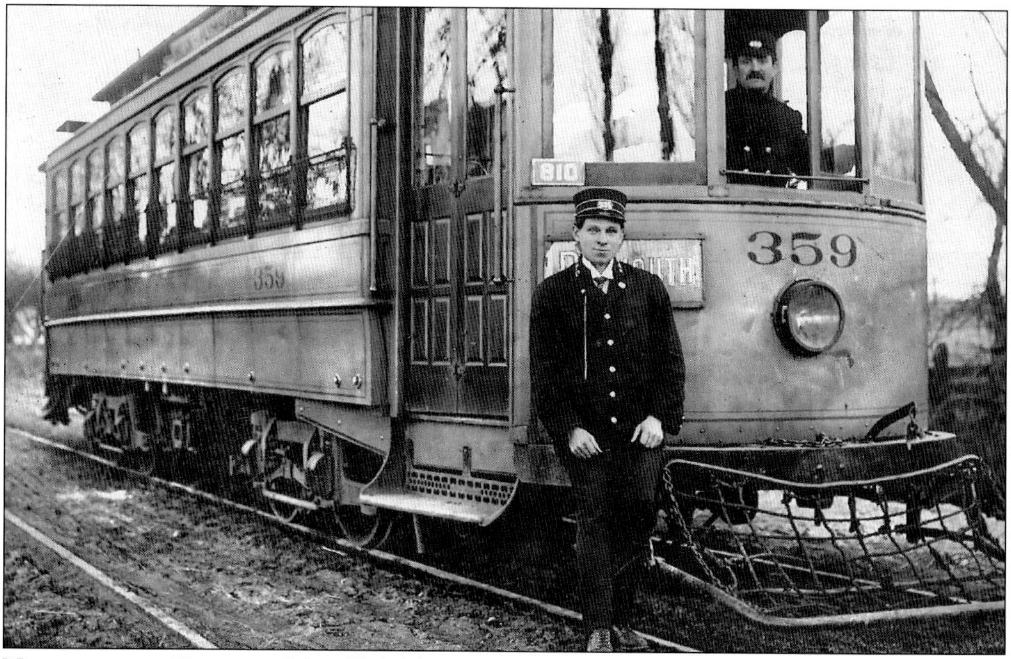

NEXT TO THE TROLLEY. John Shibilske of Bates Road stands next to the trolley while an unidentified conductor looks on, around 1920. Trolley service began about 1910. (Courtesy of John Wasnock.)

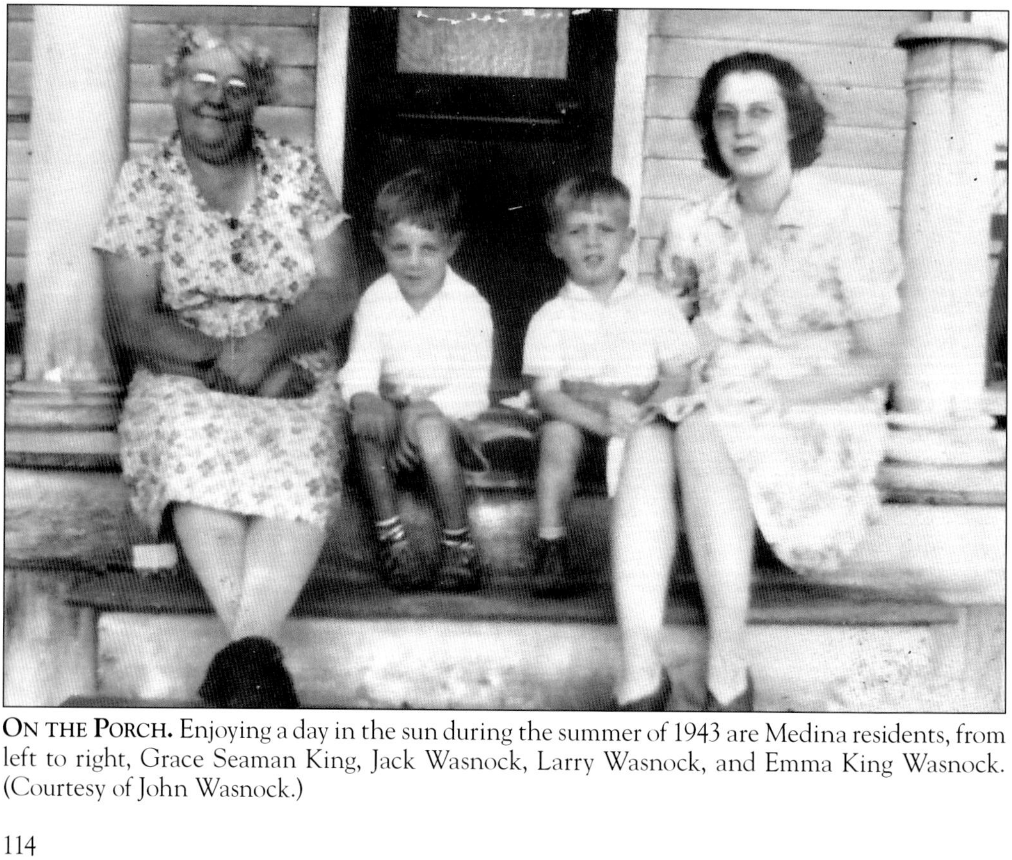

ON THE PORCH. Enjoying a day in the sun during the summer of 1943 are Medina residents, from left to right, Grace Seaman King, Jack Wasnock, Larry Wasnock, and Emma King Wasnock. (Courtesy of John Wasnock.)

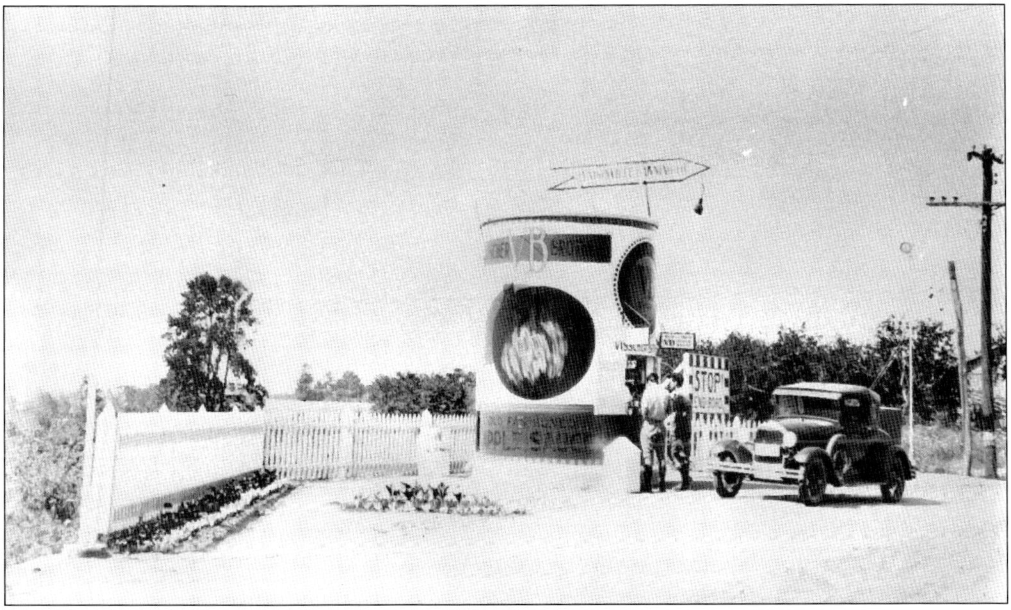

FOOD FROM A CAN. The old Lyndonville Canning Company sat on the corner of Routes 104 and 63 in Ridgeway. This roadside restaurant looked like a large can of applesauce. The two men shown here buying lunch around 1932 are unidentified. (Courtesy of Frank Berger.)

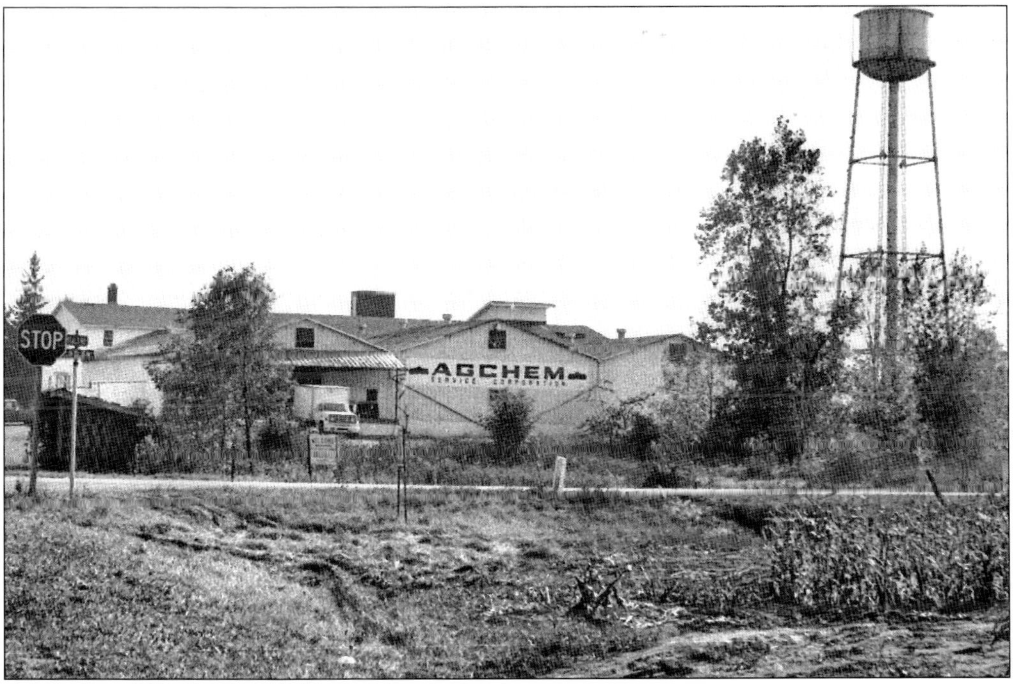

AG CHEM. This chemical plant was on the corner of Beals Road and the Million Dollar Highway (Route 31). The plant was torn down years ago, and the water tower is gone as well. (Courtesy of Richard Nellist.)

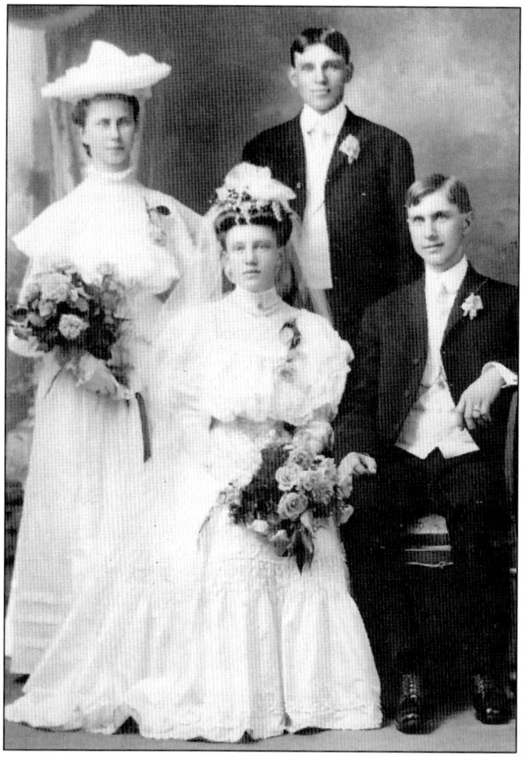

WEDDING DAY. Seated are bride and groom Catherine Shibilske and Edward Wasnock on the day of their nuptials, June 20, 1906. Behind them are their attendants, Josephine Wasnock, sister of the groom, and John Shibilske, brother of the bride. They were married at St. Mary's Church, Medina. The wedding dress was made by Mary Shibilske, the bride's older sister, and the materials for it came from New York City and Philadelphia. The flowers arrived in Medina by train the morning of the wedding. (Courtesy of John Wasnock.)

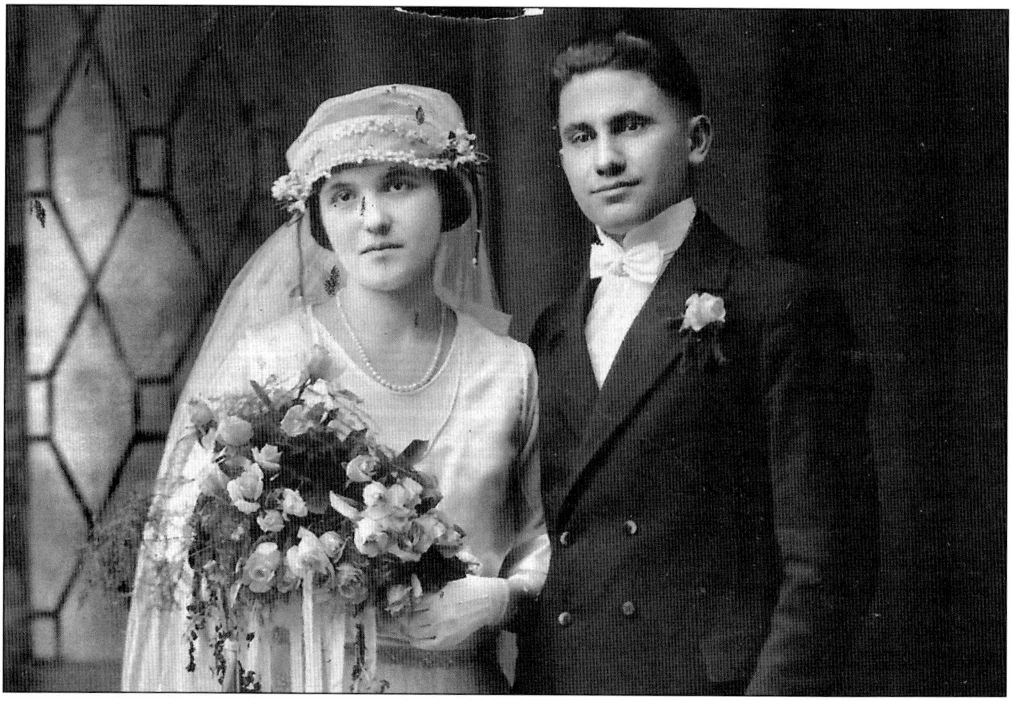

WEDDING DAY. Emily Monacelli and Gus Fortunato pose for their wedding photograph on October 18, 1922. Gus owned and operated a shoe repair shop on Medina's Main Street for many years. (Courtesy of Susan Fuller.)

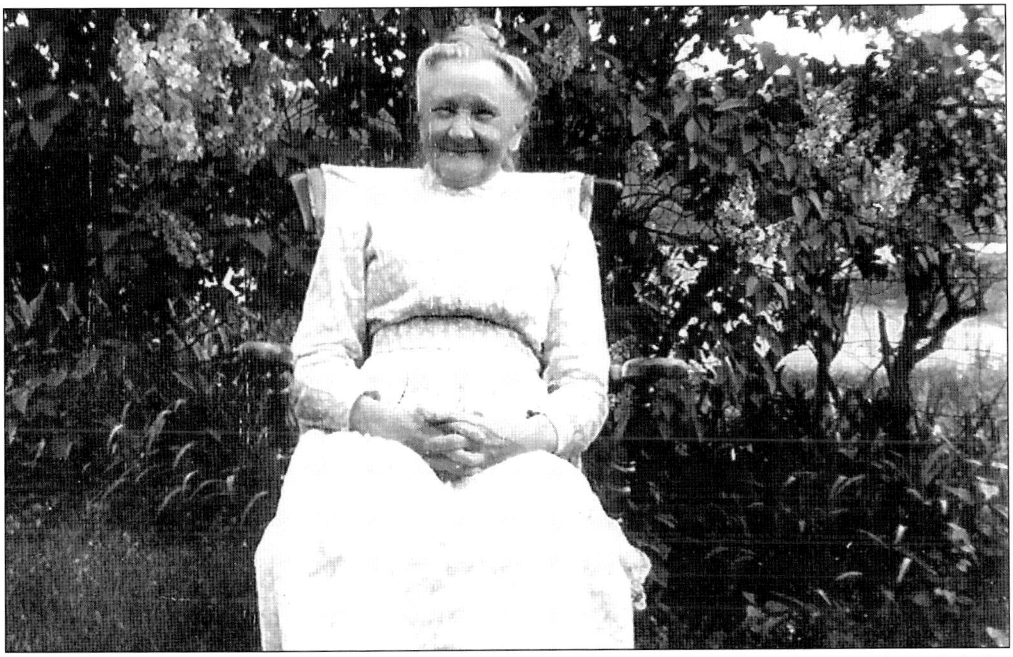

MEDINA SEAMSTRESS. Mary Shibilske made the wedding dress in the photograph at left for her younger sister. She is seen here relaxing, years later, at her Bates Road yard around 1940. (Courtesy of John Wasnock.)

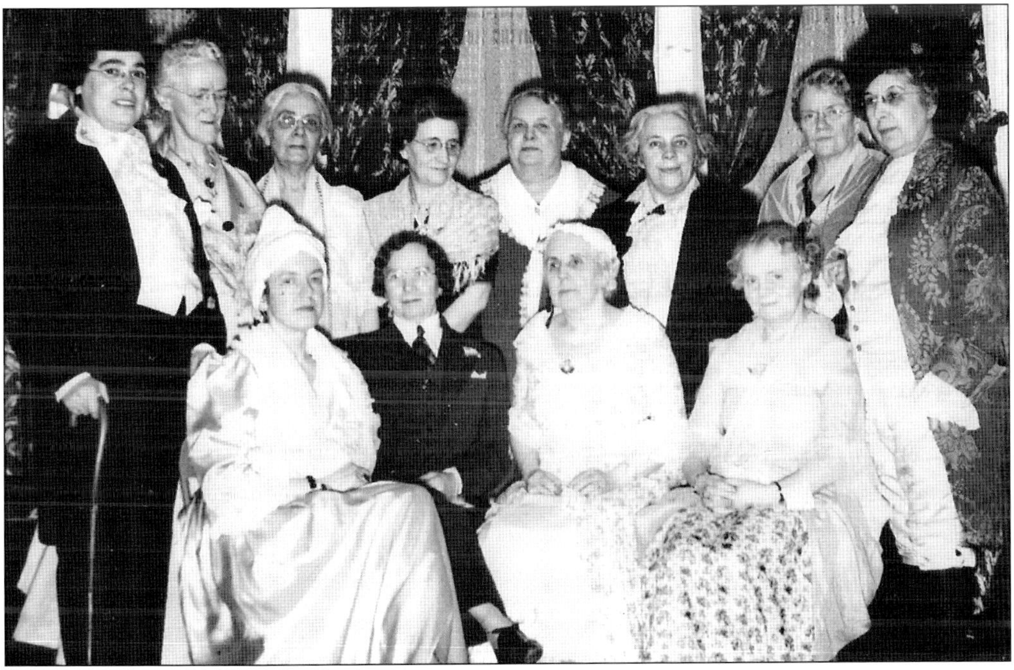

AZULIKET CLUB. This group of thespians poses for the camera in full costume around 1926. From left to right are as follows: (first row) Betty Wells, Ida Housden, Grace Rugg, and Nellie Barnes; (second row) Laura King, Bell Cooper, Jo Turner, Elsie Ferguson, Bertha Plimpton, Peg Dygert, Mary Douglas, and Dora Warren. (Courtesy of Richard Nellist.)

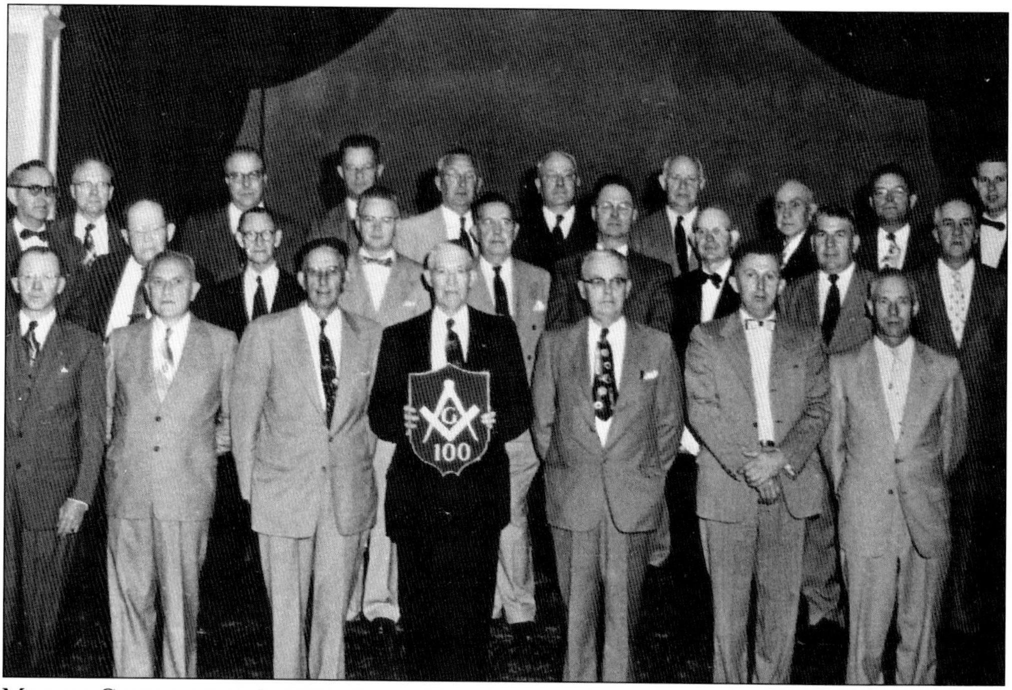

MASONS CONVENTION. In 1926, George Newell was the host of the Grand Lecturer Convention. His Medina guests are, from left to right, the following: (first row) Tim Simmons, Chester Broughton, unidentified, Dr. Harry Tanner, Claude Grinnell, and two unidentified men; (second row) Bruce Olmstead, three unidentified men, Don Acer, Elvin Eskelson, Merle Draper, and Franklin Axtell; (third row) Charles Raymond, Clyde Walters, Rockwell Kingsley, unidentified, Dr. Trolley, Hewell Maxon, Alonzo Waters, unidentified, Dr. Fulton Rogers, and Robert Waters. (Courtesy of Richard Nellist.)

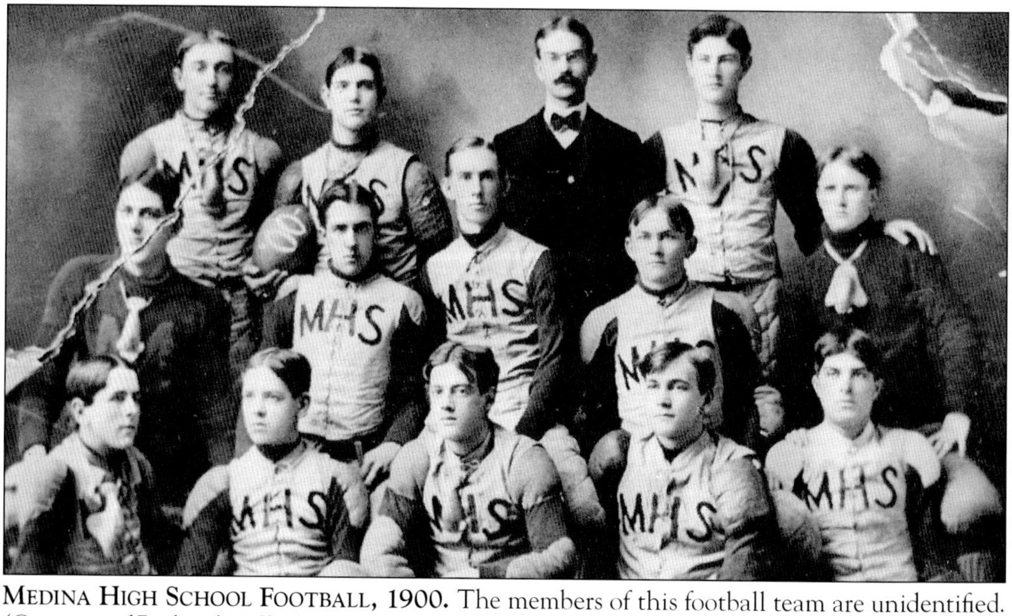

MEDINA HIGH SCHOOL FOOTBALL, 1900. The members of this football team are unidentified. (Courtesy of Richard Nellist)

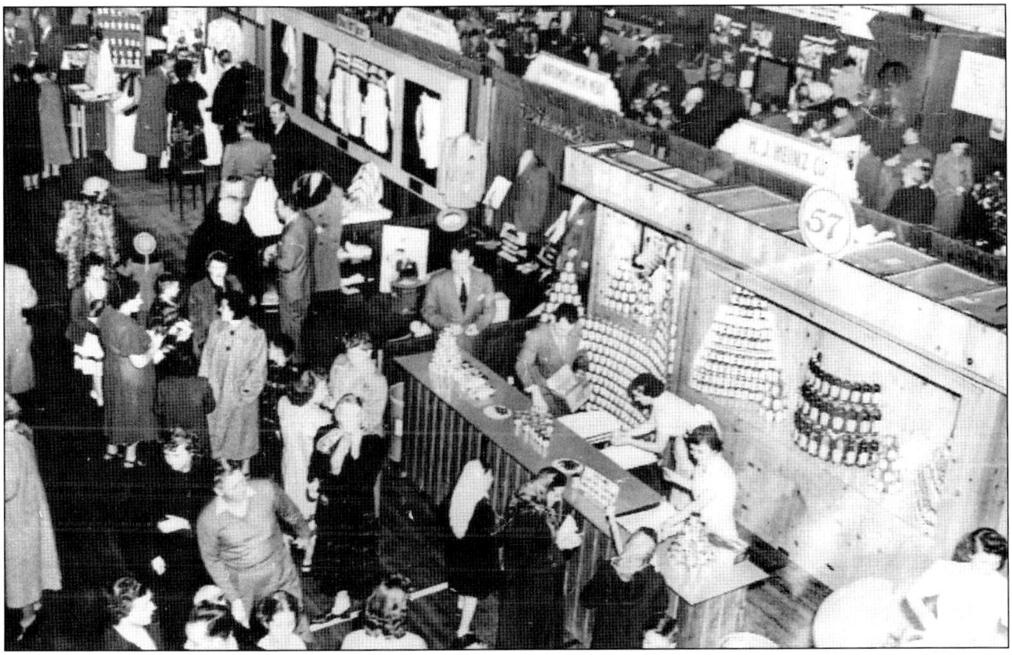

INSIDE THE ARMORY. Most every vendor in Medina reserved a spot for the annual trade show at the armory. This is a view from a show in 1950. (Courtesy of Richard Nellist.)

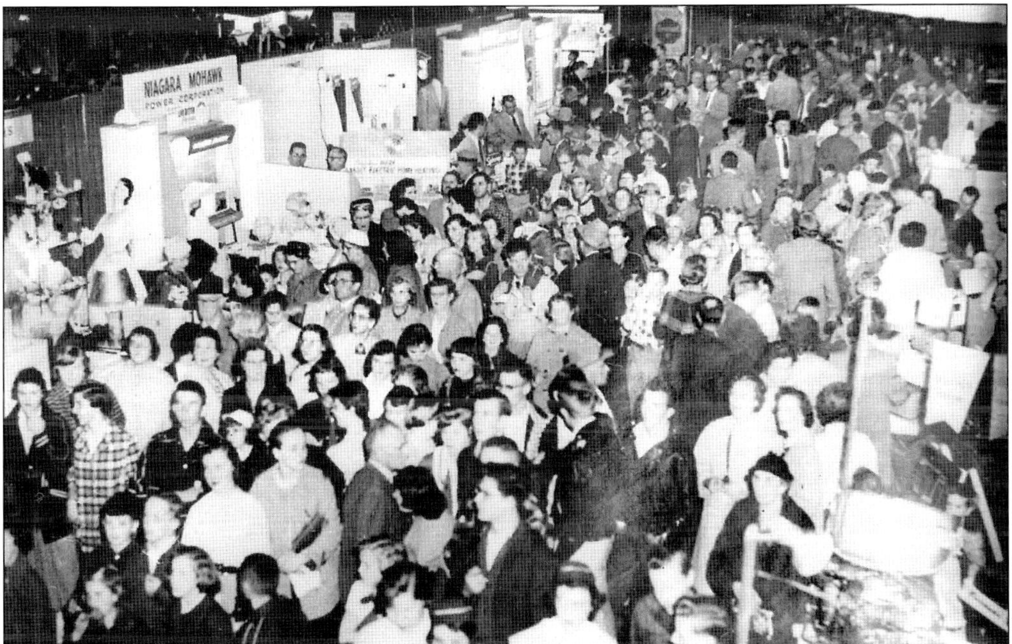

ELBOW TO ELBOW. In 1950, people flocked to the armory to see what new things Medina vendors had to offer. The trade show was an annual event for many years, but with the advent of better television, video movies, and more things to see, eventually the trade shows ceased to be successful. In the center of this photograph are Ridgeway town historian Richard Nellist and his wife. Can you find them? (Courtesy of Richard Nellist.)

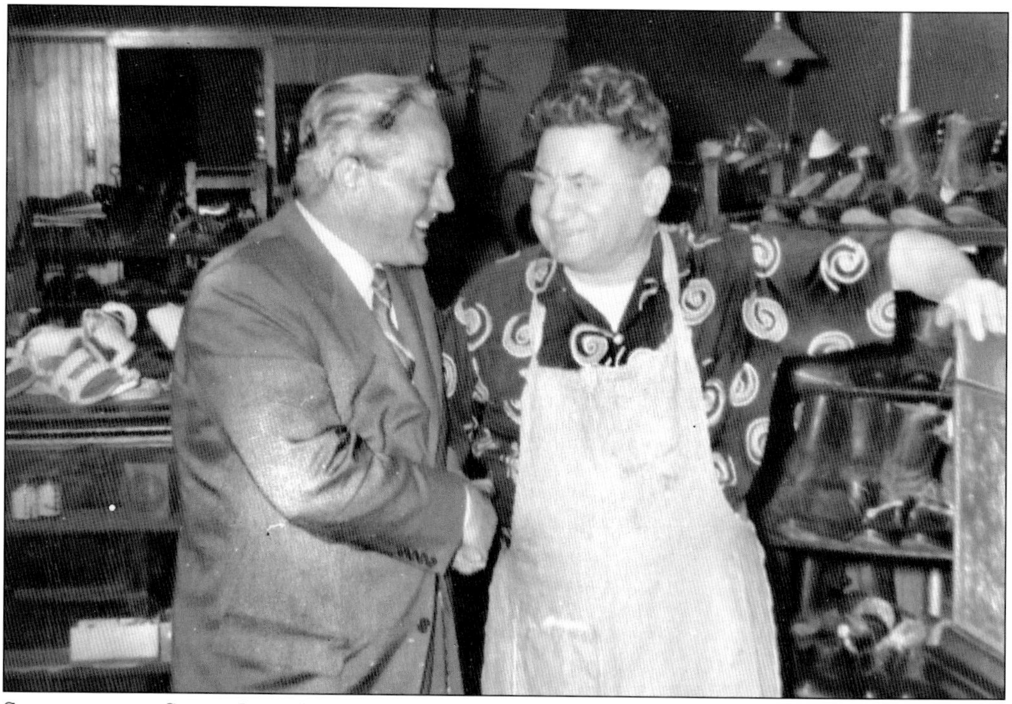

SHOES AND A STAR. In 1955, Gus Fortunato's shoe repair shop hosts Italian shoemaker and quiz show winner Gino Prato, who won the $64,000 Question game show in that year. After winning, he toured Orleans County and stopped in the shoe store. (Courtesy of Susan Fuller.)

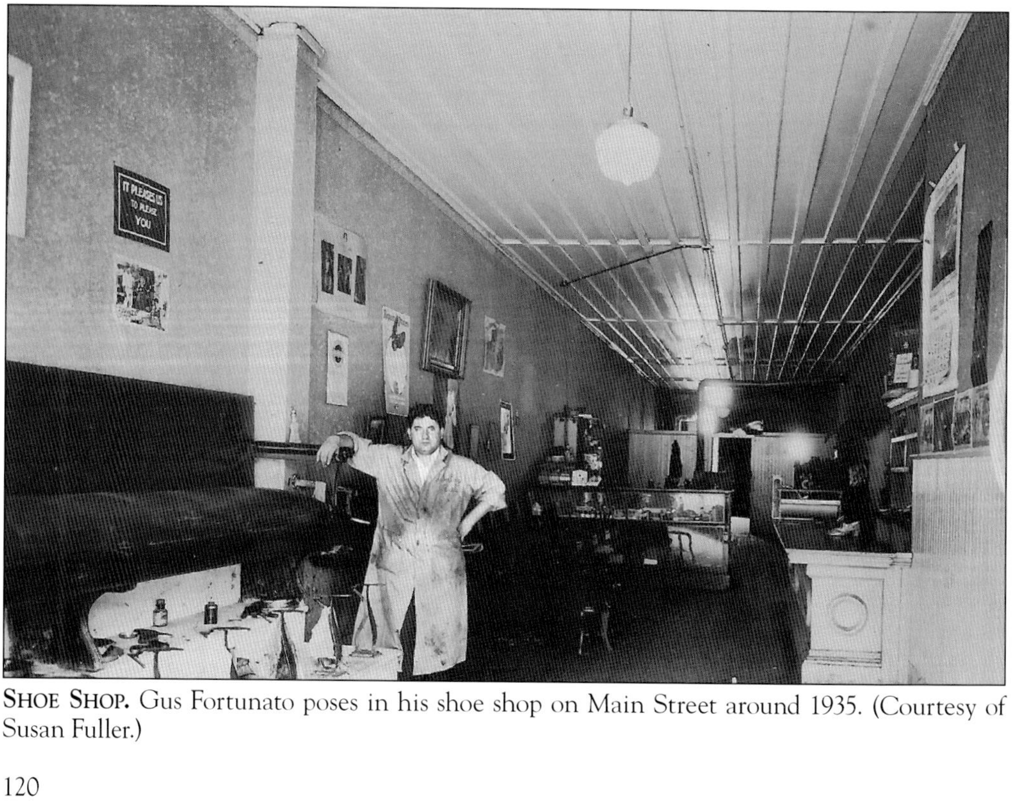

SHOE SHOP. Gus Fortunato poses in his shoe shop on Main Street around 1935. (Courtesy of Susan Fuller.)

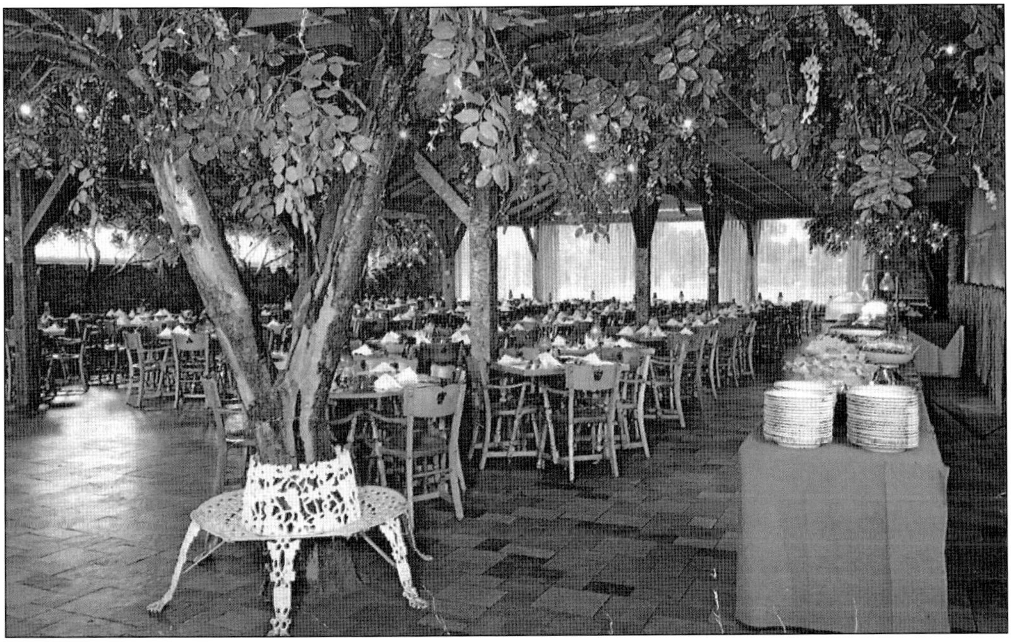

INSIDE THE APPLE GROVE, C. 1970. The Apple Grove Inn had real apple trees growing up through the floor and small twinkling lights sparkling through the branches. The restaurant was used for regular dining and hosted many wedding receptions in the Johnny Appleseed Room, seen here. (Courtesy of Bill Henderson.)

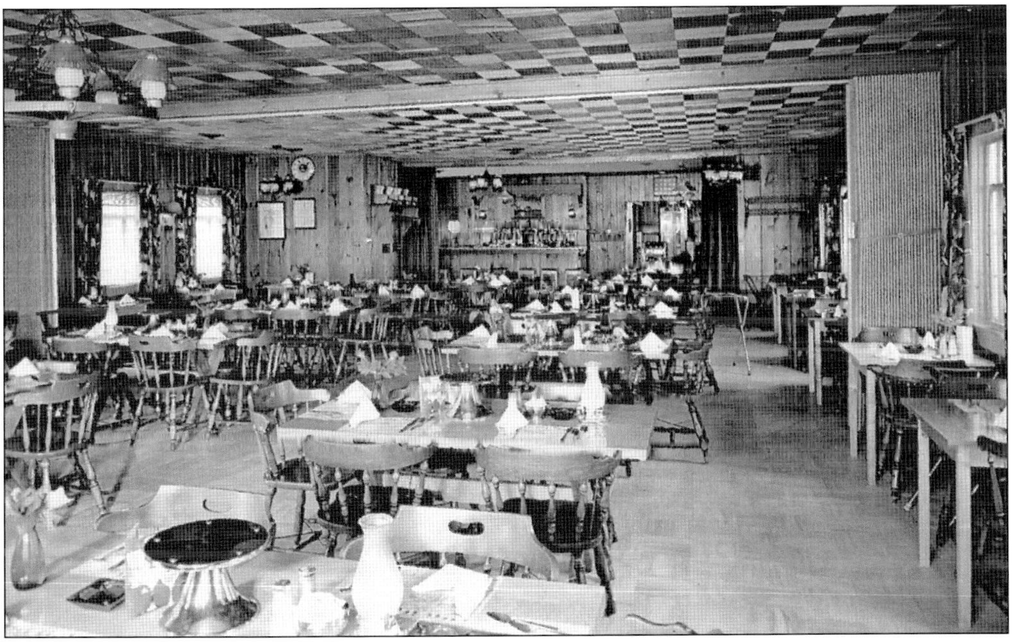

FRONT DINING AREA. This was the dining area in the north side of the Apple Grove restaurant around 1970. The restaurant burned and is now called the Apple Orchard Inn. (Courtesy of Bill Henderson.)

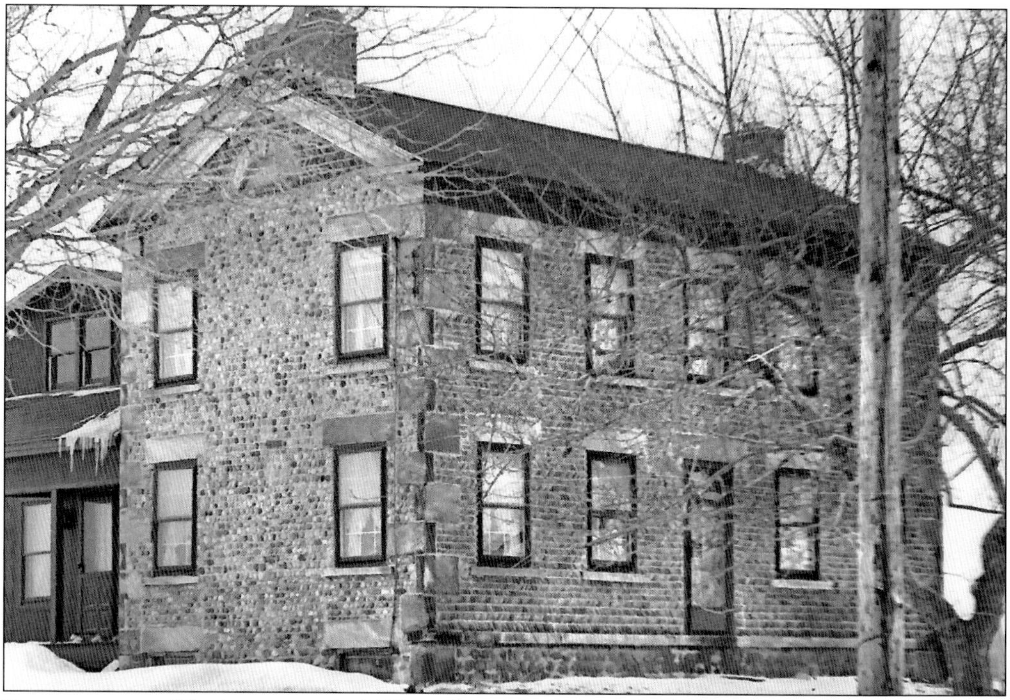

COBBLESTONES. This house was the Feldman house on Swett Road near Oak-Orchard-on-the- Ridge. (Courtesy of Richard Nellist.)

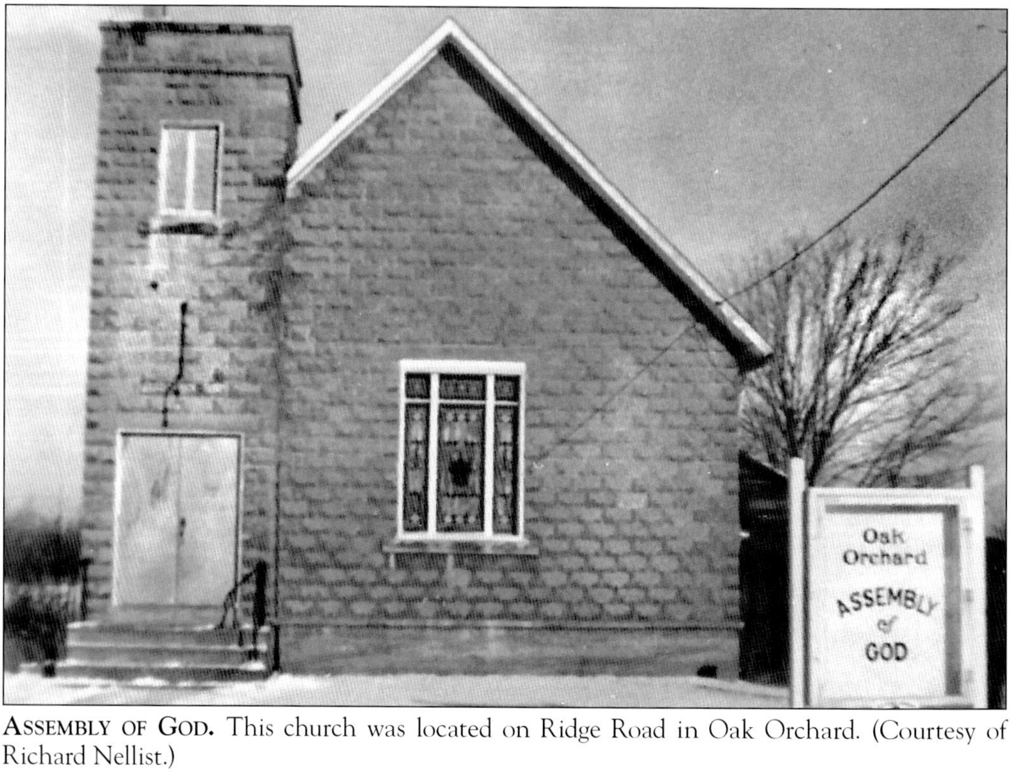

ASSEMBLY OF GOD. This church was located on Ridge Road in Oak Orchard. (Courtesy of Richard Nellist.)

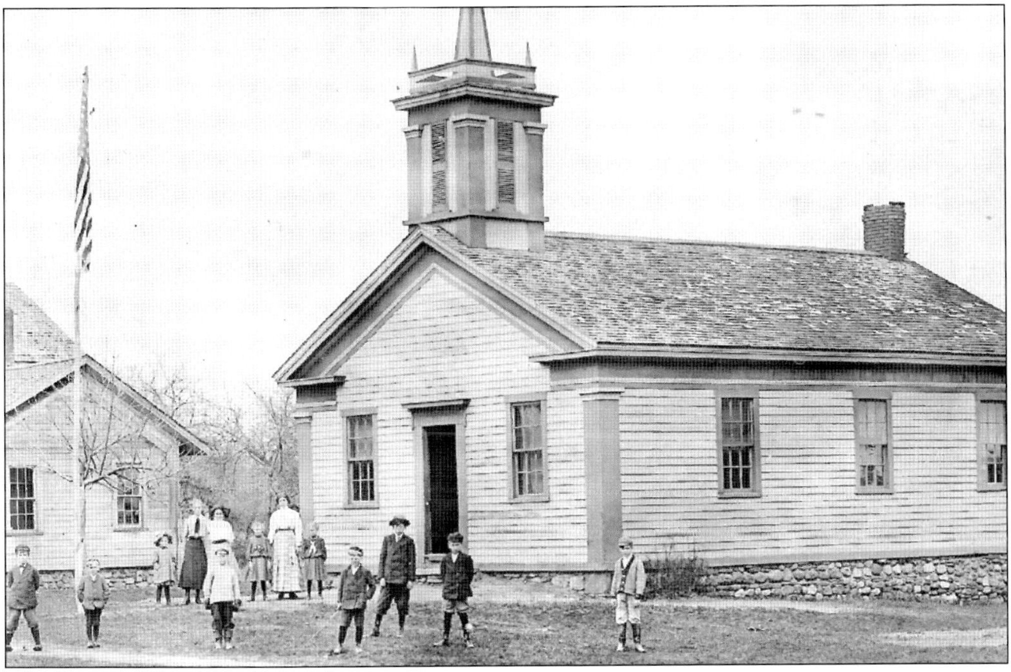

OAK ORCHARD SCHOOL, C. 1900. This was the first schoolhouse at Oak Orchard. (Courtesy of Richard Nellist.)

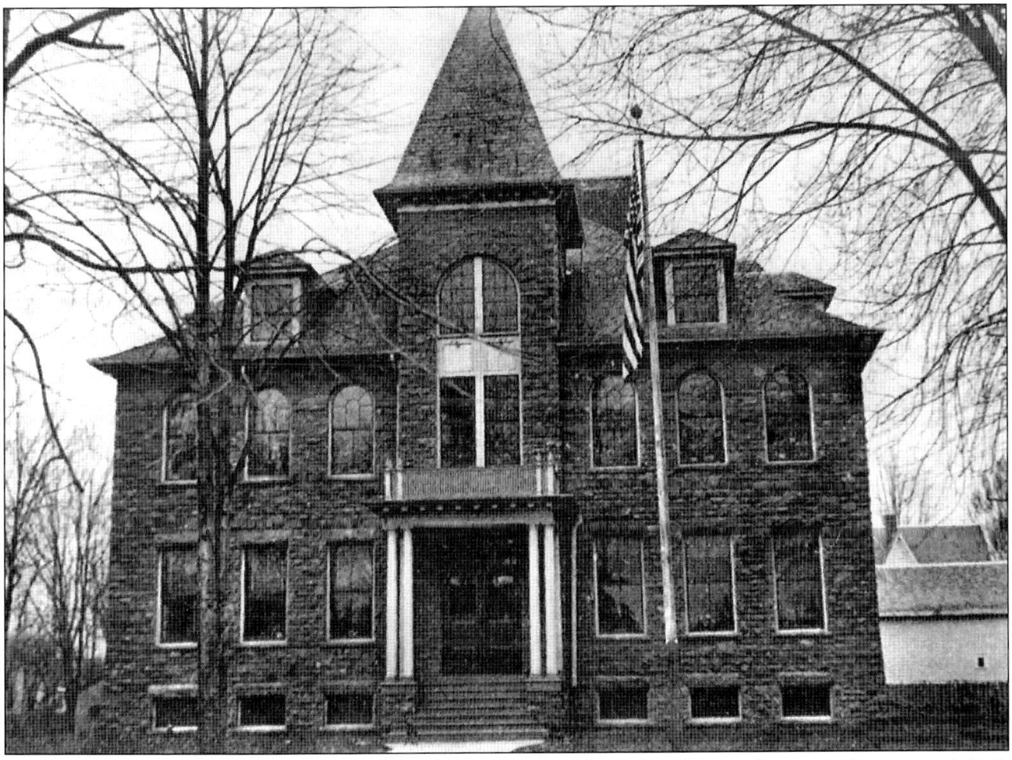

OAK ORCHARD SCHOOL. Looking similar to the Medina Academy, this was the second Oak Orchard School. (Courtesy of Richard Nellist.)

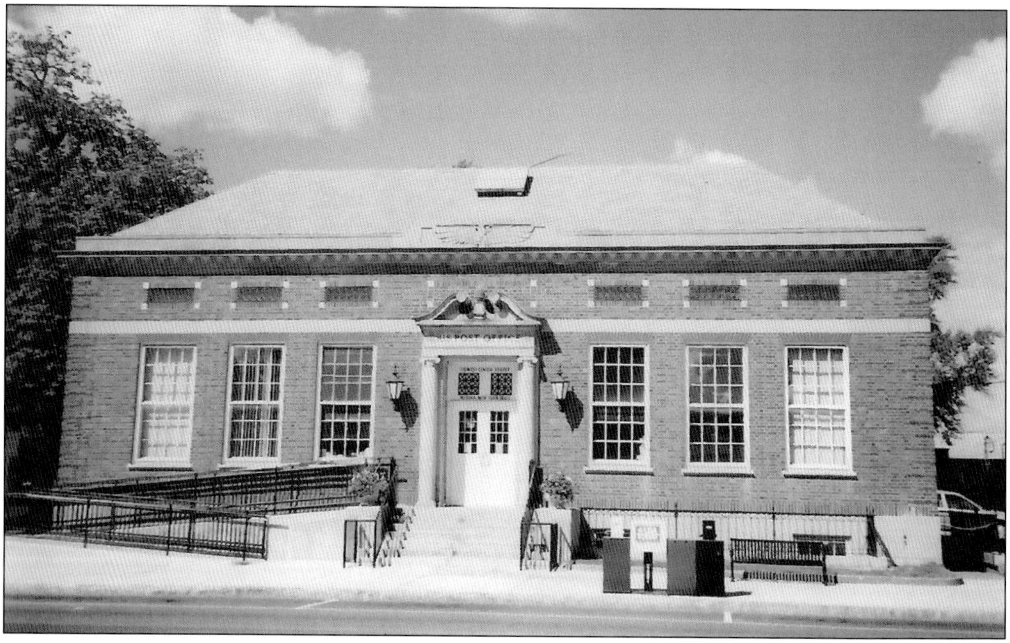

New Post Office. This post office was built on West Center Street in 1935. It not only has stairs leading to the entrance but a wheelchair ramp as well.

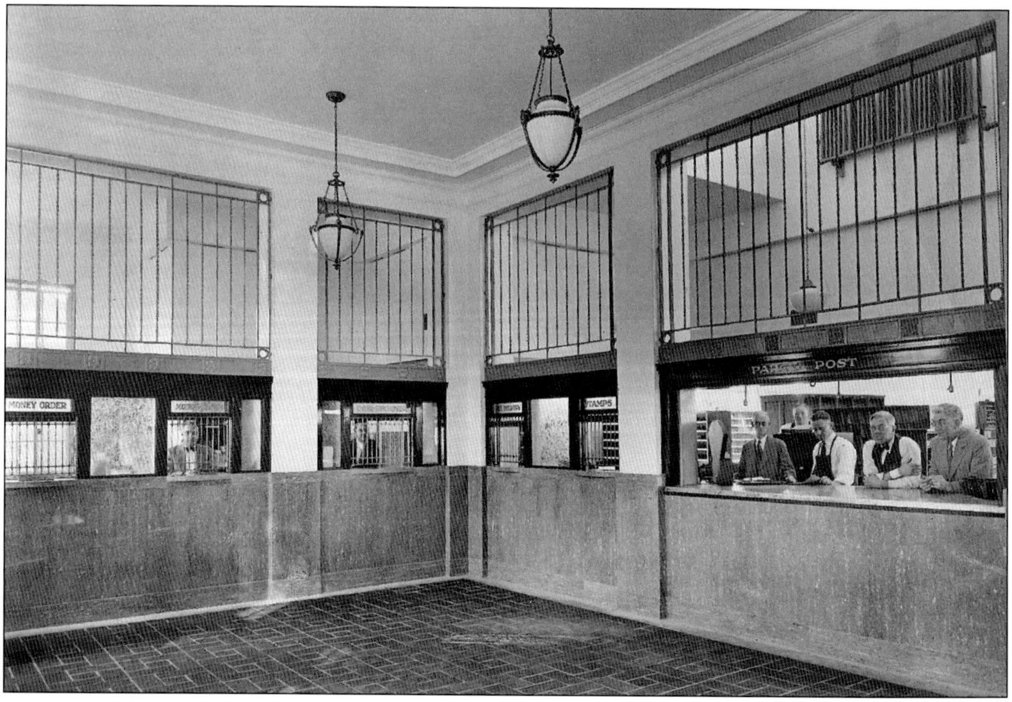

Inside the New Post Office. The postal workers man their stations for this photograph around 1935. (Courtesy of Mrs. Elmer Chatt.)

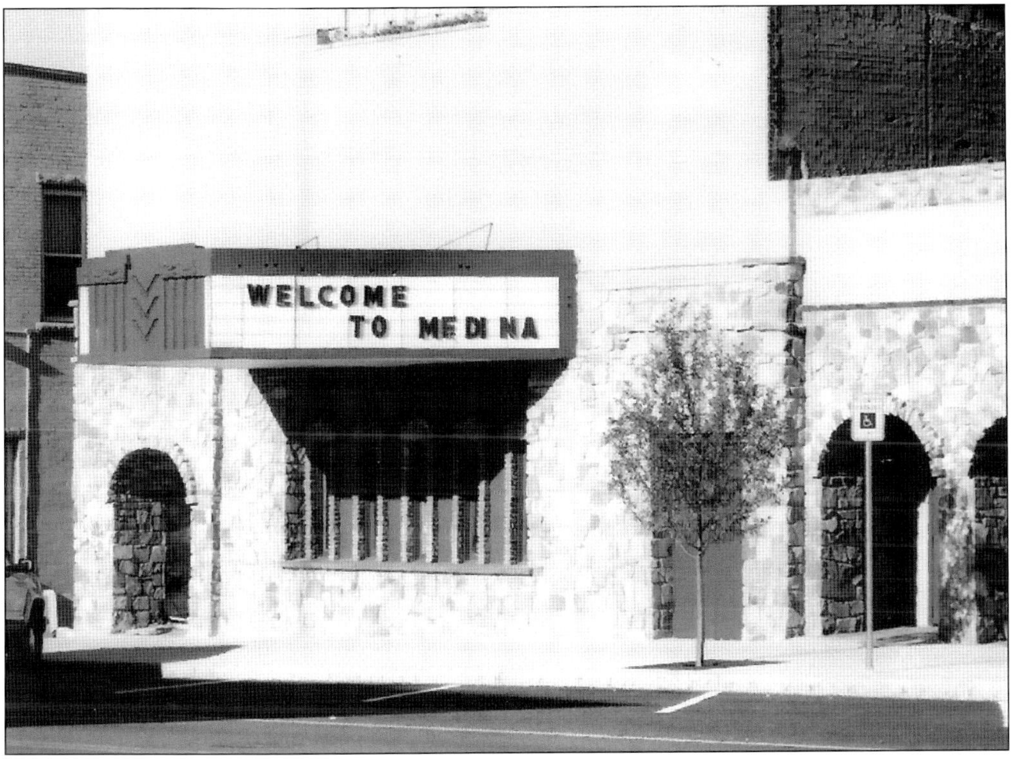

The Diana Theater. Although the theater has been closed for many years, one can still feel its dignity, imagine the ticket seller sitting at the outdoor window, and be greeted by the Welcome to Medina sign on its marquis.

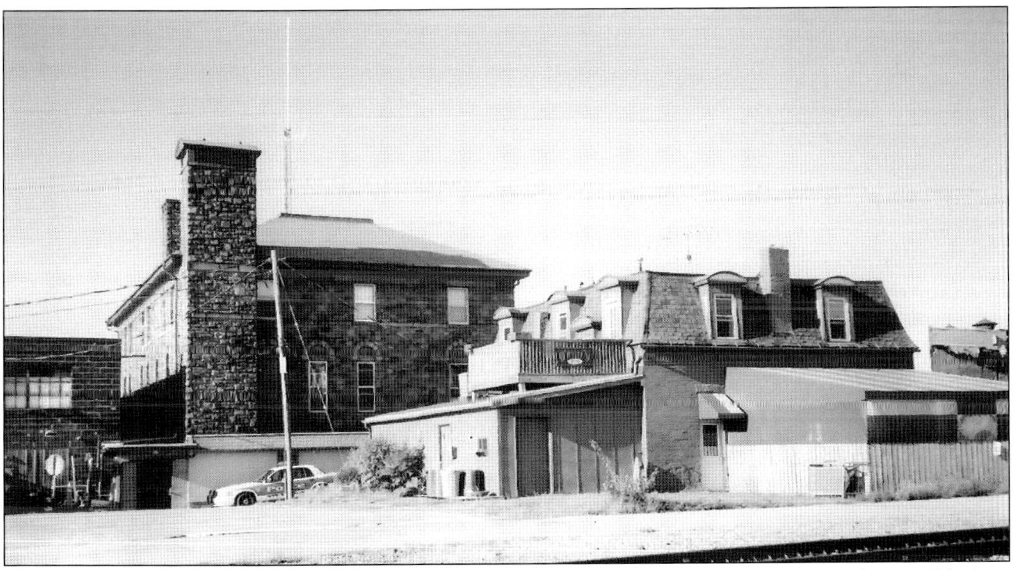

O'Brien's Today. Although O'Brien's Inn looks the same in front, new owners have added an open-air addition on the south side, where summer patrons may sit outside under a roof while listening to live music that is playing inside. This view is facing north from the railroad tracks. City Hall and a police car are next to O'Brien's.

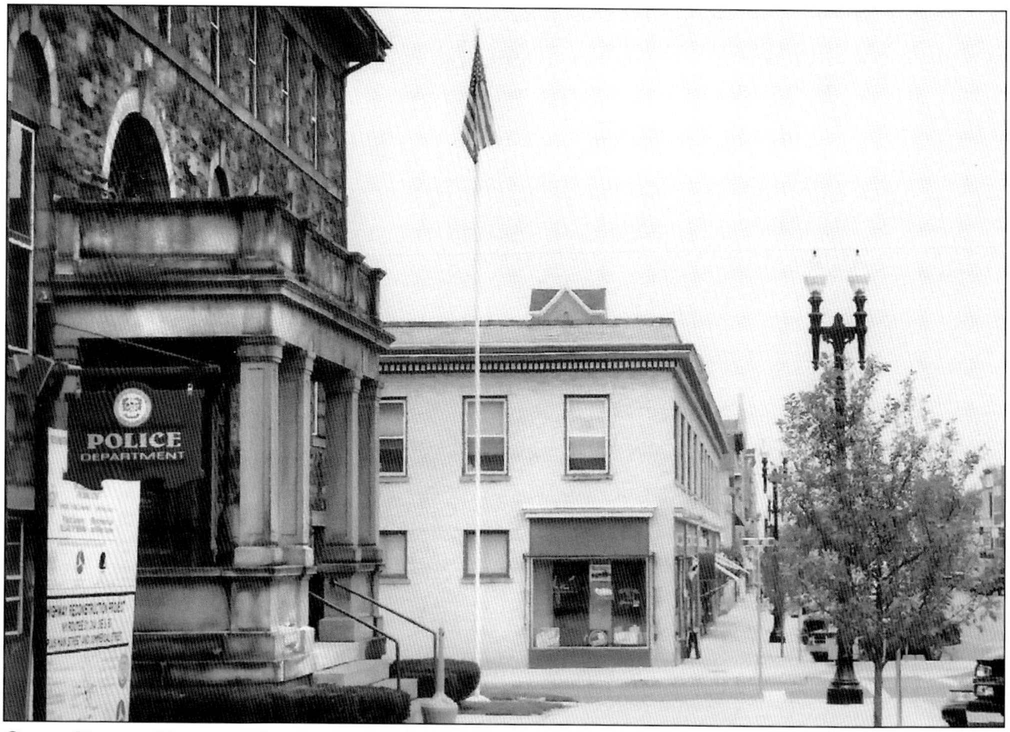

COOK BLOCK TODAY. The S. A. Cook Building is seen across the street from City Hall. The pale brick looks clean and neat, and the founding fathers were correct in demanding that the building be built securely, as it looks modern and new even though it was built over 90 years before. The streetlamps are new and stylish as well.

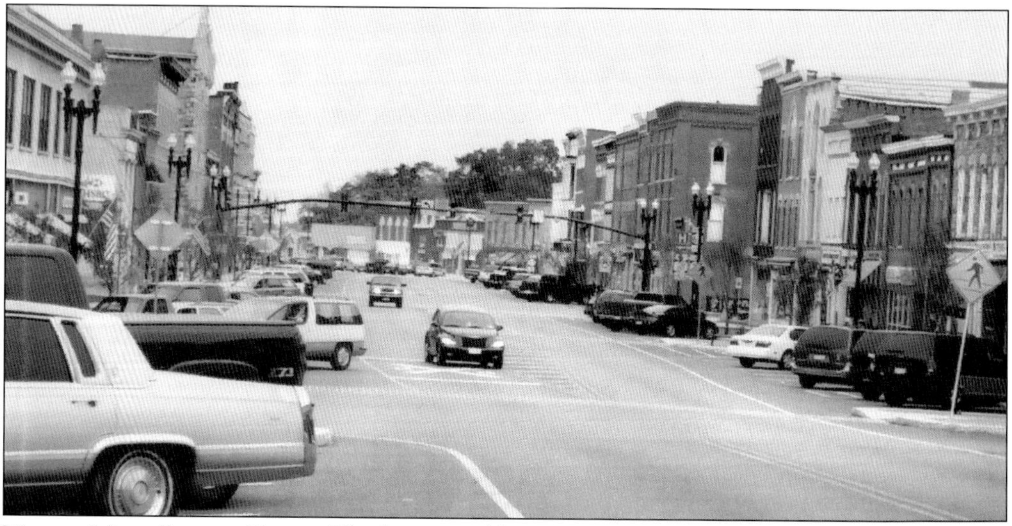

NORTH MAIN STREET TODAY. The horses and buggies are gone and have been replaced by cars and trucks. The cute pedestrian crosswalks have been replaced by yellow pedestrian crossing signs. The quaint streetlamps hung by a wire have been replaced by Victorian-style black iron lamps. Signal lights hung on wires have been replaced by modern lights suspended on long poles. But the buildings remain the same, except for the tower of the White Hotel, which was not replaced when it crumbled.

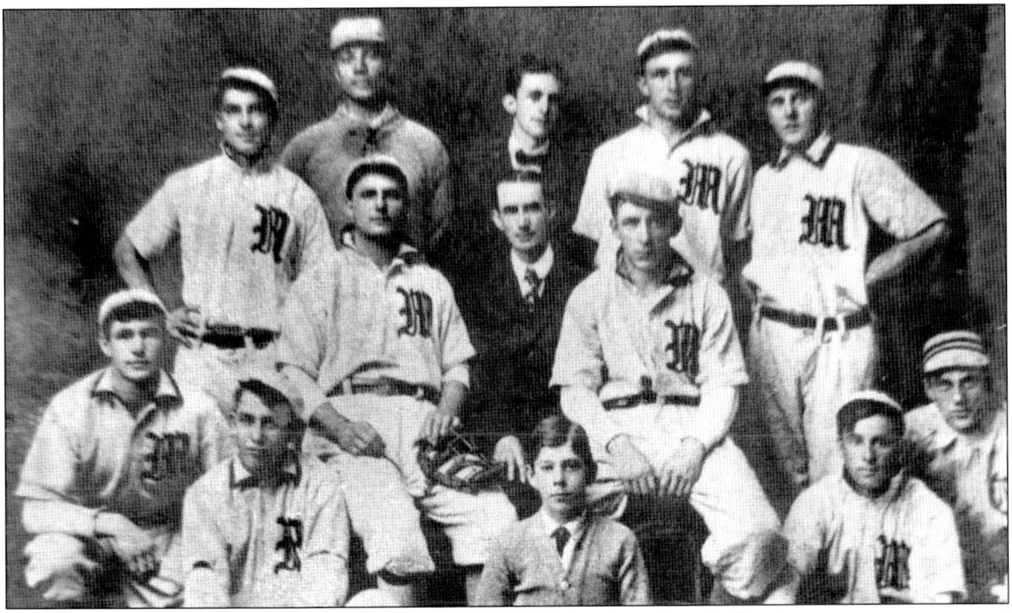

MEDINA BASEBALL, 1908. These men were the Medina baseball champion amateurs of western New York for the entire 1908 season. Shown here are, from left to right, the following: (first row) P. Burns, L. Mead (mascot), and R. Haingrey; (second row) F. Boyle, C. Bacon, J. M. Comerford (manager), I. Comerford, and L. Montgomery; (third row) F. Shultz, F. Tillman, H. Olds (scorer), J. Reil, and H. Montgomery. (Courtesy of Richard Nellist.)

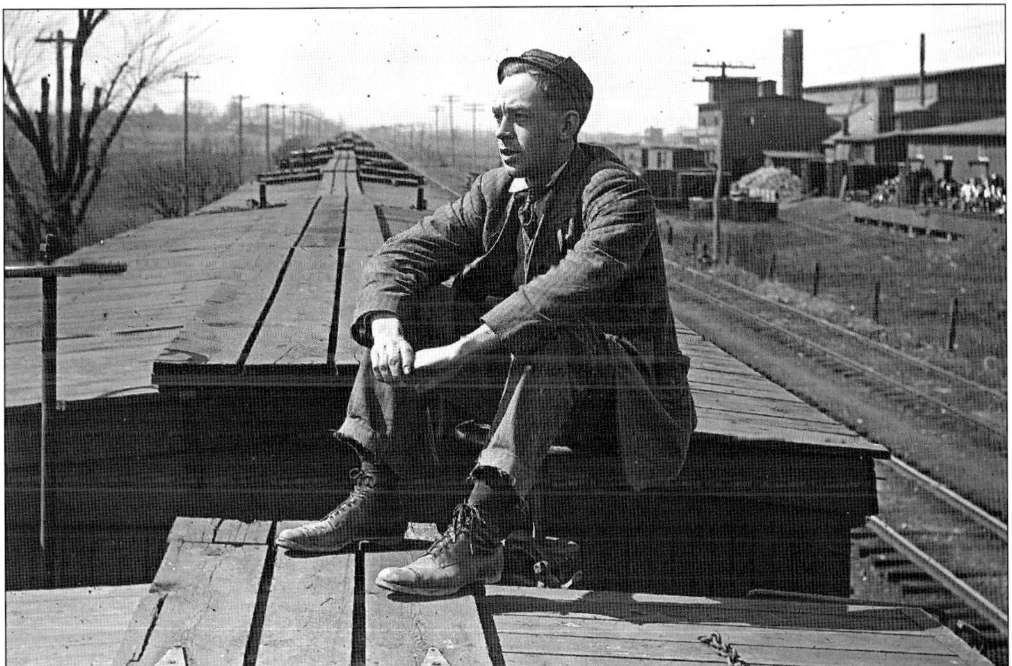

FAREWELL, MEDINA. This unidentified man with frayed cuffs and well-worn boots sits atop a boxcar, ready to ride out of town on a rail. He seems oblivious to the workers behind him. (Courtesy of Mrs. Elmer Chatt.)

ACKNOWLEDGMENTS

The following people and organizations have provided help in compiling photographs and information for this book: Mrs. Elmer Chatt, Catherine Cooper, Susan Fuller, Bill Henderson, Thomas Hickey, C. W. Lattin, Gary McCarthy, Richard Nellist, Charles Rand Penney, Sue Phillips, Amy Sanderson, Mark Tillman, John Wasnock, the staff of the Book Shoppe at Medina, the Orleans County Department of History, the Grant-Pollard Insurance Agency, the Lee-Whedon Library, the *Medina Journal-Register*, the Medina Pennysaver, and the Town of Ridgeway Historical Society.

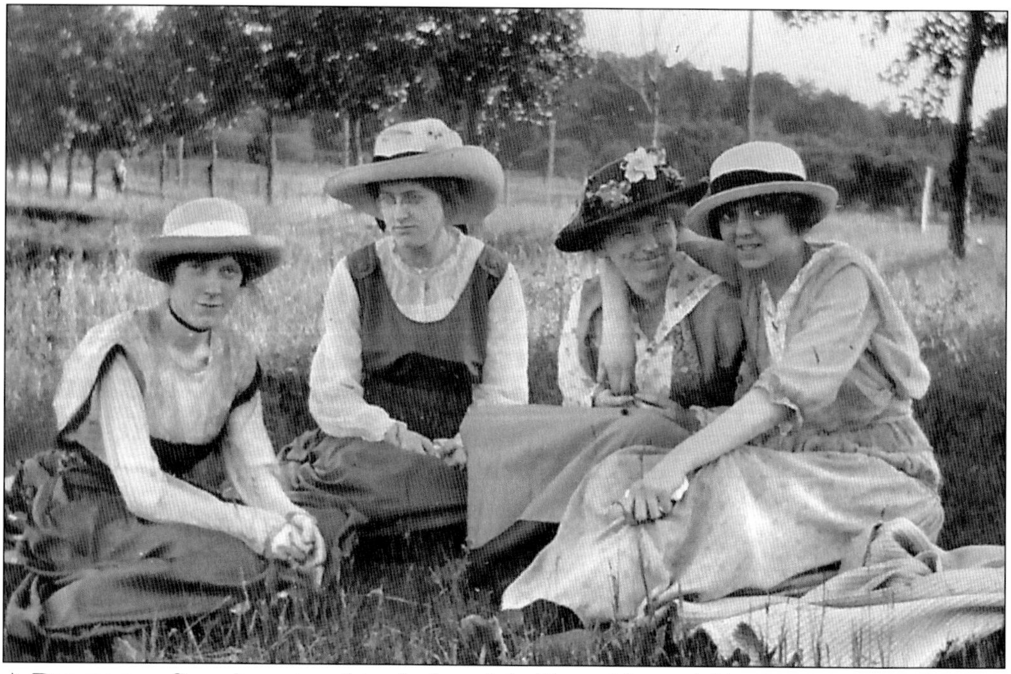

A DAY IN THE SUN. Longtime friends, from left, Elaine Hartt, Addis Hartt, June Bailey, and Alice Bailey enjoy an outing in a grassy Medina field around 1920, wearing hats to protect themselves from the sun. (Courtesy of the A. Hartt estate.)